Ethnic Labels, Latino Lives

Ethnic Labels, Latino Lives

Identity and the Politics of (Re)Presentation in the United States

Suzanne Oboler

University of Minnesota Press

Minneapolis

London

Portions of chapters 5 and 6 first appeared as "The Politics of Labeling Latino/a Cultural Identities of Self and Others," *Latin American Perspectives*, issue 75, vol. 19, no. 4 (Fall 1992): 18-36, copyright 1992 by *Latin American Perspectives*, reprinted by permission of Sage Publications, Inc.

Published by the University of Minnesota Press
11 Third Avenue South, Suite 290, Minneapolis, MN 55401-2520
Printed in the United States of America on acid-free paper
Third printing 1996

Library of Congress Cataloging-in-Publication Data

Oboler, Suzanne.
    Ethnic labels, Latino lives : identity and the politics of (re) presentation in the United States / Suzanne Oboler.
        p.   cm.
    Includes bibliographical references and index.
    ISBN 0-8166-2284-1
    ISBN 0-8166-2286-8 (pbk.)
    1. Hispanic Americans—Ethnic identity.   2. Hispanic Americans—Name.   I. Title
E184.S75027   1995
305.868'073—dc20   94-22751

Contents

Preface and Acknowledgments

Researching and writing the various drafts of this book over the past decade has been a process of intellectual and personal discovery that goes far beyond anything I could have imagined when I first began to think about the meaning and implication of ethnic labels in people's lives. It can be said that ethnicity has been the leitmotif of American history. While in recent years we have witnessed the definitive fading of the idealized image of U.S. society as a melting pot, the possibility of recasting it in multicultural terms has proven to be problematic. What was being sought by the proclamation of ethnic diversity has become a matter of increasing concern in contemporary politics and educational debates.

I knew that unraveling the meaning of this process entailed understanding the history of various civil rights movements that first mobilized around issues of citizenship, race, and national origins. But perhaps more important, it seemed to me that it also involved grasping the meaning of an ethnic label as it is strategically incorporated and reformulated in the lives of individuals.

Words, names, social labels can take on a life of their own beyond the control of those who coin them or to whom they are applied. Using the term *Hispanic* as a case study, I wrote this book in an attempt to explore the racialization of a population since the nineteenth century and its historical demarcation as a homogenized ethnic group. In undertaking this subject, I wanted to examine some of the varying ways that socially constituted identities are in turn appropriated by different people according to their individual race, class, and national origins. This seemed to me to be the first step toward mapping a framework from which to analyze the social meaning of ethnic labels.

The term Hispanic began to be disseminated as early as 1970 by government agencies. It has since been adopted for self-identification by various sectors of the population with ties to Latin America in several regions of the country. In the course of my research on this ethnic designator, the term *Latino* began to emerge among grassroots sectors of the population, coined as a progressive alternative to the state-imposed bureaucratic label Hispanic. The term Latino has since been increasingly adopted, primarily in urban areas in which various Latin American national-origin groups are represented. For reasons that will become apparent in this book, my own preference is for the term Latino. Nevertheless, I am aware that it—like the words *Hispanic, ethnic, minority, marginal, alternative,* and *third world*—is also "inaccurate and loaded with ideological implications," as Guillermo Gómez-Peña and several other scholars have increasingly pointed out. In this book I use both terms throughout. Generally speaking, I use the term Hispanic to signal the official and institutional designation of the group; the term Latino corresponds to my understanding of its common use as self-referential by some but not all sectors of this population. In short, my aim is not to "advocate" for the adoption of one term over the other, or even to repudiate the use of ethnic labels. Rather, it is to understand the role they play today in the current reformulations of the debate on race and class in the name of ethnic diversity and multiculturalism, and in the struggle for citizenship rights and social justice in contemporary U.S. society.

Numerous people have contributed to my intellectual and personal growth in the process of completing this project. First, I am deeply indebted to the people in the education program who shared their lives and thoughts with me. Their support and willingness to participate in this project allowed me to gather data through which to think more concretely about the otherwise intangible relationship between the social construction of identity and its meaning in people's individual lives.

I want to express my gratitude to Alberto Sandoval Sánchez for his careful readings and comments on this manuscript, and for his intellectual and personal courage, friendship, and support; to Elitza Bachvarova for our many discussions over the years, for her challenging comments on this manuscript, and for helping me to clarify my ideas on race, culture, and politics; and to Keitha Fine for her probing questions and close readings of this project throughout its various stages. I also want to thank Frances Aparicio, Anani Dzidzienyo, Juan Flores, Jim McIlwain, the late William McLoughlin, María-Elena Mujíca, Silvia Spitta, and Josh Wallman—my friends and colleagues who read different chapters and gave me many helpful comments.

Some of the ideas I present here became clearer to me as a result of earlier discussions with my dissertation advisers, Faye Ginsburg and Henry Perkinson, as well as with Elaine Abelson, Silvia Arellano,

Maria do Carmo Campello de Souza, Marilyn Hamilton, John Hammond, William Kelly, Jaime Manrique, Beatríz Morales, Hilda Mundo López, María Celia Paoli, Fredy Roncalla, Nick Unger, Dicxon Valderruten, and James Willimetz. *Muchas gracias a todos ustedes* for your comments, support, and encouragement. I would also like to thank my editor, Janaki Bakhle, for her helpful suggestions and great sense of humor, both of which were fundamental in completing this manuscript; and the anonymous readers of my manuscript, for their thoughtful questions, observations, and remarks.

Last, but certainly not least, this book has benefited from many lively discussions with my students at Eugene Lang College, the New School for Social Research, and Brown University—among them Melissa Coss, Jaime Delgado, Alicia Diaz, Elizabeth García, Johanna Fernández, José Herrera, Sheila Maldonado, Lyla Materón Arum, Maricruz Ponce de León, and Irma Valdez. I thank them for their intellectual curiosity, their often brilliant contributions to our class debates, their creativity, their research support, and their warmth and encouragement. In many ways they have helped me, both in my thinking and in my efforts to make this book a more nuanced reading of race, class, and the complex meanings that ethnicity has acquired in shaping the shifting boundaries of our lives and identities today. This book is dedicated to them, *la nueva generación de Latinos y Latinas, y a mis hermanos queridos, Thomas y Elizabeth, que entienden cómo es la onda por aquí y por allá en el Perú.*

Hispanics in the United States: "We All Sing a Different Song"

On a bright summer day in early February 1985, a group of fourteen Peruvians left their country to begin what was to be a long and arduous journey by air, sea, and land to the United States.[1] The group was made up of men and women, none of whom knew each other. Some were couples, most were single; some were liberal professionals, others manual laborers; three were housewives; and one or two were unemployed. All of them had been hit by the downturn of the economy, the fear of the guerrilla war, the feeling that things in Peru could only get worse. They had never met each other, but they all shared a "travel agent," who promised to help them through the tortuous visa and customs bureaucracies of the various countries they would have to cross to reach their destination.

The group flew first to Ecuador, and then went by bus into Colombia. Even before they took the boat to a nearby island off the Colombian coast where they were to wait for their visas into Panama, the travel agent had already disappeared. She took with her much of their money, forcing three of them to give up the journey before it had actually begun. Only two managed to get a visa before boarding the boat to Panama. The rest decided to take their chances at the Panamanian border. Half of the group was turned back in Panama, but, undaunted, the others continued on their way, taking buses through Costa Rica, Nicaragua, Honduras, El Salvador, Guatemala, and finally Mexico. In each, they were forced to stay anywhere from two weeks to two months as they waited for their visa applications to cross the border into the next country:

> Every time we showed the border patrol our visa to enter a new country, we were scared we'd get sent back to Peru. So while we

waited for the visas in each country we would learn the customs, and their use of language, and change our way of dressing, and walking. Then at the border we'd say we were living in the country before the one we were asking to get into. That way if they deported us, we'd only get set back one country. . . . Each country was so different. For example, everyone spoke Spanish, but each country's Spanish was different. You know how it is: we all sing a different song. . . .
(Julián, Peru)

From Mexico, each eventually found his or her way across the border to the United States, from where they hoped to find the means to help the families they had had to leave behind. Throughout their journey, their sense of national identity had, if anything, been affirmed. For in the continuous confrontation with the cultural and linguistic differences between their own use of language, customs, ways of dressing, and walking and those of other nationalities, the travelers had established to themselves that they were indeed Peruvians. After all, as the British historian, Eric Hobsbawm, once pointed out, departure from one's homeland means that immigrants "can no longer take themselves for granted as people who do not require definition."[2] Once in the United States, however, and to their eventual surprise, they also discovered that their newly asserted national identity was of little relevance to the society at large. Instead, they found out that they were now U.S. "Hispanics," a term whose meaning(s) and social value, *as these have evolved in this country*, they were expected to learn and assimilate—just as they had had to learn and adopt the meanings and customs of other foreign cultures on their journey through the hemisphere's various nations.

Like Julián and his fellow Peruvian travelers, thousands of people from Latin America have made their way to the United States since the passing of the Immigration Law of 1965. Once here, they have joined other immigrants or exiles from South and Central America, the Spanish-speaking Caribbean, and Mexico. They have also encountered Puerto Ricans and sectors of the Mexican-American/Chicano communities who have long lived in this country as U.S. citizens.[3] Unlike the more recent arrivals, the historical relationship of these two population groups to the United States was not originally shaped either by immigration or by forced exile but rather by conquest and colonization. The various populations of Latin American descent have thus found themselves living in the United States as a result of varying historical processes and at different periods of the nation's history.[4] Yet, regardless of these historical differences and variations in each national-origin group's time and way of arrival, their lives are today affected directly or otherwise by the use of the term Hispanic to characterize them in the United States.

The ethnic label Hispanic began to be widely disseminated by state agencies after 1970. Unlike the increasingly heard alternative term Latino, the ethnic designator Hispanic *officially* identifies people of Latin American and Spanish descent living in the United States today.[5] This book explores the emergence of the term Hispanic and its implications in the U.S. context and examines the meaning(s) and social value(s) that people of Latin American descent in turn attribute to this ethnic label in their lives.

The adoption of the ethnic designator Hispanic is commonly understood in terms of Spain's presence in the hemisphere for over three hundred years. Yet, as I discuss in the following pages, the names by which groups and individuals become known acquire political, social, and personal significance in the context of the debates on ethnicity and race in the United States. Thus, it is important to ask to what extent the appeal to the legacy of the Spanish colonial rule can justify the homogenization under the label Hispanic of the subsequent experiences of at least 23 million citizens, residents, and immigrants of Latin American descent. Can this appeal account, for example, for the legacies of Mexican Americans/Chicanos and Puerto Ricans, whose respective post-Spanish colonial histories and cultures have since been differentially shaped by their experiences in the United States? Does it help us to understand the relationship between these two historical minorities and sectors of the Cuban exile community, for instance, whose presence has increasingly affected U.S. diplomatic relations in the hemisphere? And is it rooted in an accurate perception of the diversity of Latin American populations in their *own* countries of origin?

It is important to note that contact and relations among Latin Americans and between them and the United States have historically been limited primarily to the interactions between and among their state representatives. In this respect, this book is an attempt to address the emerging historical phenomenon of the unprecedented coming together in one nation of millions of representatives of all the *pueblos americanos* understood in a hemispheric sense, and the issues this encounter raises in the process of constructing the political unity of Latinos in the United States. Julián's narrative of his travels up the Latin American continent, for example, points to how his particular group came to discover the implications of some of the national and cultural elements that distinguished their own identity as Peruvians from those of other Latin Americans. Others have noted the ethnic and racial differences *within* each country, exploding the myth of cultural and national homogeneity among Latin Americans in their own homelands:

> The term [Hispanic] fails to recognize the extremely rich ethnic and racial diversity of Latin Americans, for example, Argentines of Italian, German or French descent; Mexicans of Irish or Japanese ancestry; Cubans with Spanish, Lebanese, African or Chinese forebears; Peruvians of English, Russian-Jewish or Inca lineage; Venezuelans of Polish or Uruguayan stock; Brazilians of Korean or Greek heritage— the varieties go on and on. And, of course, there are those many Latin Americans who are entirely or partly of African and American Indian ancestry with some of the above thrown in.[6]

This diversity in itself raises the issue of the role of the national cultures, the racial and class differences, the customs and language of first-generation Latin American immigrants for understanding their relationship both to "being Hispanic" and to Chicanos and Puerto Ricans who are historical minorities in the United States. While Latinos' commonalities are often recognized in the U.S. context, the acknowledgment of their internal diversity includes examining the implications of the historical differences that shaped the experience of incorporation of the various national-origin groups encompassed by the term Hispanic. This is the point of departure of this study, along with the observation that our linguistic and cultural commonalities notwithstanding, people included under this label do not always choose to identify themselves primarily as Hispanic. More specifically, insofar as people of Latin American descent do not necessarily share social, national, or historical backgrounds, it cannot be assumed that all believe that they have to have a common identity *in the U.S. public sphere* with people of other nationalities who are labeled Hispanics. Indeed, as I argue throughout this book, differences in social and racial backgrounds, personal life experiences, and political beliefs are key to understanding not only the meaning of the ethnic label Hispanic in people's lives but also Latinos' decisions to participate actively under an umbrella term in movements for social justice in the United States.

A key component of the specificity of the populations identified as Latinos in the United States is the fact that they have always been and continue to be constructed by themselves and others in the context of both international and U.S. historical referrents. Certainly, sectors of the populations of Latin American descent have lived in what is now the Southwest, California, Florida, and other parts of the country for centuries. Like many Latinos today, they too forged their own real *and* "imagined" communities in the United States, with clear recognition of their ties to specific Latin American regions. Writers and scholars have documented the mutual support, for example, of sectors of the Cuban and Puerto Rican populations living in the United States during the nineteenth century, who collaborated in the struggle to achieve the independence of their respective islands from Spain. Similarly, researchers have documented the varied community organizations of Mexicans, Chicanos, and others of Latin American descent throughout various regions in the Southwest and California. These self-help organizations long served to support the maintenance of the language and cultures Latinos inherited from the Spanish empire in the Americas, as well as to fight against discrimination and the persistent exclusion from access to full and equal rights in this society.

What has changed in the past two decades, then, is *not* Latinos' sense of ourselves as communities bound by language, by cultural heritage, by an acknowledgment of our Latin American heritage, by the common goal of expanding and protecting Latinos' rights, by the aim of improving our lives and the communities' standards of living. Rather what is at issue is the different emphasis in U.S. politics on ethnic categories and their changing attributions and the state's distribution and withdrawal of resources on the basis of those terms since the 1960s. Even the brief overview I present in chapter 1 of the various issues involved in defining the term Hispanic and evaluating its social value suggests that it is important to take seriously the implications of the fact that this ethnic label was, at least originally, an artifact created and imposed by state administrative agencies.

It is important to note that ethnic labels, like all names, are by their very nature abstractions of a reality—in many ways, a necessity of speech in a society as large and complex as the United States. As such, their usage perhaps inevitably includes singling out particular socially constructed attributes, whether related to race, gender, class, or language. The attributes are imputed to be common to the group's members and are used to homogenize the group. Yet this schematic designation does not necessarily correspond to the reality of the group to whom the label is attached. Speaking Spanish, for example, is one of the attributes used to differentiate Latinos from other groups in the society. The popular perception is that "all Hispanics speak Spanish." Yet studies have shown that not all Latinos in the United States are Spanish dominant. In fact, increasingly, a significant number among the second and later generations are English dominant, and there are some, although relatively few, who do not speak Spanish at all.[7] Similarly, the assumptions that all Latinos are racially mestizo, that all are Catholic, or that all are lower class are examples of other common misperceptions used to justify homogenization under a common ethnic label. Popular (mis)conceptions about these or any other specific characteristics attributed to a particular group often serve to explain a particular ethnic label and to justify differentiating the group from others in the society. In the process the obvious diversity of individual people's lives, social experiences, and political beliefs are set aside.

It could easily be argued that given that labels *are* abstractions, accuracy about a particular group to whom a label is attached will inevitably be sacrificed for the sake of expediency in social communication. In this particular sense, it is important to emphasize that the use of ethnic labels in and of itself is not necessarily problematic. Yet, precisely because labels presuppose the sacrificing of accuracy, the meanings attributed to them over time are inherently decontextualized and their usage is ahistorical. While the homogenizing nature of ethnic labels is perhaps inevitable, the lack of historical memory that often accompanies their use means that there is often very little understanding of the conditions under which each label was created and through which its meanings and social value have been shaped and change over time. Lack of historical contextualization and of recognizing the shifting meanings of a term becomes particularly important when the label in question connotes that the group has or is assumed to have a presumed negative attribute of some kind—a "social handicap" (lack of English skills, for example) or a perceived or real cultural, social, or racial difference. In this case, ethnic labels do become a problem, particularly for the members of the group to whom they are attributed. Far from being merely a method of social categorization, they become the means of stigmatization. In short they become *stigmatizing labels*.

In disseminating and using a stigmatizing ethnic label to distinguish a particular group from others, the dominant ideology differentiates it from the rest of the population. The label's negative connotations become manifested in the discriminatory practices that in turn designate the group's status in the society. Ethnic labels incorporate the specific social contradictions that their creation and dissemination may originally have intended to quell. It is in this sense that all social constructions, labeling among them, can be seen as both strategic and referential. Labels are proposed from a political position and used by a particular social grouping according to the particular and changing social value attributed to them within specific contexts.

In the context of political dynamics, ethnicity, more particularly ethnic labeling, is directly related to the distribution of resources and opportunities. Ethnic labels serve to point to the practices of political inclusion or exclusion of the group's members from full participation as first-class citizens in their nation. By their very political and social usage, stigmatizing labels confirm the existence of a distinction in the society between full civil rights guaranteed to all and the definition of rights as social privileges extended to certain groups and denied to others. Although their original meanings have been long forgotten or are unknown by their users, ethnic labels become part of the struggle of both the socially privileged and the discriminated groups alike. Each seeks to redefine the process of establishing the social value of the group(s) with respect to the distribution of social resources and thus also the distance that separates one from the other. The struggle to point out the stigmatizing quality of the label becomes part of the struggle for social justice, as the black movements of the sixties, for example, made clear in demanding that the terms "Negro" and "colored people" be replaced by that of "Black" and later "African American."

While public policy imposes stigmatizing ethnic labels and reinforces a particular group's inferior status in society, from the point of view of the group itself, adoption of a common name is inseparable from political mobilization. A common name, no less than a stigmatizing label, may demand a homogenization, a uniformization of the group. In so doing, the group's constituency can become narrowed, whether as a function of the demands for political mobilization proper, of the character of the conflicts within the community and the larger social context, or of the demands and structure of the leadership. The effectiveness of a label such as Hispanic disseminated by government institutions, and indeed of all labels, relies at least partially on ensuring that both the broader society and the group members themselves internalize the connotations attributed to it. As a result, the group members have to overcome the larger political and social effects of the stigmas attached to the label in shaping their lives and relations with the broader society. But just as important, they must confront the label's negative connotations and stereotypes, which they too have invariably internalized. Some of the difficulties raised by this confrontation can be seen, for example, in Latinas' struggle to affirm themselves within the context of the predominantly white, middle-class women's movement. As Gloria Anzaldúa has noted, "We no longer allow white women to efface us or suppress us. Now we do it to each other." And she goes on to explain, "Even those of us who don't want to buy in get sucked into the vortex of the dominant culture's fixed oppositions, the duality of superiority and inferiority, of subject and object."[8]

Thus, because ethnic labels homogenize the group's internal diversity, factionalism may arise, combated by a rigid orthodoxy of unanimity. Conversely, special needs by segments of the constituency articulated to social, racial, national, gender, sexual preference, or age issues may well serve or bring about the very redefinition of the aims of the social movement. For ultimately what distinguishes a social label from a politically relevant community is the very nature of the latter's organization, as well as the history of its constitution as reflected in the lived experience and relations among the labeled population. The present dynamics within the Latino groups sometimes seem to suggest that the continued lack of recognition of the implications of differences within the group may ultimately hinder efforts to unite in the various and ongoing struggles for social justice.[9]

Thus, in undertaking this study my aim was to begin to think about a framework that might contribute toward disentangling our personal and cultural identities as Latinos in the United States (including allegiances to our particular national-origin groups) from the need to forge the political unity of our various groups under one umbrella term (whether *Hispanic* or *Latino*) in the search for full citizenship rights and social justice. Indeed, when Latin American immigrants' experiences of incorporation are examined against the historical presence and specific experiences of Chicanos and Puerto Ricans, one cannot help but wonder *why* such varied national-origin populations came to be lumped together as a homogeneous group in the early 1970s, such that their diverse nationalities, races, classes, histories, and languages are today subsumed under the "Made-in-the-U.S.A." label "Hispanic." To what extent, for example, does the Hispanic ethnic group actually exist as a distinct community *in the terms assumed by* the label's homogenizing connotations? And what meanings and social values do Latinos themselves attribute to the term Hispanic, through which they are invariably perceived as soon as they cross the border?

These are some of the questions that led to my research on the meaning(s) attributed to the ethnic label Hispanic and on the construction of the often different connotations and social values that non-Latinos and Latinos alike attribute to "being Hispanic" and "Hispanic ethnicity" in the United States. Political and cultural beliefs, like the customs and traditions shaped by race, class, gender, sexual preference, language, and national origins, are indeed significant for understanding Latinos' daily lives and relations with one another in the U.S. context. While scholarly works, for example, often briefly acknowledge the internal diversity of the group, its implications still remain largely unexplored: relatively little is known about Latinos' self-referential use of the term Hispanic in their daily lives, both in relation to people from Latin American nationalities not their own and to the non-Hispanic populations in the United States.

This book is thus motivated by several concerns, foremost among which is the need to think more deeply about the meaning of what Félix Padilla has called "Latinismo"[10]—the forging of unity among Latinos in the struggle for full citizenship rights and social justice in the United States. Equally important is the need to provide second and later generations of Latin American descent with a broader framework for examining the meaning and implications of their respective national, racial, linguistic, class, and gendered diversity in the process of constructing that unity. Regardless of their own birthplace or the time or way that their parents' respective national-origin groups were incorporated in this society, those born after 1970 represent the first generation born and raised in this country who have been specifically designated by mainstream institutions as "Hispanics" in the United States.

In the following chapters I explore the experience of biculturalism, bilingualism, and binationalism in the context of a society that has historically denounced social privileges even while in practice tolerating discrimination under the ideology of pluralism. Over the years, curiousity, research, study, and personal experiences in various national settings have led me to formulate questions about the differentiated interactions of race, class, and citizenship in shaping daily life throughout the Americas. What follows, then, is my understanding to date of how these dynamics were shaped by the dominant culture and society of the United States since the early contacts with Mexican and Puerto Rican populations, and how they are translated today by Latin American immigrants into the ethnic and racial hierarchy of the nation.

I focused the first part of this book on some historical aspects of the societies of Latin America and the United States in an attempt to locate and understand the roots of the conflict between the national and cultural identities of Latinos born or raised in the United States today, particularly as it affects their access to full citizenship rights. These aspects I believe can illuminate how culturally homogeneous perceptions and representations of the experiences of populations of Latin American descent could become commonplace today among scholars, government agencies, the media, and the public at large. Grouping populations from long-established Chicano and Puerto Rican communities with more recently arrived Latin American immigrants or political exiles under a homogenizing label raises various issues related to Latinos' citizenship and rights, and affects our understanding of diversity and of the implications of multiculturalism in U.S. society as a whole and in the Latino community in particular.

The second part of this book presents a study that stems from my observation that in the eyes of non-Latinos, Latin American immigrants seem to become "instant Hispanics" in the terms described above as soon as they cross the border into the United States. I wanted to examine how personal and social identities, marked as my own has been by previous socialization in Latin America, are affected by grouping diverse individuals as "Hispanics" in a particular setting in the ethnic and racial context of the United States. I interviewed men and women from nine different countries and Puerto Rico currently living and working in New York City. My focus here is on the ways that first-generation Latin Americans draw on their past experiences in their homelands as well as on their current social status and position to understand the meaning and social value of the label Hispanic in their lives in U.S. society. But as I explain more fully in the introduction to the study itself (see chapter 5), it is important to note that this research data and findings are by no means intended to be understood as representative of all Latinos in the United States. The study was undertaken as part of my doctoral degree work in which I used the qualitative techniques and methods drawn from the fields of anthropology, literature, and communication studies. My aim was specifically to examine the implications of class and race heterogeneity of a particular group of individuals *who had come together, by chance,* in the setting in which I conducted the study and who were defined as Hispanics in relation to the "non-Hispanics" therein. The need and decision to limit the size of my sample in this way was not without some consequences, however. I am aware, for example, of the absence in my research site— and hence in my study—of representatives of the significant Cuban community in the United States. The post-1960s establishment of this exile community, as well as its early racial, social, and political composition, contributed toward shaping this population's trajectory in U.S. society. And there is no doubt that the Cuban and Cuban American community is playing a more significant role both within the Latino population and in the nation as a whole—even as its own internal dynamics point to the increasing racial, social, linguistic, and ideological diversity within the group. Nevertheless, in undertaking this study I chose to focus on the larger consequences that the label Hispanic has in determining the lives and survival strategies of these particular people—arbitrarily grouped and small in number—in order to examine the validity of suggesting further research on the extent to which the use of the label obscures the class and racial dynamics of the interaction both within each group and between them and the society at large. I conclude with a discussion of the impact of homogenization on second and subsequent generations of Latinos and on the creation of new Latino identities in the United States. I also make some suggestions for further research to meet the consequences of the changing demographics of the nation.

This study was shaped by my continuing concerns about the meaning of citizenship and the need to broaden access and develop strategies to ensure full participation and social justice for all in the United States. I hope this book will in some way contribute to the dialogue on the meaning of Latinos' experiences as U.S. citizens and, more generally, toward broadening the understanding of the social value and implications of ethnic labels in shaping identity in the United States today.

Chapter 1

"Hispanics? That's What *They* Call Us"

A person is of Spanish/Hispanic origin if the person's origin (ancestry) is Mexican, Mexican-Am., Chicano, Puerto Rican, Dominican, Ecuadoran, Guatemalan, Honduran, Nicaraguan, Peruvian, Salvadoran; from other Spanish-speaking countries of the Caribbean or Central or South America; or from Spain.[1]

In the past two decades, the term *Hispanic* has come into general use in the United States to refer to all people in this country whose ancestry is predominantly from one or more Spanish-speaking countries. As a result, millions of people of a variety of national backgrounds are put into a single "ethnic" category, and no allowances are made for their varied racial, class, linguistic, and gender experiences. The term ignores, for example, the distinct and diverse experiences of descendants of U.S. conquest, such as the Chicanos, and those of the Puerto Rican populations, colonized by the United States at the turn of the century. Its users often neglect to contextualize the specific histories and cultures that differentiate these two groups, both from one another and from more recent immigrant arrivals, whether from Mexico, Central or South America, or the Spanish-speaking Caribbean nations. In so doing, longtime native-born U.S. citizens and residents are combined with more recently arrived economic immigrants who may have crossed the U.S. border yesterday.

The term Hispanic also lumps together recent political refugees from El Salvador with past political exiles like the first wave of Cubans who arrived in the early 1960s. The latter's upper- and middle-class status and racial composition in turn masks the differences between their entry process and experiences and those of the nonwhite working-class Cuban "Marielitos," for example, who arrived in 1980. Moreover, some exiles have today become economic immigrants like the contras and upper- and middle-class Nicaraguans who originally left their country soon after the Sandinista victory of 1979.

While most scholars limit their policy-related research on Latinos to populations with ties to Latin America, the U.S. government census definition that begins this chapter also includes European immigrants from Spain. In addition, the perceptions of the general population compound the sources of definitional confusion about the term Hispanic. Unlike government agencies and scholars, many are not aware of the political and cultural implications of the diverse backgrounds of those whom public opinion also unofficially classifies as Hispanics. Among these are the Brazilians who, because of their Portuguese heritage, share neither the language nor the culture of Spanish America, and hence rarely self-identify as "Hispanics."

In addition, the term homogenizes class experiences and neglects many different linguistic, racial, and ethnic groups within the different nationalities themselves: various indigenous populations, the descendants of enslaved Africans, waves of immigrant populations from every country in Europe, Asia, the Middle East. Members of these populations too are increasingly making their way to the United States, ensuring the growing visibility of Latin America's heterogeneity within the Latino populations in this country.[2]

In the current usage by the U.S. census, government agencies, social institutions, social scientists, the media, and the public at large, then, the ethnic label Hispanic obscures rather than clarifies the varied social and political experiences in U.S. society of more than 23 million citizens, residents, refugees, and immigrants with ties to Caribbean and Central and South American countries. It reduces their distinct relations among themselves and with U.S. society to an ethnic label that in fact fails to do justice to the variety of backgrounds and conditions of the populations to whom it has been applied. As Martha Giménez put it, the term Hispanic "strip[s] people of their historical identity and reduc[es] them to imputed common traits."[3]

Like other ethnic labels currently used to identify minority groups in this country, the term Hispanic raises the question of how people are defined and classified in this society and in turn how they define themselves in the United States. It points to the gap between the self-identification of people of Latin American descent and their definition through a label created and used by others.

The Label Hispanic: Problems of Definition

Insofar as the ethnic label Hispanic homogenizes the varied social and political experiences of more than 23 million people of different races, classes, languages, national origins, genders, and religions, it is perhaps not surprising that the meanings and uses of the term have become the subject of confusion and debate in the social sciences, government agencies, and much of the society at large. As C. Nelson and Marta Tienda noted, "Hispanic as a label combines colonized natives and their offspring, foreigners and political refugees under one ethnic umbrella, but the coherence of this label is questionable on theoretical and historical grounds."[4]

While some scholars have pointed to the political consequences of the debate on the term, others have analyzed the demographic implications of the various census definitions since the 1930s. Teresa Sullivan, for example, pointed to at least five elements, other than class, that also structure the diversity of the experience of this group, namely, national origins, time of arrival, language, race, and minority status.[5] Gender issues, too, continue to strongly affect the debates on the value of indiscriminately grouping people diversified by their sexual preferences, their race, and their class.[6] Addressing the elusiveness of the definition of the label Hispanic, Joan Moore and Harry Pachon raised the issue of whether the concept refers to a "racial minority or simply another predominantly Catholic ethnic group like the Italians for example."[7] And in assessing the policy implications of the term Hispanic, Pastora San Juan Cafferty and William McCready noted that today, "policies are created for Hispanics which help some and harm others because there are, in one sense, no generic Hispanics." They suggest that had policies for the new "Euro-ethnics" been established at the turn of the century in the same terms as they have been today, "it is likely that such a policy would have done more harm than good."[8]

Although many scholars have pointed to the inadequacy of the "umbrella" term Hispanic, there have been very few debates on the actual need for a "standardized terminology." Among the recent exceptions is the debate in the *Journal of Public Health* on the virtues of the government's use of "Hispanic" and the grassroots alternative designator "Latino." Yet this debate, too, shows that neither side questioned the merits of standardized terminology. Instead, the discussion focuses on *which* of the two terms is more accurate for describing populations of Latin American descent to health practitioners and policymakers.

In this debate, David Hayes-Bautista and Jorge Chapa defend the use of the term Latino and convincingly argue that the main unifying factor among the peoples of Latin American descent in the United States is political:

> The current debate over terminology of Latinos in the U.S. continues this 160-year-old conflict, sometimes verbal, sometimes armed, over Latin American identity. Only now, it is further recognized in Latin America, that a major element in current Latin American identity is the relation to the US. . . . In sum, we propose using a nationality-derived term, "Latino," to describe a geographically derived national origin group, that has been constantly and consistently viewed and treated as a racial group, in both individual and institutional interaction while in the United States.[9]

By suggesting the conscious choice of the term Latino they differentiate it from the imposed label Hispanic. At the same time, they use historical examples to recall that the Monroe Doctrine of 1823 effectively unifies Latin Americans, for to this day it determines the history of U.S. political and economic domination of the continent. They thus defend the use of "Latino" as a substitute for "Hispanic" in an attempt to embrace all Latin American nationalities, including those which neither have ties to Spain nor are necessarily Spanish-dominant groups—for example, Brazilians; second- and third-generation English-dominant U.S. citizens, particularly within the Chicano and Puerto Rican populations, as well as among the second and later generations of Latin American descent; English-speaking Panamanians; and various non-Spanish-speaking indigenous groups from diverse Latin American regions.

In his response to the arguments in favor of the term Latino, Fernando Treviño points to the advantage of continuing to use the now-known category Hispanic in ensuring the community access to much-needed resources and in making demands from the ethnically based policy structure of U.S. government. As a result, he argues for the maintenance of the term Hispanic, "so long as all the major national statistical data systems in this country identify Hispanics and not Latinos."[10] According to Treviño, the adoption of a new term would merely "add to the confusion" and would ultimately hinder Hispanics' competition with blacks and other groups for much-needed government resources. As he affirms, "My point here is that the continual suggestion of new labels only hurts our people." Treviño thus strongly advocates the continued use of the term Hispanic in spite of the confusion it perpetuates: "Like Representative Martinez [Democrat, California], I believe that after 30 years we have a pretty good idea of what a Hispanic is."[11]

But as Giménez suggested in her response to both sides of the terminology debate, some scholars have explicitly stated that there is no consensus on who or what a Hispanic is. She notes that critics of the label have argued instead that "this statistical construct has hardly any relation to the real world," and that "it vastly oversimplifies the situation. The heterogeneity of the Hispanic population reduces the term to a merely heuristic device."[12] Not surprisingly, Giménez is led to ask, "What can this or any other 'umbrella' term identify?" More important, she raises the question, "What is the meaning of the data gathered about this population?" Pointing to significant differences in the class and socioeconomic status both within and among the various nationality groups, Giménez strongly criticizes the assumption of homogeneity among Latinos and the search for a standardized term:

> The problem facing social scientists and public health specialists in trying to make sense of the data collected by federal, state, and other agencies is a problem not only of comparability but of meaning. . . . To speak about "Hispanic" fertility, child-rearing habits, health subculture, migration patterns, etc. is to engage in empty talk, at best, or in stereotyping. The heterogeneity of national origin groups, in turn, undermines generalizations about the entire group.[13]

At the same time, the reality and significance of ethnicity in structuring minority groups' access to better housing, to improved socioeconomic and educational resources, and to political power has also fostered recognition of a much-needed panethnic unity, or in Félix Padilla's apt expression, of "Latinismo," among sectors of the various groups. Indeed, notwithstanding the differences among the various groups under the ethnic label Hispanic, the post-1960 distribution and withdrawal of resources by the state in ethnic terms has led some scholars to identify the common grounds on which Latinos can and do forge panethnic unity. Padilla's seminal *Latino Ethnic Consciousness*, for example, explored the importance of Latinismo in the collaboration between Chicago's Mexican-American and Puerto Rican populations in the political struggle for equality and social justice. His work convincingly shows that "the expression of Latino ethnic conscious behavior is *situationally* specific, crystallized under certain circumstances of inequality experience shared by more than one Spanish-speaking group at a point in time." Padilla argues that the various national-origin sectors within the group can mobilize their communities through pointing to the inequalities they share. He notes that panethnic political unity among Latinos is also fostered by a state that has expanded through an emphasis on ethnicity and the competition for resources in those terms: "State expansion . . . has provided otherwise ununited, culturally distinct, resource-poor groups with clear objects for efficiently focusing their collective hostility and frustration." Yet Padilla is also careful to distinguish between situational Latinismo and the attribution of a fixed, static, and homogenizing identity of "Hispanic" to the populations of Latin American descent. As he says, "The Latino-conscious person sees himself as a Latino sometimes and as Puerto Rican, Mexican American, Cuban and the like at other times."[14]

Similarly, other scholars, like B. E. Aguirre and Rogelio Saenz, have recognized the political need for a panethnic unity among Latinos. In their assessment, "Latinismo is a historical fact, an outgroup label, and a dream of union which will never become a reality without social planning." Their focus is thus on the "organizational imperative" of Latino social movements, the need to construct the grounds through which the various groups come together under an umbrella term.[15] The works of these scholars raise questions about the role that ethnic labels such as "Hispanic" are playing today in challenging or reinforcing the social and political positions of the populations they encompass in U.S. society. Indeed, ethnic designators such as Hispanic, like terms such as black or African American, Native American, Arab American, Jew, Asian American, white European, point to the need to reexamine the ways in which the specific historical and social experiences of various groups have actually been shaped and interact in the present context.

Issues of Latino Integration: Historical Antecedents

The controversy and issues raised by the meaning and social value of the label Hispanic can best be understood in the context of recent debates in the area of ethnic and race studies. A key issue in the debates on ethnicity has been the role played by race as it is articulated with class and gender in the incorporation of various groups as "Americans" throughout the history of the nation. Scholars such as Werner Sollors, for example, argue that "ethnicity includes dominant groups and . . . race, while sometimes facilitating external identification, is merely one aspect of ethnicity." Others, like Michael Omi and Howard Winant, have focused more specifically on racial and racialized minorities to suggest that race, together with class and gender, has always been "at the very center of America's social and political history," stressing that at issue is the fact that the concept "has varied enormously over time without ever leaving the center stage of U.S. history."[16] In this book, I argue that race, as it is articulated with class and gender, is indeed essential to consider in understanding the shaping of ethnicity, as well as the varied meanings and social values that Latinos and non-Latinos alike have attributed both to being "Hispanic" in different historical periods and, more recently, to the ethnic label Hispanic.

There is no doubt that scholars and researchers in the field of ethnicity have made important contributions to the understanding of various aspects of past immigrants' integration into American society. In many cases, for example, they have provided significant historical data on particular old ethnic groups or case studies of their cultural processes of assimilation or integration.[17] Yet many working within the ethnicity paradigm today continue to use the assimilation experiences of the European immigrants of the past to argue in support of what Moynihan has called "patterns of ethnic succession." This perspective envisions the eventual integration and upward mobility of nonwhite groups.[18] In so doing, however, its proponents neglect the specificity of African Americans' historical experience in the United States, as well as several factors that are essential to consider when addressing the populations identified as Hispanic and that differentiate them from other groups in this country.

Indeed, recent works on various groups within the Latino populations have made clear that at least three major sources of differentiation between their experience and that of other groups in the United States must be acknowledged.[19] The first is the historical specificity of the Puerto Rican and Chicano populations within the Latino group. The second is the importance of recognizing the implications of the geopolitical factors in the hemisphere. And the third is the particular historical and economic conjuncture during which each group entered the United States—whether by conquest, colonization, or immigration.

Mario Barrera, for example, has detailed some of the implications of the regional nature of the American economy during the conquest of the Southwest, noting that until the 1830s, "it was not clear that the United States would be able to develop into a major industrial country." Thus, the Mexican-American War (1846-48), the conquest of Mexico's lands, and the annexation of Texas occurred during a period when the United States was seeking to expand its territory, to forge a national economy, and, in Barrera's words, "to establish the base for its future role as a major world power."[20]

Almost overnight, Mexicans living in northern Mexico's territories found themselves in the United States and confronted with the option of becoming U.S. citizens. Their role in building the transportation infrastructure of the emerging nation and in developing its mining and agricultural resources ensured that their early insertion into the nineteenth-century U.S. economy was to differ significantly from that of the Puerto Ricans, whose island and population were colonized fifty years later at the end of the Spanish-American War by the United States, which subsequently imposed U.S. citizenship on its population in 1917.

The military occupation of Puerto Rico after 1898 coincided with a period when the search for markets for its growing industrial production was of increasing concern to U.S. government officials and entrepreneurs alike. As one historian documented, "The Department of State explained that 'It seems to be conceded that every year we shall be confronted with an increasing surplus of manufactured goods for sale in foreign markets if American operatives and artisans are to be kept employed the year around.' "[21] Thus, according to Adalberto López, following the war, American capital quickly penetrated the island, "commercial relations between the United States and Puerto Rico grew rapidly, and the island quickly became one of the metropolis' most important overseas markets." By the mid-twentieth century, the effects of constant U.S. exploitation of the island's human and material resources had led to the massive migration of unemployed Puerto Ricans, lured by the postwar demand for labor on the eastern seaboard of the United States.[22]

The three decades following World War II were again characterized by economic growth and industrial expansion in the United States. Increasingly, manufacturing industries and plants relocated to other countries in search of both cheap labor and labor conditions unencumbered by government restrictions related to environmental concerns. Particularly since the early 1980s, the restructuring of the international economic order has caused U.S. society to experience the effects of a shrinking economy and a consequent gradual dwindling demand for unskilled labor. Annette Fuentes and Barbara Ehrenreich pointed to the changes in the global economy, noting their impact on women: "There are over one million people employed in industrial free trade zones in the Third World. Millions more work outside the zones in multinational controlled plants and domestically-owned subcontracting factories. Eighty to ninety percent of the light-assembly workers are women."[23]

The changes in the global economy and their impact on the U.S. labor market have significant implications for today's new immigrants from Latin American nations. They confront a steady decline of industries such as garment manufacturing, which have traditionally provided unskilled, entry-level jobs to newly arrived populations in the United States. Thus, these more recent immigrant groups cannot follow the kinds of labor market insertion open to earlier European groups—a significant historical difference that is often overlooked when comparing the integration of turn-of-the-century immigrants with those arriving today. In short, then, and beyond the specific cases of Puerto Rico and sectors of the Mexican-American populations, the particular historical and economic conjuncture during which the various Latin American populations are entering the country today has also differentially shaped each national group's experiences in the United States.

In addition, it is important to consider the effects on the post-1960s immigrants of political and geographic factors specific to the history of all the nations in the Western Hemisphere. These have also differentiated the experiences of more recent Latin American immigrants both from one another and from those of the European immigrants of the turn of the century. Unlike the populations arriving from Latin America, for example, past immigrant groups did not have to experience the effects of the historical presence and overwhelming impact of U.S. capital in their countries' economic development. They never had to confront the constant threat and sometimes reality of U.S. military intervention in their native lands (for example, Guatemala, 1954; Cuba, 1961; Dominican Republic, 1965; Nicaragua, 1980s; Panama, 1989), the overthrow or undermining of their democratically elected leaders (Chile, 1973), or the constant policing of their governments.[24]

Rather, the fate of more recent Latin American populations in this country has shown how deeply their immigration experience has been marked by the political relationships between the United States and their respective countries. The experiences of the Cuban community represent perhaps the clearest example in this respect, marked as it is by the differentiated treatment received by the early and later waves of immigrants from Cuba. It is a unique community among the Latino groups, in the sense that unlike the individualized immigration experiences of other Latin American populations, a large number of Cuban refugees arrived simultaneously at the beginning of the 1960s. Unlike other Latin American groups, the first wave of Cubans was largely composed of upper- and middle-class white Cubans who left their country after Fidel Castro came to power and who received a financially supportive welcome from the U.S. government. This allowed the Cubans from early on to establish the economic and political basis of a strong Cuban ethnic enclave in Miami, and contributed to their subsequent ability to integrate later waves of refugees, including the 125,000 working-class, nonwhite Marielitos, in many ways obviating the more hostile reception the latter received from the U.S. government in 1980.[25] Whether rich or poor, the relatively positive incorporation experiences of Cubans differ significantly from those of immigrants from other Latin American nations, such as the more recent Salvadoran refugees, who until recently were fleeing a U.S.-backed war in their country. Similarly, the Dominicans, who began to arrive in the New York area in increasing numbers following the 1965 revolution, were received in the United States as economic immigrants rather than political refugees. Their reception was conditioned by the role played by the United States in the 1965 revolution and, along with their class and racial composition, served to differentiate their immigration experience from the early Cuban community in Miami.

Once in the United States, then, political and geographical factors also differentiate the experiences of immigrants, residents, and citizens with ties to Latin America from those of previous immigrant groups. At the same time, those factors contribute to the complex relationship that Latinos establish today both among each other and with the state, government agencies, social institutions, and the non-Latino populations of the United States.

In view of their varied historical, economic, and geopolitical experiences and relations with the United States, as well as of their national, racial, linguistic, and class heterogeneity, the ethnic assimilation paradigm as a model for the study of Latinos as a homogeneous group must be reassessed. Referring to the terms of the debate on acculturation and pluralism as it applies to Puerto Ricans and Caribbean immigrants in New York City, Juan Flores has argued that "the problem is clearly more than a terminological one, for it has to do with detecting a developmental pattern leading neither to eventual accommodation nor to 'cultural genocide.' Beyond these two options . . . a more intricate structuring of ethnicity is evident."[26] Latin American elements in the Puerto Rican culture of New York, for example, are perceived as indicative of a broader expression of a third world colonial history of resistance. The different Latin American nationalities currently represented in the U.S. setting recognize this history as the root of their common heritage.[27] Highlighting the significance of recognizing the historical presence of Puerto Ricans and Chicanos in U.S. society, the authors of one report explain, "Hispanic resistance to assimilation is fueled by a consciousness of the wrongs of recent history. . . . Other migrants have never had to swallow the memory of territorial loss of their homeland to the United States to become committed United States citizens."[28]

Thus, some analysts emphasize the geopolitical and historical considerations that impinge on traditional expectations of what Omi and Winant have called the "immigrant analogy." Within this perspective, far from viewing the Latino experience as a continuation of the assimilation patterns of past European immigrants, various new interpretations of Latino ethnicity are emerging, some of which focus on what Gloria Anzaldúa first identified as the culture of the borderlands, to suggest the impact of transnationalism, multiculturalism, and bilingualism in people's lives.[29] The Spanish Caribbean and Latin American populations in this country, as Flores has noted, manifest instead "a markedly different process, one which is indeed pluralist and confluent in nature and perhaps for that reason even more challenging to established thinking on ethnic relations."[30]

Defining the Social Value of the Label Hispanic

Added to the specific historical, geographical, and political experiences that differentiate the Latinos from each other and from previous immigrant groups in the United States are new institutional trends related to ethnicity that also have an impact on the society as a whole and, specifically, on the construction of a homogeneous Hispanic group. The term Hispanic is used, for example, in formulating government policy; in designing advertising, media, and business strategies; and in elaborating educational and language policies.

The language issues raised by the growing presence of Latinos in the United States provide an extreme example of the potentially explosive impact on American institutional life of the label Hispanic and of the homogeneous ethnicity it attributes to people of Latin American descent. Indeed, the present battle over the English language, as exemplified by the English Only movements and the bilingual education debates, are indicative of the extent to which language choice and usage are increasingly significant in defining both social relations in contemporary U.S. society[31] and the debate on the grounds for affirming the nation's identity today. For while bilingualism, language policy, and usage have historically been issues of contention long evident in the educational system, language skills at the turn of the century were not as essential for jobs and survival as they are today.

Fueling the debates on the English Language Amendment, a 1986 special report by the Council for Inter-American Security emphasized that "Hispanics in America today represent a *very dangerous, subversive force* that is bent on taking over our nation's political institutions for the purpose of imposing Spanish as the official language of the United States."[32] Nevertheless, many policymakers and researchers stress that Latinos rarely support bilingual programs that do not also include English language learning—as Mr. Corrado told the House of Representatives in 1984:

> Whenever the debate centers on the issue of bilingual education, we repeatedly hear the insidious myth that most Hispanic children do not want to learn English and that their parents want them educated only in their native language. . . . I for one have never met a Hispanic parent or student who stood in favor of delaying acquisition of English.[33]

Specifically, the bilingual education debate and English Only movements have raised two related issues. The first concerns the role that language is playing in constructing or affirming the identity of the Hispanic ethnic group, for the Spanish language is commonly used as an identifier of Hispanics. The second concerns the role that language is increasingly playing in constructing representations about what constitutes an "American" national identity: this is a question that schools must address as they socialize not only the children of immigrants but also those of residents and citizens into U.S. society today.[34]

At the same time, the unprecedented valorization of the Spanish language and of the concept of Hispanic by both non-Latino and Latino advertising and business sectors shifts the social and cultural impact of the language, and the label, in a different direction. Gone are the days of the "Frito Bandito," an advertisement created by the Frito-Lay company in the late 1960s. As described in a U.S. Civil Rights Commission report, it featured a character who had "a Spanish accent, a long handlebar mustache, a huge sombrero, a white suit tightly covering a pot belly and he used a pair of six-shooters to steal corn chips from unsuspecting victims."[35]

Particularly in the past decade, an increasing number of established non-Hispanic businesses—such as large advertising agencies and the American corporate media—have begun to court the "Hispanic mar-

ket" aggressively. Corporate interests like AT&T and airline companies, as well as Hollywood, surveyed the Hispanic ethnic group and
courted its market through Spanish media and advertisements. Thus,
in spite of the alarmist views of English Only interest groups lobbying
for an English Language Amendment and against bilingual education,
U.S. businesses and advertising concerns are learning, as one study's
title put it, "to speak Spanish—the hard way."[36] As a recent, widely
used advertising study on Hispanics in the United States concluded,
"More of them think of themselves as 'Hispanics first, Americans second.' They place greater importance on perpetuating the Hispanic culture and language throughout succeeding generations, and are expressing a greater need for Hispanic media. . . . The results of the study
indicate that . . . the marketer could consider all Hispanics in aggregate
as a consumer segment."[37]

Statements such as this raise the issue of who is actually involved in
homogenizing the Hispanic ethnic group. Are marketers merely taking
advantage of an existing "group" as a potentially lucrative target
population? Or are their advertising strategies in fact helping to "de-
sign" the group, "invent" its traditions,[38] and hence "create" this homogeneous ethnic group?

The surge of Hispanic-related themes in Hollywood films such as
Fort Apache the Bronx, *Latino*, and *Crossover Dreams*, to name only three,
also points to a 1980s trend in Hollywood's interest in Hispanics—a
trend partially explained by Carlos Cortéz in terms of the mid-1960s
era of "ethnic revival." Carlos Cortéz notes that Hollywood realized
that "ethnicity is good box office, particularly when tinged with sen-
sationalism," adding that the result was the emergence of "the greatest
boom in ethnic theme motion pictures since the early days of the twentieth century."[39]

While advertising and business concerns are actively seeking entry
into what they perceive as a "lucrative Hispanic market," Hispanics
are simultaneously being categorized as "low-income people" who
confront "unusual poverty and unemployment."[40] Indeed, Latinos are
increasingly associated with high numbers of school dropouts, rising
rates of teen-age pregnancies, crime, drugs, AIDS, and other social ills
of this society, leading the New York State Governor's Advisory Committee on Hispanic Affairs to state, "As the full public hearings re-
vealed, and this report describes, the situation of the majority of Hispanics in New York State is extremely troubling. The same basic issues
emerge again and again."[41]

While social labels may be relatively inoffensive in and of themselves, they clearly point to the varied ways in which group representations are constructed by different sectors within the society. From the perspective of the dominant society, for example, Hispanic ethnicity is perceived as welfare-ridden, AIDS-ridden, drug-ridden, dropout-ridden, teen-age-pregnancy-ridden—hence, "Hispanics" become a "social problem." From the perspective of business entrepreneurs, however, the term "Hispanic ethnicity" identifies a lucrative market segment and good box office—in this context, then, those labeled as Hispanics are created as consumers. Moreover, some scholars have pointed to the growing numbers of the Hispanic community as indicating that Latinos constitute "a growing force to be reckoned with," suggesting that its potential unity makes it a powerful voting block.[42] In this situation, the label constructs "Hispanics" as citizens. In short, Hispanic ethnicity has shifting political, economic, social, and cultural meanings and values. Latinos are perceived primarily in terms of assumed patterns of cultural behavior, of stereotypes reinforced by vaguely defined and ahistorical interpretations of the meaning of "Hispanic ethnicity" in the U.S., whether as consumers they actually consume "Hispanic products" or not, whether as citizens they vote for politicians who happen to be Latinos or Latinas, or whether those who are forced to drop out of school in fact do so because of the socioeconomic context of their lives.

Even many among those who recognize the need for specificity in the interest of scientific accuracy and policy-oriented data research often seem to neglect the empirical evidence of significant socioeconomic and cultural diversity among the populations labeled Hispanics. As Giménez put it, "It is fascinating to observe how those writing about 'Hispanics' (discussing policy issues, or reporting research findings and vital statistics) do so while fully cognizant (with exceptions) of intrapopulation variations of such magnitude as to render statements about 'Hispanics' in general either meaningless or suspect."[43]

The broad, undefined usage of this ethnic label by sectors of the Latino and non-Latino populations alike points to at least two phenomena in American life today:

1. The use of ethnicity in shaping the understanding and trends of the institutions and social life in the United States; and its corollary:
2. The importance of a Hispanic "ethnic-community" context, *albeit undefined*, into which a heterogeneous immigrant, resident, and citizen population is expected—by government agencies, social institutions, the media, the non-Hispanic public, and even longtime resident

Hispanics—to mold itself as an indicator of its integration into U.S. society.

In view of the seemingly obvious discrepancies between the homogeneity assumed by the term Hispanic and the diversity of the population it encompasses, I examine in the following chapters the relationship between the emergence of this ethnic label, its use as a way of categorizing the populations it encompasses, and the value attributed to it by both Latinos and non-Latinos alike.

The approach I have adopted is thus quite different from one traditional perspective on U.S. society and seeks to dialogue with another one: The first refers to the melting pot concept, which assumes that immigrants shed their cultural values and ways and adopt a putative Anglo-American identity. It is an approach that, as I argue in chapter 2, is quite problematic, given the shifting boundaries of national identity and its meanings in this country.

The second approach with which I dialogue is the idea that the United States is made up of a plurality of ethnic groups. My framework parts company with this perspective's essentially sequential understanding of ethnic groups' integration into U.S. society. As I argue in chapters 3 and 4, it is important to take into account two additional dimensions that are not always fully considered by ethnicity theorists: the first is the dynamics forged by the *articulated interaction* of class, race, and gender in shaping people's access to citizenship rights and political inclusion; the second is the contemporary transnational context within which national identities are being reconstituted and ethnic identities are being shaped in the United States.

In the first part of this book, then, I have sought to demonstrate the need to examine the specificity of the experiences of Chicanos and Puerto Ricans in the United States. I argue that following the 1960s movements by both groups, their respective experiences as historical minorities in the United States were in fact thrown back into invisibility through the emergence of the label Hispanic in the early 1970s.

In the second part of the book, I look at the effects of the term Hispanic in the lives of other Latinos, who are *not* members of these two historical minority groups. Specifically, I present the results of a study I conducted in New York City on the meanings and social values that a group of Latin American immigrants and Puerto Ricans (both island- and mainland-born) attributed to the term Hispanic in their lives. Thus, their responses to the ethnic label Hispanic were shaped by their backgrounds in Latin American countries. I argue that differences in the ways that race and class are understood by more recently arrived Latin American immigrants are important to consider in assessing the issues that contribute toward or hinder the fostering of what B. E. Aguirre and Rogelio Saenz have called a "Latino Culture" in the U.S. context.[44]

As I suggested in the Introduction, ethnic labels by their very nature are used ahistorically, yet they incorporate specific social contradictions that their emergence and dissemination may originally have intended to quell. The study shows that insofar as all people of Latin American descent are today identified by the state as Hispanics in the United States, the experiences of more recent Latin American immigrants cannot be understood without serious consideration of the context of historical discrimination shaped in relation to Chicanos and Puerto Ricans.

Ultimately, as I argue throughout, it is in recognizing the specificity of the diverse histories and experiences of the population identified as Latinos in the United States that we can begin to better understand our own multiculturalism. It will also more forcefully contribute to addressing the future of Latinos in the United States.

"So Far from God, So Close to the United States": The Roots of Hispanic Homogenization

Given the diversity of the various population groups both in Latin America and in the United States, how *did* the culturally homogeneous representations of people identified as Hispanics become commonplace among scholars, government agencies, the media, and the public at large in this country? Popular reasoning about the origin of the term Hispanic usually locates it within the legacy of the Spanish conquest and colonization of the New World.[1] After all, the justification goes, Spanish colonial rule lasted for over three centuries, certainly long enough for the social, ethnic, linguistic, racial, and national experiences of the populations of Latin America and the Caribbean to establish a homogeneous heritage.

But in Latin America itself, the role of the Spanish legacy in shaping a common cultural identity on the continent has been the subject of ongoing debates since that region's independence in the early nineteenth century. Underlying these discussions is the recognition that in spite of the shared Spanish colonial heritage, there are profound differences in the various nations' postindependence histories and populations that often override cultural or linguistic commonalities they may also share. In many ways, then, the issue of the creation of a unified cultural—and even political and economic—"Hispanic identity" in the United States actually transports to this country a debate that Latin American intellectuals have themselves waged since the nineteenth century in historical essays, social science texts, and their respective national literatures.[2]

Thus I suggest that the definition and uses of the term Hispanic in the United States cannot be sought in its Spanish colonial heritage or even in Latin American antecedent debates. Instead, its meanings and social value must be found through exploring the specific context of U.S. society that fostered the emergence of this ethnic label as an ideological construct—a label that is thus specific to the political and daily life of this nation, to its past ideological self-image and identity as a "melting pot" of immigrants, and to its current redefinitions as an "ethnic mosaic."[3]

I begin with a brief overview of the racial and social dynamics developed during Spain's rule in the Americas, to explore the ways these shaped the social and racial hierarchies of colonial society, such that they continued to differentiate the image, status, and relations of various ethnic, social, and racial groups in postindependence Latin America. Although a historical account is certainly not the aim of this chapter, it is important to note some of the ways that the significance of these differentiations were manifested in relation to the United States at different points during the nineteenth century—how varied social sectors within the Mexican and Puerto Rican populations, shaped in the context of the Spanish colonial heritage, responded to the expansionism of the United States in Mexico and the Caribbean, respectively. As I suggest in this chapter, internal social and racial group differentiations notwithstanding, people of Latin American descent in the United States have long been perceived homogeneously as "foreign" to the image of "being American" since the nineteenth century, regardless of the time and mode of their incorporation into the United States or their subsequent status as citizens of this nation.

Indeed, insofar as the understanding of the U.S. national identity is invariably defined and shaped in relation to those conceived as "foreign Others" in the hemisphere, it is perhaps not surprising that in a period in which an increasing number of new nations were being established in the Americas, the contacts between this country and the newly formed Latin American national populations contributed toward creating representations in the United States of a unified image of the "American national community." Thus, I argue that the nation's identity was forged in the nineteenth century *partially* through the creation of racialized perceptions that homogenized Latin America's populations and that in turn set the context for the later emergence of the label Hispanic in the twentieth century. Based on the development of ideologies that justified the expansionist actions of the United States in Latin America and the Caribbean, these perceptions reflected a peculiar fusion of the social status, race, and nationality of "foreign Others" in the hemisphere.

Domestically, and particularly in the years following the Civil War, imagined boundaries of inclusion and exclusion in the national community were also being institutionalized through legalizing segregationist practices and customs in relation to previously enslaved African Americans. Thus, the community of *Americans* came to be imagined as white, Protestant, and Anglo-Saxon, despite the presence not only of non-Anglo-Saxon and Catholic Europeans, but also of native Americans and African Americans, as well as Asians, Caribbeans, and Latin Americans of varying classes, races, and national origins.

The nineteenth-century fusion of the race and nationality of "foreign Others" both at home and in the hemisphere as a whole thus came to justify the systematic exclusion of nonwhite, non-Anglo-Saxon minorities from "being American." By the twentieth century, this was to ensure that regardless of citizenship status, non-white-European racial minorities born in the United States could continue to be conceived in the popular mind as outside of the "boundaries" of the "American" community.[4] It is important to reiterate that what follows is not intended to be a history of the period and that I am wary of oversimplification in intergroup relations, which perhaps inevitably arise from trying to synthesize complex ideas about the past. I am fully aware, for example, that the following discussion omits both the complex diversity within the "white European" population and an account of the multiple links and nuances that have always existed in individual relationships between white Europeans and minority groups in the United States. Similarly, I have omitted discussion of the complex relations between Mexicans and the various indigenous populations in the region. I want to emphasize, however, that my aim here is in no way to provide a history of the period or of the various groups' interrelations but rather to suggest some of the nineteenth-century issues that I believe should be considered in seeking to understand both the grounds for the mobilizations of the Chicanos/Mexican Americans and Puerto Ricans during the civil rights period and the emergence of and response(s) to the label Hispanic. More specifically, I want to show that the early fusion of race and nationality was to provide important grounds for defining the particular forms of mobilization that non-white-European minorities adopted in their struggles to achieve political and cultural inclusion during the 1960s.

The Legacy of Spain in Latin America

There is no doubt that the newly formed Latin American republics of the early nineteenth century inherited a highly stratified social order from three hundred years of Spanish colonial rule.[5] The conquistadores who went to the New World were not the hidalgos or Spanish lords who, as unquestioned rulers of their feudal estates, owned large tracts of land and oversaw the labor and lives of serfs who in turn were born and died in servitude on their estates. But neither were they members of the poorest sectors in the Spanish society of their day. Rather like the law-school dropout Hernán Cortés (conqueror of Mexico) or Francisco Pizarro (conqueror of Peru), the son of a pig-herder, they were members of a small emerging middle sector of peasants and artisans who basically had very little, if anything, to lose and much to gain from leaving Spain to go to the New World.[6]

Once in the New World, the Crown provided them with both temporary land grants and indigenous laborers in recognition of their honor and bravery in their conquest and settlement of far-off lands. As Carlos Fuentes has noted, it is perhaps not surprising then that the Spaniards who settled in Latin America sought the privileges and status of the hidalgos and recreated the semifeudal hierarchical arrangements of the society they had left behind. But it is important to note that "*hidalguia* does not mean hard work. Quite the contrary, it means not having to labour with your hands; it means winning glory in the field of battle and then receiving the reward for your effort in lives and lands that should work for you."[7]

The Crown's control of this "new aristocracy" in the New World was partially guaranteed by its imposition of limits on the land grant terms, which meant both that these could eventually revert back to the Crown and that not all Spaniards remained at the top of the social hierarchy.[8] But it also meant that complex, regionally specific racial, social, and cultural arrangements were developed over three hundred years of colonial rule as the settlers and their descendents sought ways of reinforcing property ownership patterns and semifeudal labor relations on the agricultural haciendas, ranches, and mines.[9]

For the most part, distinctions between Christians and pagans had been erased early on by the relatively quick conversion of the indigenous populations. As these early religious grounds for separation between the ethnic groups disappeared, colonial master-slave relations were superimposed on a racial order that became increasingly diversified through both miscegenation and the introduction of the African slave trade.[10] Thus, exploitation of both the indigenous populations and the enslaved Africans was not limited solely to their labor, for the presence of both these groups also served to reinforce the class and racial status they and their offspring afforded the New World's Spanish rulers. Throughout the colonial period, factors such as the higher ratio of men to women and various laws addressing intermarriage and interracial relations as a whole did nothing to diminish the ongoing raping and violation of indigenous and black women.[11] As Richard Morse and others have noted, however, they did ensure that the racial composition and the consequent rigid hierarchies of colonial Spanish America were ultimately determined not by strict segregation, but rather by *miscegenation*, the mixing of white Europeans, Indians, and Africans.[12] Indeed, to the extent that Spain's conquest of the Americas can also be seen as the conquest of women, as Magnus Morner suggests, the large numbers of "half-breeds" meant that the term *mestizo* in a deeply Catholic context was negatively appraised as a synonym for "illegitimate."[13]

As a result of extensive miscegenation throughout the colonies, racial classifications, social status, and honor evolved into a hierarchical arrangement that Alejandro Lipschütz has called a "pigmentocracy."[14] As Ramón Gutiérrez has described, this was a racial system whereby whiter skin was directly related to higher social status and honor, while darker skin was associated both with "the physical labor of slaves and tributary indians" and, visually, with "the infamy of the conquered."[15] Morner has explained that this extreme color consciousness was often accompanied by equally complex legal and social restrictions concerning marriage, taxes, residential settlement, and inheritance. Intermarriage among whites, "pure mestizos," and Indians, for example, was permitted—increasingly so, toward the end of the colonial period—but marriage of "pure bloods" to blacks and mulattoes required the authorities' permission. And, insofar as miscegenation, particularly among the lower sectors of the hierarchy, was also perceived as a real or potential threat to the established order, Afro-Indian marriages were strictly forbidden.[16] The Spanish notion of *pureza de sangre* or purity of blood was thus embedded in the New World aristocracy's understanding of the interrelated concepts of race, social status, and honor. And, although upper-class families adhered to it more rigidly, as Richard Griswold del Castillo notes, the patriarchal authority men derived from it, regardless of race or social status, was maintained through the corporativist ideology of the family's honor and respect—ensuring in the process the subordination of the women of all races and classes.[17]

As a result, Morner concludes that miscegenation in Latin America never necessarily meant either social or racial assimilation. Rather, as

Morse explains, the gradated system of color prejudices was interwoven with the perceived status of different groups' social function in a highly rigid and entrenched corporativist hierarchy. Many of its remnants are still in evidence in Latin American societies even today.[18] Similarly, the colonies' semifeudal hierarchies and status arrangements, the disdain for racial and social inferiors, the continued violation of indigenous and black women, and the prevailing dominant ideology of contempt for manual labor ensured that the rancor between the races—although often disguised as class prejudice—was not to be so easily dismissed, even by the new Latin American republics formed in the early nineteenth century. Although at the end of the wars of independence several of the new national governments abolished all laws that made distinctions among the various ethnic and racial groups and some made concerted efforts to integrate their respective nations, the assessment of one Mexican intellectual in 1865 was to hold true for much of Latin America well into the twentieth century:

> The white is a proprietor, the Indian a proletarian. The white is rich, the Indian poor, and miserable. The descendants of the Spaniards have all the knowledge of the times within their reach . . . the Indian is ignorant of everything. . . . The white lives in the city in a splendid house, the Indian lives in isolation in the countryside in a miserable hut. . . . There are two peoples in the same territory. What is worse, these peoples are to a certain degree mutual enemies.[19]

Almost one hundred years later, the commentary of race and ethnic relations in Peru by the famous novelist and anthropologist José María Arguedas reinforced this earlier observation and in many ways summarizes the racial, ethnic, social, linguistic, and regional divides that today continue at least partially to hinder both the integration of Latin America's respective nations and the construction of the unity of the continent's populations: "I believe there would be less distance between the czar of Russia and a peasant than between [an Andean] villager of Andahuaylas (my native village) and any of the presidents of Peru."[20]

It is perhaps not surprising then that several contemporary noted scholars insist that the unity of the continent hinges both on the social and economic incorporation into the Latin American nations of populations marginalized since colonial times and on the political recognition of the ethnocultural diversity of the region. While most agree that integration is an imperative, as Juan Odonne has stated, the "regional reality of the continent is a goal that is still far from being achieved."[21]

In many ways, Latin Americans' understanding of the racial and social hierarchy continues to be based on "a black-white continuum," to
borrow Peter Wade's expression, one in which money can "whiten"
people through intermarriage.[22] Yet this perception often undermines
the extent to which lack of citizenship rights and continued discrimination has remained tied to historical prejudices against the racial and
social status of indigenous people and blacks. The consequent articulation of race, social status, and religiously grounded beliefs of family
honor and respect has thus at least partially contributed to the current
problems in achieving the continent's full integration.

The Clash of Cultural Hierarchies: Race and Class in Latin America and the United States

The significance of the attitudes and perceptions about race and social
status shaped in colonial Latin America for understanding the sudden
and violent incorporation of Spanish-speaking populations into the
U.S. social hierarchy can perhaps best be exemplified through pointing
to some of the differences in the ways that rich and poor Mexicans responded to the conquest and penetration of what were once Mexico's
territories in the Southwest. After all, the 1846-48 Mexican-American
War and its aftermath contributed to setting the stage both for what has
since become a continuous clash in the construction and cultural perception of the racial and social hierarchies of the United States and
Latin America, and the consequent homogenizing of "Hispanics" in
this country.

In political and economic terms, land ownership was certainly one
key point of contention between Anglo settlers and conquered
Mexicans—rich or poor—in the aftermath of the war. Many of the
Mexicans who had decided to accept U.S. citizenship and stay in the
United States, as stipulated by the Treaty of Guadalupe Hidalgo,
sought to retain ownership of their lands, appealing to the U.S. courts
of law to uphold their property rights. While many won their cases,
hundreds were ultimately displaced from their lands—whether as a result of unscrupulous lawyers and unfair judicial practices, of pressure
to give up the land, or of confusion about their titles and the new land
laws and language.[23] At the same time, "Mexican hating" (to use Ronald Takaki's expression) also justified the systematic expropriation of
many Mexican small village farmers' communally owned grazing
lands (*ejidos*) and underlay the eventual political and social subordination of large sectors of the Chicano populations.[24]

But, as Mario Barrera noted, insofar as all Mexicans were not members of the upper echelons at the end of Spanish colonial society and thus did not have "an equal stake" in the land, "not all Mexicans were seen or treated as inferior" in the immediate aftermath of the war. In southern California, New Mexico, Arizona, along the Texas border, and elsewhere, sectors of the landed elite families (*los ricos*) struggled in different ways to remain in control of their power and wealth, reinforcing their commitment to the traditional castelike social hierarchy inherited from Spain. Early nineteenth-century Yankee immigrants in California, for example, had had to contend with the political and economic power of the two hundred ruling *Californio* families who controlled 14 million acres of land and thus the lives of a considerably larger number of agricultural laborers.[25] Many of the *ricos* forged alliances with the growing numbers of "Anglos," whether through their collaboration and political alliances with the new Anglo officials, through strengthening their economic ties with the emerging Anglo business classes in urban areas, or through intermarriage or court cases or both. Others essentially sought to become brokers for the communities of small farmers, shepherds, serfs, and villagers in the rural Southwest.[26]

Sectors of the latter in turn sometimes banded together to prevent the enclosure of their traditional communal lands by Anglos and their allies among the Mexican elites.[27] But by the end of the century, as Sarah Deutsch has recently shown, structural economic changes had forced many of the poorer Mexican populations to become seasonal migrant workers, establishing in the process new villages in which both kinship and shared economic and cultural ties were reinforced, particularly by women, in regional communities spread out over hundreds of miles. This too contributed to the development of villagers' strategies of resistance to the presence of Anglos throughout the Southwest, as the regionally based autonomous communities and economic systems allowed *los pobres* a relative independence from exploitative labor conditions, as well as the survival of their culture and language.[28]

Anglos in Texas, whether merchants or officials, were for their part, as David Montejano has noted, "quite adept at drawing the distinction between the landed 'Castilian' elite and the landless Mexican."[29] But although the old ruling families tried to protect their status and power in their respective communities, by the 1920s the continuous flow of new Anglo settlers in the region, along with the period's changed economic context, had made even this distinction obsolete. *Los ricos* often incorporated the prevailing Spanish-American "aphorism about color and class"—"money whitens"—in the strategies they developed to cope with the increasing decline of their fortunes during the second half of the nineteenth century and with the racial, segregationist-based attitudes that had developed in Anglo society. But it is important to note, as Montejano suggests, that this also meant that "the only problem for upper-class Mexicans was that this principle offered neither consistent nor permanent security in the border region."[30]

As their wealth decreased toward the end of the century, sectors of the elites of New Mexico increasingly began to refer to themselves as Hispanos—perhaps the earliest period in which the term was widely used in the United States, specifically as a response to the American social and racial context. Although, as Gonzales suggests, they were not to fully deny their Mexican origins until the early years of the twentieth century, in adopting the term Hispano they were emphasizing not their racially miscegenated, mestizo origins, but rather their specific class-based descent from the original "pure-blooded" Spanish conquistadores who settled in New Mexico. The translation of Hispano in this case would thus *not* be Hispanic but rather, as Rodolfo Acuña states, "Spanish American," for "according to them, New Mexico was isolated from the rest of the Southwest and Mexico during the colonial era; thus, they remained racially pure and were Europeans, in contrast to the mestizo (half-breed) Mexicans."[31]

In this sense, what Carey McWilliams called the "fantasy heritage" of racial purity adopted by *los ricos* was, as Acuña suggests, more likely a strategy to retain power and status based on their understanding of the Anglo racial hierarchy than actual fact for, as in the rest of Spanish America, New Mexico's colonizers, too, had mixed with and exploited indigenous populations such as the Pueblo in the region.[32] By the early part of this century, prejudice and discrimination against Mexicans had increased such that the term "Spanish American" had become widely used among the Spanish-speaking elites in the United States, particularly by the New Mexican *ricos*. "Money whitens," and thus, insofar as they were rich and considered themselves to be white, by the early twentieth century the *ricos* had adopted it to distinguish themselves in the context of Anglo society from the *mexicanos pobres*: "You don't like Mexicans, and we don't like them either, but we are Spanish-Americans, not Mexicans."[33] Similarly, as David Montejano notes, the influx of Mexican farm laborers recruited to work in the expanding commercial farming industry of Texas ultimately "eroded the centuries-old class structure of the Mexican ranch settlements," reducing the Mexican populations of the region "to the status of landless and dependent wage laborers." He goes on to describe the bitterness of the Mexican elite as they responded to their process of exclusion from the national community. The cumulative effects on upper-class Texas Mexicans in the early decades of the century were recorded by Jovita Gonzales:

> We, Texas-Mexicans of the border, although we hold on to our traditions, are proud of our race, are loyal to the United States, in spite of the treatment we receive by some of the new Americans. Before their arrival, there were no racial or social distinctions between us. Their children married ours, ours married theirs, and both were glad and proud of the fact. But since the coming of the 'white trash' from the north and middle west we felt the change. *They made us feel for the first time that we were Mexicans* and that they considered themselves our superiors.[34]

Given the Spanish colonial legacy in the Americas, it is perhaps not surprising that the general disdain of some ruling elite families for "Mexicans"—understood in the pejorative class-based terms adopted from the Anglos—also prevailed in what were once Spanish colonies and later Mexico's northern territories. In cultural and racial terms, then, the postwar period was to bring a shift from an initial confrontation to a gradual overlapping of two very different social hierarchies, which reflected differences in the ways race relations and social status were understood. The postindependence Latin American hierarchy within which Mexican *ricos* and *pobres* were socialized was based on rigid social and racial hierarchical arrangements stemming from the Spanish and Catholic colonial heritage.

The social and status hierarchy in the United States was instead forged concomitantly with the construction of the nation's identity based on the belief in white, Anglo-Saxon, and Protestant superiority. As a result, and notwithstanding Mexicans' adherence to the social and racial dynamics that once differentiated their status and power in Spanish colonial and postcolonial societies, they, like other Latin American populations, came to be perceived homogeneously, and as culturally and racially inferior in the U.S. context. As Leonard Pitt noted, eyewitness accounts of the gold rush years in California, for example, documented the prevalence among Anglos of condescending Protestant attitutes toward Catholics, of the republican traditional loathing of aristocratic attitudes such as those held by the Mexican ruling elites, and of the idea of the nation's "manifest destiny," the upholding of the Protestant work ethic, and the general discomfort with interracial settings.[35]

In fact, as I argue in the following sections, this was partially due to the domestic boundaries of membership in the national community. These had been largely shaped by the presence and legalized segregation of native-born blacks, such that the nation's self-definition and public image in relation to "foreign Others" could be invoked primarily in white-only terms. The subsequent forms of incorporation of Mexicans and later of Puerto Ricans were also defined in these terms. At the same time, they simultaneously excluded people of Latin American descent from the black/white framework through which the national community of citizens came to be imagined, and differentiated their experience from that of African Americans after the Civil War.

The underlying religious, racial, and social bases of colonial Latin America's history of miscegenation and consequent racial continuum were in sharp contrast to the black/white divisions. As Peter Wade points out, the latter divisions were to legitimize the oppression of blacks as a specific group in the United States and also to allow for their subsequent politicization in those terms in the 1960s.[36]

Considerations on Images of Community of the United States

As more new nations joined the United States in the hemisphere during the early nineteenth century, the problems of establishing the imagined community of the United States, defining its boundaries, ensuring its national integration, and constructing the identity of its racially diverse and hierarchically structured population also had to be addressed by the United States. Indeed, as Benedict Anderson suggested, nations are culturally constructed artifacts, imagined as communities by their populations. The way in which people imagine their national community is thus just as important in determining their experiences in their society as is their recognition of the limits of their nation set by its boundaries and the sovereignty that ensures them their freedom.[37]

But contrary to the nation-building policies adopted by some of the other emerging nations in the hemisphere, the issue of defining an American nationality was actually compounded by the fact that being an American had never really been solely conceived in terms of birthplace. The melting pot, a term first coined in 1909, had initially served to encapsulate the belief that the combined effects of the egalitarian ideals of the United States and the mixing of all immigrant and ethnic cultures during the previous centuries had in fact created a *new* "American" culture. But in the course of the twentieth century, it became increasingly clear that being "American"—and hence American culture, as symbolized by the term *melting pot*—had long been imagined exclusively in white Anglo-American cultural terms.[38] Insofar as "Anglo-conformity" had been the prevailing ideology of assimilation throughout much of the nation's history, as Milton Gordon suggested in 1964, the (racial) terms of exclusion of African Americans and Native Americans had in fact been established long before the term *melting pot* was actually popularized.[39] Hence, it is perhaps not surprising that the rejection by racial minority groups of the melting pot metaphor during the 1960s represented the *beginnings* of a struggle to shift the way the U.S. community of citizens had come to be imagined. "In the blunt words of one black intellectual: 'There never was a melting pot; there is not now a melting pot; there never will be a melting pot; and if there ever was, it would be such a tasteless soup that we would have to go back and start all over!' "[40]

Two years after Gordon's study, Joshua Fishman explained why the belief in assimilation and de-ethnization of immigrant populations has persisted for so long, suggesting that as a society of immigrants, the United States was essentially representative of a nation whose ("American") nationality had no ethnic roots itself. As a result, for all immigrants after the Puritans, "the Americanizing process itself takes on a central role in the formation of the national identity and the national self-concept of most Americans." Hence the relevance of negotiating the role of ethnicity in ensuring "assimilation," in creating an *American* national identity, an *American* ethnic-nationalism.[41]

Becoming an American has always also been, to use Eric Hobsbawm's apt phrase, "an act of choice" both by the individual and by the national society. But, while the former may decide to make the ideological choice to become Americanized, the latter could also "choose" whether to accept him or her into the national community and to support the extension of full citizenship rights. Throughout the nation's history, representatives of the society's institutions have emerged again and again with the power to recreate the "American public" and its "opinion" in their discourse. In the process they contributed toward setting the terms of the debates on individuals' inclusion or exclusion from various aspects of the national community and its social and political life.

Key to understanding these debates, as they were to affect both the meaning and value of ethnicity more generally and the development of the racialized basis of the incorporation of Latin American populations in the United States, is the role played by the particular form of exclusion of African Americans from the nation's population.[42] Unlike all other groups in this country, the very basis of African Americans' historical struggle for human and civil rights is rooted in slavery. Thus, the specificity of their history contrasts markedly with the terms of the historical public debates on inclusion of people of Latin American descent. Regardless of the prejudices and racialized discrimination against the latter, they did not have to contend with the political and socioeconomic consequences of enslavement. Instead, the situation of Latinos entailed the disentangling of the conflation of their race and national origins in their political struggle for political and civil rights. These have long been identified with various social and economic policy issues, particularly as these impact on public opinion about their presence in the United States. As a report to the secretary of labor detailing each Latin American country's racial composition concluded in 1925:

> It is the economic argument which chiefly has made a welcome to these immigrants to the United States and the economic argument for immigration has always been dangerous. No man is a worker alone. He is also a citizen and must further be viewed as the father of more citizens also. The years of his service as a wage earner are limited; not so the span of time in which those of his blood will play their parts in the country."[43]

And, more recently, educational questions closely tied to the historical debates on the national language have been added to long-held concerns about immigration. Ernest L. Boyer, president of the Carnegie Foundation for the Advancement of Teaching, appealed to American public opinion to once again rethink its stance on allowing non-English-speaking foreigners to immigrate into the United States. He noted that the national community's social tensions in the mid-1980s were now signified by bilingual education—a "code word," he argued, that had turned the schools into the "battle ground" of the nation.[44]

Although appeals to public opinion have often been used to cultivate national pride in the nation's self-image as a land of immigrants, instilling fear of the real or imagined consequences of introducing foreign ways into American life has at times also contributed to defining the national identity of the United States. In this sense, Hobsbawm's historical perspective perhaps provides a more useful approach than Boyer's to explain the issues involved in past and current debates on the question of immigrants and the "making of Americans," as well as in understanding the incorporation of racial minorities as "Americans" into the "national community." Focusing on the 1870-1914 period, Hobsbawm argues that the concept of Americanization as "an act of choice," as a "decision to learn English, to apply for citizenship—and a choice of specific beliefs, acts and modes of behavior"—implied the concept of "un-Americanism." Emphasizing the significance of distinguishing between people's status in the nation and their lack of patriotism, he notes that unlike the case in many other countries during that period in the United States (as in Germany), a person's lack of patriotism "threw doubt on his or her actual status as member of the nation"[45]—a doubt, one might add, that has often been raised throughout this century, regardless of the style in which the American nation's "public opinion" has variously reimagined "un-Americanism" over time.[46]

The forms of mobilization that minority groups adopted during the 1960s exemplify the response by specific racial groups to their status in the nation. While originally conceived in different ways, the response was embedded in the style in which mainstream society had imagined its boundaries in white Anglo-Saxon terms, and ensured their exclusion from full participation in the national community. Referring to the racial violence of the 1960s, Hannah Arendt pointed out that "the obvious dangers of domestic violence" in a multinational society such as the United States had historically been contained "*by making adherence to the law of the land, and not national origin, the chief touchstone of citizenship* and by tolerating a considerable amount of mutual discrimination in society." Consequently, she argued, the struggle of African Americans for political inclusion during the sixties raised the need to acknowledge that nationalism and racism are not the same. The solution to the racial violence could not be approached in the same way as it had been in the past.[47] Thus, while the civil rights and black liberation movement during the 1960s were certainly a struggle to get the "community of Americans" to *recognize* the political and civil rights of African Americans as equal citizens under the law, they also represented an attempt to shift the notion of *how* one is defined as an American with full citizenship rights away from ideological choice to one of native-born right to membership as citizens in the nation.

Indeed, although African Americans had been legally excluded from social mobility and freedom for centuries, there has not been any doubt—at least since the Civil War—that they were born in the United States.[48] For, however reluctantly and in spite of their political and legal exclusion, the dominant society has acknowledged their existence—albeit negatively, through the Civil War, the passing of segregationist laws and practices, and consequent persistent discrimination. The question of ethnicity in the United States is thus rooted in the segregationist policies of the nineteenth century. These had the effect of excluding African Americans from the way the national community was imagined and simultaneously establishing the domestic "boundaries" in ethnic terms for those who *would* be included as members of the nation. As a result, the "black issue" in the United States became a question of trying to define empirically the distinction between nationality as their native-born right in relation to the society's right to exclude them (based on ideological notions of racial and moral superiority) from the national community's self-image.

In 1896, for example, in spite of a few attempts to protect the rights of African Americans (through, for example, the Civil Rights Act of 1875, revoked by the Supreme Court in 1883), segregation became "an established fact, *by law as well as by custom.*"[49] The *Plessy v. Ferguson* case challenged the constitutionality of an 1890 Louisiana law that reestablished segregation of blacks and whites in the state's railroad trains. Based on the Fourteenth Amendment guaranteeing equality to African Americans, this case was brought to the court by Homer Adolph Plessy, a man whom Richard Kluger has described as "exceedingly light-skinned," in a part of the country where the racial mixture of blacks, French, Indians, and Anglo-Saxons had created "a racial *bouillabaise* unlike any other state in the union." The "separate but equal" decision thus brought to light issues of racial passing and the difficulties in disentangling racial origins. At the same time, it served to legally acknowledge the presence of blacks and simultaneously justify their segregation on the grounds that "social equality" could not be reached in the national community through what the court referred to as "laws which conflict with the general sentiment of the community upon whom they are designed to operate."[50]

Domestically, then, until the 1954 *Brown v. Board of Education* decision, the presence of blacks in the United States was acknowledged through the *Plessy v. Ferguson* decision, which legalized nineteenth-century customary practices of discrimination. As the next section illustrates, the enforced segregation of African Americans was paradoxically also to signal their partial political incorporation into the nation. At the same time, it contributed to establish the internal boundaries of the "national community" such that the public self-image of the American nation could be invoked primarily in white-only terms. In this sense it is not surprising that in demanding full participation and rights in the nation, the black movements of the sixties reinforced the "adherence to the law of the land" as one means of combating long-held "general sentiments" of the "national community."

Forging the Exclusion of Latin Americans from the American Imagined Community

The struggle of Mexican Americans and Puerto Ricans for civil rights and equality before the law has necessarily taken a different form from that of African Americans, precisely because, at least since the Civil War period, the exclusion of blacks has not been couched in distortion stemming from xenophobic portrayals of them as foreign born. Indeed, the experiences of Mexican Americans and Puerto Ricans in the United States (legally fellow citizens of Americans since 1848 and 1917, respectively) exemplify the ways that xenophobic nationalism and domestic racism have been conflated since the early nineteenth century.[51] This fusion has forged a public self-image of the "American people" in relation to racially perceived foreign "Others" not only in the United States but in the hemisphere as a whole.

The conflation of Latin Americans' race and nationality has shaped a different relationship between Mexican Americans and Puerto Ricans and the American imagined community—a relationship based primarily on de facto (rather than de jure) exclusion. Indeed, the Treaty of Guadalupe Hidalgo, signed at the end of the 1846-48 Mexican-American War, had ensured Mexicans, unlike African Americans, the full privileges of U.S. citizenship, including the right to appeal to the courts to maintain their ownership of their lands—making them the first non-Anglo-Saxons to have the rights and privileges previously reserved only to white, European men. As Tomás Almaguer recently suggested, legal access to these citizenship rights was to have important implications in the subsequent development of the various Mexican-American communities in the United States and was certainly a key factor differentiating their experience from that of African Americans and other racial groups—at least in terms of their legal recognition as members of the "national community."[52]

Nevertheless, while both citizenship rights and legal recourse to the courts of the nation were guaranteed, the fact that the populations of the Southwest were persistently perceived as foreign to the style in which the "national community" was imagined meant that, fifty years after the Treaty of Guadalupe Hidalgo, "the Anglo still considered the Mexicans as aliens and made attempts through the courts to exclude them from citizenship. In 1896 Ricardo Rodriguez was denied his final naturalization papers."[53] Thus although legalized segregation of African Americans had shaped the *domestic* definitions of exclusion from the imagined community of Americans, segregationist customary practices were gradually extended to ("foreign") Mexicans and sometimes even served as the basis from which to challenge the dictates of the "laws of the land."

It is ironic that Rodriguez brought his case to the courts in 1896. For as discussed above, it meant that the very year the Plessy verdict legally sanctioned the segregation of African Americans in the society was also the year when the recognition that blacks were present—albeit segregated—in the national community was clearly being affirmed in the courts against "foreign" Mexicans who sought to assert their legal right to become naturalized. As Acuña notes, in making their case against Rodriguez "the authorities argued in court that *Rodriguez was not white or African and 'therefore not capable of becoming an American citizen.'* " Noting that "they wanted to keep 'Aztecs or aboriginal Mexicans' from naturalization," Acuña tells us that nevertheless Rodriguez himself eventually won his case for naturalization through invoking the terms prescribed by the Treaty of Guadalupe Hidalgo.[54] But the very fact that he had had to assert his right to citizenship against a prosecution using racial terms shows that the definition of the domestic boundaries of the national community in black/white terms had also become a legitimate justification for reinforcing nationality to render Mexican Americans invisible both as *citizens* and as *native-born members* of the nation.

By the turn of the century, this definition, initially shaped in relation to Mexican Americans, was further reinforced through the relations the U.S. established with all the Latin American nations. In fact, the form in which nationality and race were fused in the treatment of Mexican Americans, Puerto Ricans, and indeed of all Latin Americans in the United States is best exemplified in some of the expansionist policies and ideologies of the nineteenth century. As early as 1823, the Monroe Doctrine determined that the entire hemisphere was to come under the sphere of influence of the United States. Initially an economic rather than political declaration, the doctrine aimed at preventing the intervention of European nations in the affairs of the hemisphere. But as Victor Valenzuela bluntly states, "By the end of the XIX century, the Monroe Doctrine was used freely by the United States to seize, to control or to intervene openly in the affairs of Latin American countries."[55] Thus the Monroe Doctrine had in effect early on begun to establish a homogeneous approach to relations between the United States and Latin American nations and was to have far-reaching implications in forging a public American identity in relation to the other emerging nations in the hemisphere.

At the same time, the fusion of Latin Americans' race and nationality was also furthered by the development of the ideology of the nation's "manifest destiny," which substantiated the doctrine's clearly expansionist intent at home.[56] The term was initially coined in 1845 by John O'Sullivan, then editor of the *Democratic Review*, who apparently drew his own conclusions about the nation's future mission and destiny from early Puritan beliefs of Providence. In so doing, he provided the Polk government with the rationale for both the Mexican-American War and the subsequent annexation of more than half of Mexico's territory.[57] Effectively declaring the superiority of the white Anglo-Saxon, the ideology of the nation's manifest destiny was widely used by journalists to spread the justification of expansion and the subsequent exclusion of "foreign" Mexicans from the way the national community was imagined.[58] While competing commercial concerns and economic interests were, as Mario Barrera has argued, more probable causes for the conquest of Mexico's northern territory than the pure adherence to the belief in the nation's manifest destiny, the ideological terms of the debate are also essential for explaining the process through which popular support for the war was galvanized and justified by politicians and journalists to the American public.[59]

Among politicians, there was much discussion about the merits of declaring war on Mexico and on its aftermath. Both those in favor and those against the war and annexation struggled with the conflict between economic interests and the racial concerns about Mexico's Spanish and Indian *mixed* populations. According to Reginald Horseman, the latter seem to have caused much soul-searching among some antiexpansionists, particularly among those who were not English but rather of proud Scottish and Irish descent. Confronted by the serious issue of what to do with the "mongrel" Mexicans, they were nevertheless not willing to accede to the claims of Anglo-Saxon superiority. This led them to affirm the superiority of "Americans" of northern European descent, thus relegating the Spanish southern European heritage of Mexicans to "second place" in the white European hierarchy in the hemisphere. Thus, while some could then praise the European side of Mexico's heritage in these terms, almost all could use racial arguments to deny their rights as equal citizens of a national community in which the superiority of white northern Europeans was rarely challenged.[60]

In setting the style for establishing the boundaries of the nation of Americans, nineteenth-century American opinion makers came to construct a "white only" public, which, whether as northern Europeans or in more specific "Anglo-Saxon" terms, included "every American." Having defined the national community in those terms, an image of a coherent, powerful nation unified against the foreign "enemy" could then be evoked by those who "viewed the conflict as a manifestation of the national future." As the editor of *Scientific American* wrote, "Every American must feel a glow of enthusiasm in his [*sic*] heart as he thinks of his country's greatness, her might and her power."[61] Buttressed by the justifications of the Monroe Doctrine and manifest destiny of the United States, popular perceptions of foreign "Others" also fused their races and nationalities. The grounds of the earlier debates on the mixed heritage of Mexico's population seem to have been put aside to some extent in the latter decades of the century as myths of the racial superiority of "Americans"—now reinforced through victory and the social Darwinism of the times—fed the perception of the inferior homogeneous identity of all people of Mexican, and later of Latin American, descent.

The extent to which these images were disseminated in ways that contributed toward erasing the racial and class distinctions among Latin Americans can perhaps best be seen in the attitudes of the forty-niners during the gold rush. In 1849 alone, 100,000 newcomers from all over the world arrived in California, including 8,000 Mexicans and 5,000 South Americans. As seen earlier, because of their social class standing as well as their length of residence, the established Mexican elite families had made a point of distancing themselves from more recently arrived lower-class Mexican *cholos* (or "half-breeds," as they were derogatorily called) following Mexico's independence from Spain. But now they suddenly found that the thousands of Yankee Anglo-Saxons pouring into the gold-mining regions made no such social distinctions among the varied Latin American national groups. Instead, as McWilliams notes, "whether from California, Chile, Peru, or Mexico, whether residents of twenty years' standing or immigrants of one week, all the Spanish-speaking were lumped together as interlopers and greasers." Thus unceremoniously and indiscriminately brought together under the "Mexicans" label, Latin Americans—regardless of race, class, or nationality—became the potential and real targets of robberies, murders, rapes, and lynchings, and hence the butt of the often-violent repercussions of the American "glow of enthusiasm."[62]

Similarly, the homogenization of the social and racial differences among Latin American populations is also exemplified in the colonization of Puerto Rico following the Spanish-American War. As in the case of the conquest of Mexico's lands, the 1898 war was largely fueled

by the need for external markets. And again, the ideological justifications provided for the economic interests in the society were also to
further shape the boundaries of the U.S. imagined community. On the
eve of the war, a *Washington Post* editorial, for example, galvanized
public support for the war in the following terms:

> A new consciousness seems to have come upon us—the consciousness
> of strength—and with it a new appetite, the yearning to show our
> strength. . . . Ambition, interest, land hunger, pride, the mere joy of
> fighting, whatever it may be, we are animated by a new sensation. We
> are face to face with a strange destiny. The taste of Empire is in the
> mouth of the people even as the taste of blood is in the jungle.[63]

But if the American people were being asked to imagine the taste of
their "strange destiny," it was the populations of the countries affected
by U.S. expansionist actions who were actually to swallow the nation's
cultivated self-image as an empire after 1898. The war finally sealed
Cuba's century-long struggle for independence, bringing to a close
Spanish colonial rule in the hemisphere. In the course of the war, however, U.S. troops had also landed on the nearby Spanish island-colony
of Puerto Rico, which, given its location in the Caribbean, was significant in military terms and thus was included, along with the Philip-
pines, as part of the gains of the United States in the Treaty of Paris that
ended the war.[64]

The transfer of Puerto Rico to the United States was generally welcomed by the island's population, although the reasons varied according to the social sectors. The propertied classes, for example, were anx-
ious to benefit from both the ideals of democracy and the closer ties
with the U.S. economy, while sectors of the poorer classes were convinced that their scores against the corruption of the island's ruling
classes would finally be settled and the Spanish colonial castelike hierarchy in which they had for so long been forced to live would be dis-
mantled.[65] These misperceptions were to prove as misinformed as
those the U.S. troops held about Puerto Ricans: some Americans found
a population that, particularly among the working class and the poor,
seemed "patient" and "docile," their very gentleness permitting "the
unjust scale of wages they receive to become the custom." Others,
however, saw "the natives" as "lazy and dirty, but . . . very sharp and
cunning," and found that "the introduction of American ideas disturbs
them little, they being indifferent to the advantages offered."[66]

Notwithstanding either the intercultural and political misperceptions on both sides or the island's various social sectors' expectations,

Puerto Ricans' sigh of relief at the end of Spanish colonial rule proved to be short-lived. For in contrast to the fate of Mexico's territories, which following annexation were eventually incorporated as states of the union, in the case of Puerto Rico, the U.S. Congress adopted a measure largely aimed at exacting tariffs on the island's agricultural products. Known as the Foraker Bill, it also denied, for the first time in U.S. history, both territorial status and constitutional protection and citizenship to a newly acquired territory. This initially provoked heated partisan debate between Democrats and Republicans alike, both of which favored the bill's economic advantages while seeking to avoid blame for what were clearly colonialist implications of the new territorial status created for Puerto Rico. One senator poignantly summarized its potential implications for the nation's identity as well as for the future image of the national community at home and abroad:

> It will end the history of the Republic and open the history of the empire. It dethrones the Goddess of liberty and elevates the demon of power. It destroys constitutional government and creates a Congressional despotism. It is but the forerunner of countless other bills to follow in order to inaugurate the new imperialistic regime. It is antagonistic to all the traditions of our country, to all the principles of our Government, and will, I believe, be the commencement of much disgrace and much disaster. (Applause)[67]

Nevertheless, the bill's tariff-related economic advantages were apparently to outweigh its political ramifications, for it was signed into law by President McKinley in 1900. Although, as Benjamin Ringer notes, varied political and economic concerns made it inexpedient for members of either party to raise the issue of race as part of the debate, it was apparently on the minds of at least some of the congressmen, for their concerns about it are also recorded in no uncertain terms:

> I am opposed to increasing the opportunities for the millions of negroes in Puerto Rico and the 10,000,000 Asiatics in the Philippines of becoming American citizens and swarming into this country and coming in competition with our farmers and mechanics and laborers. We are trying to keep out the Chinese with one hand, and now you are proposing to make Territories of the United States out of Puerto Rico and the Philippine Islands, and thereby open wide the door by which these negroes and Asiatics can pour like the locusts of Egypt into this country.[68]

As the acquisition of both Puerto Rico and of Mexico's territory exemplify, the justifications of expansionism into Latin America had from

early on been furthered by racial explanations that, overtly or otherwise, homogenized the complex and heterogeneous class and racial hierarchies that had evolved over more than three hundred years of
Spanish colonial rule.\The combined effects of the Monroe Doctrine
and the idea of the manifest destiny of the United States contributed
toward shaping the boundaries of the American community in relation
to the Spanish-speaking populations south of the Rio Grande. Moreover, the creation of the *image* of a unified "national community" contributed toward erasing the complex differences in the ways that race,
culture, and nationality were understood by the Spanish-speaking
people who lived in the United States in the years following the Mexican-American War.

Key to the process of exclusion of people of Latin American descent
from the American imagined community was the fact that newly and
often violently created customary practices frequently came to define
their lack of citizenship rights and to shape their experiences more
clearly than the "laws of the land." As Montejano has emphasized,
class-based distinctions within the Mexican community were recognized, for example, in Texas. Yet this did not prevent individual Anglos
in the Southwest from imputing in their "less dramatic, daily encounters" the same segregationist attitudes they customarily invoked *in relation to blacks*:

> In her first trip to Corpus Christi in 1870, Mrs. Susan Miller of
> Louisiana stopped at the State Hotel and "was horrified to see
> Mexicans seated at the tables with Americans. I told my husband I
> had never eaten with Mexicans or negroes, and refused to do so. He
> said: *'Mexicans are different to negroes and are recognized as Americans.*
> However, I will speak to the manager and see if he will not put a
> small table in one corner of the room for you.' He did so and we
> enjoyed the meal."[69]

In spite of legal rights, Puerto Ricans and Mexican Americans have remained largely unacknowledged as "fellow citizens" of Americans
throughout much of the twentieth century. Denied full citizenship and
human rights by the customary practices of exclusion, they could be
routinely bounced in and out of the "national community" according
to the ever-changing political and economic needs of the nation. This is
exemplified in their differentiated incorporation into the U.S. economy.
Notwithstanding internal social and racial differentiations, their respective communities have also since been variously affected by the
nation's political needs in war and peace, by its employment practices,

and by the racial and immigration policies that reflected the nation's economic laws of supply and demand.

The 1917 Jones Act, which imposed U.S. citizenship on Puerto Ricans, for example, allowed for their massive participation in World War I, while simultaneously denying the island's population the right to vote for the presidents who have since sent them to every war. Later, "Operation Bootstrap," and specifically the passage of the 1947 Industrial Incentives Act, combined a massive industrialization program on the island based on long-term tax breaks for U.S. corporations and the export of thousands of displaced workers to the United States. As a result, between 1948 and 1965, Puerto Rico witnessed "the unusual spectacles of a booming economy with a shrinking labor force and . . . shrinking unemployment." During the same period, the number of Puerto Ricans displaced to the United States has been estimated to run from nine hundred thousand to one million, including the children born abroad.[70]

Similarly, U.S. government policies also contributed to the increase in the Mexican American population between the 1940s and the 1960s and determined both the fate of the more established Chicano communities—most of which, by the 1940s, were in urban areas—and their interaction with the thousands of Mexican immigrants in the United States. As a result of labor shortages during the war, for example, the bracero program, begun in 1943, brought 4.8 million Mexican workers across the border between 1943 and 1964. Soon after the war, "Operation Wetback" was begun, ostensibly aimed at tracking down and deporting "illegal" Mexican workers. The bracero program was simultaneously extended, however, this time including a provision for industrial workers, but also effectively keeping rural wages down and ensuring an ample supply of strike breakers in the fields of the western and southwestern states.[71]

Exclusion from full rights of citizenship has reinforced the *public* perception of Chicanos, like that of Puerto Ricans, as outside of the boundaries of the popular image of the national community. This explains, for example, Mexican Americans' treatment by U.S. officials, who, at various times throughout the twentieth century, felt no qualms in deporting them at will, regardless of their U.S. citizenship and length of time in this country. Ironically, throughout the twentieth century, this same perception often left Mexican Americans with no other recourse than to appeal to the Mexican consulate for protection against discrimination from officials of their own country, namely, the United States. As for the Puerto Ricans, they could not even resort to this option, insofar as they had been declared citizens of the United States in 1917, in the context of the transfer of the island from one colonial power to another.[72]

The Fusion of Race and Nationality: Imagining the "Hispanic Other" in the Customs and Laws of the Land

Rooted in the nineteenth-century search by newly formed nations to define their identities in the hemisphere, the United States relied on a series of ideological assumptions rather than birthplace in forging its population's self-definition as a nation. As a result, the American self-image developed largely from ideological beliefs of superiority and inferiority and hence from the denial of what Todorov in a different context called "the existence of a human substance truly other" in its relations to foreign Others in the hemisphere.[73] To a large extent, these assumptions have since ensured the exclusion from the memory of mainstream U.S. society of knowledge about the lives and diverse historical experiences of Chicanos, Puerto Ricans, and the descendents of Latin Americans in the United States. They have thus served to perpetuate homogenizing popular perceptions of these populations as foreign to the way the national community of Americans is imagined.

The differentiated experiences and responses to the conquest of the Southwest, for example, reduced both rich and poor to a homogeneous image of all Latin American populations as "Mexicans," who were "idle," "shiftless," "fatalistic," and "resigned." Nineteenth-century politicians described native New Mexicans as "a hybrid race of Spanish and Indian origin, ignorant, degraded, demoralized, and priest-ridden,"[74] an image that, as McWilliams suggested, was projected nationwide, as indicated in letters, journalistic accounts, and travelers' reports:

> Essentially this same impression was formed by a wide variety of observers: men and women; officers, miners, surveyors, trappers, mountainmen, sea captains, and journalists. Passed along to those who were about to leave for the borderlands, repeated by all observers, *these stereotyped impressions were national currency during the Mexican-American war and the patriotic sanction long continued.*[75]

Moreover, these portrayals were extended to include all Spanish-speaking people in the hemisphere and continued to shape both the direction of U.S. policy and popular prejudices toward people with ties to Latin America well into the twentieth century.[76] One hundred years after the conquest, the conflation of race and nationality still underlay the public exclusion of Mexican-American War veterans from celebrations of the imagined community of the United States. Although by this time Mexicans were officially classified as "white" by the U.S. census, during Fourth of July celebrations in two Texan towns in 1943, for example, local newspapers reported:

> Several hundred citizens of the United States of Mexican extraction were told over the loudspeaker that they should go home because the dance being held in a public square was for white people only. Among the persons ejected were many wearing United States soldiers' uniforms. At still another place, again on the Fourth of July, at an American Legion dance, Spanish-name veterans of World War I were asked to leave because the dance was for "whites" only.[77]

And in the late 1960s, the conflation of nationality and race still exemplified the ways that the gap between the laws and customs of the land continued to shape the style in which public officials "imagined" the national community, such that Mexican Americans were excluded as foreigners in U.S. society:

> It was the quiet discontent and the foreboding of an electoral revolt in the barrios that led to the formation by President Johnson in 1967 of the Inner-Agency Committee on Mexican American Affairs. The "benign neglect" of the Chicanos has since progressed from the vulgar to the sardonic. In the autumn of 1969 a bill, introduced by Senator Montoya to extend the life of the President's committee (rechristened the Cabinet Committee on Opportunity for the Spanish Speaking), passed the Senate and was sent to the House. It was "lost" for four months. Embarrassed by this denouement, its Senate sponsors instituted a hectic search for the missing bill. It was found in the House Foreign Affairs committee. *Someone had assumed that "Mexican-American Affairs" was a "foreign problem."*[78]

The marginalization and invisibility of Chicanos and Puerto Ricans has distorted the ways in which U.S. history is presented to schoolchildren, and thus also affects the way they are taught to imagine their "national community." This was noted as recently as 1970 in a study of the treatment of minorities in forty-five junior and senior high school social studies textbooks, which concluded:

> A significant number of texts . . . continue to present a principally white, Protestant Anglo-Saxon view of America's past and present, while the nature and problems of minority groups are largely neglected. . . . Even less attention is paid to America's increasingly

significant minority groups of Spanish-speaking peoples. In social studies textbooks the Mexican American has replaced the black man as the "invisible American." Puerto Ricans fare only slightly better.[79]

And even in the 1980s, Frank Bonilla could still point to the extent to which invisibility and negative stereotypes about Puerto Ricans have persisted. Reviewing some of the early statements made by U.S. military observers about the Puerto Rican people in 1898, cited earlier, he asks:

> What are we to make of the fact that 70 years of increasingly elaborate social science research on Puerto Rico and its mainland offshoots have added practically nothing to the imagery of the Puerto Rican current among our U.S. overseers that could not readily be inferred or extrapolated from the 1900 impressions?[80]

Drawn from the dominant definitions of the manifest destiny of the Anglo-American peoples, the nineteenth-century "laws of custom" thus do not seem to have disappeared in the late twentieth century. Instead, the early fusion of race and nationality had ensured that Chicanos and Puerto Ricans—regardless of race, class, birthplace, or citizenship status—were explicitly excluded *as foreigners* from the style in which the white Anglo-Saxon public opinion was encouraged to imagine the national community of the United States.[81] Insofar as the public dominant image of "Americans" was forged in white Protestant Anglo-Saxon terms against the created image of people of Latin American descent as "foreign Others," it is not surprising to find that throughout the twentieth century the latter's images continued to be reinforced in the popular mind as foreign to the style in which the American national community is imagined.[82]

Finally, it is important to note that since the nineteenth century, the public "racial" style of imagining the nation in relation to foreign others was also reinforced by a civil war, which ultimately led to establishing the national community's domestic boundaries in strictly black and white terms. Thus, as in the case of African Americans, the relationship between the American imagined community and Mexican Americans/Chicanos and Puerto Ricans (subsequently extended to embrace Latin Americans as a whole) stems from the historical lack of recognition of the latter groups' membership as citizens of the nation. But, unlike African Americans, it is also based on continually denying their native-born presence and participation in setting the boundaries and constructing the image of the "national community" of the United States.[83]

The boundaries of the national community were "imagined" in white Anglo-Saxon Protestant terms. Yet it is important to note that once "imagined" in those terms and institutionalized through segregationist laws and customs, the reality of the boundaries of inclusion and exclusion were to long affect, albeit in different ways, every aspect of the daily lives of Mexican Americans, Puerto Ricans, African Americans, and other racialized minorities in the United States.

The effects of the nineteenth-century fusion of nationality and race were still strongly visible in the 1960s. They became manifest in the particular forms of mobilization adopted in the struggle against the differentiated exclusion that long determined the lives of various groups in the United States. As the following two chapters suggest, in the process of shaping the respective struggles of Mexican Americans and Puerto Ricans for political inclusion in the late 1960s and early 1970s, they also established the terms of the recent debates to clarify the meaning and social value of *both* "being American" and its corollary, "being Hispanic," in U.S. society today.

Chapter 3

"Establishing an Identity" in the Sixties: The Mexican-American/ Chicano and Puerto Rican Movements

Although much has been written about the sixties, as Elizabeth Martínez notes, the history of the period is yet to be fully told. Questions about periodization, issues related to the black/white paradigm in U.S. historiography, and a continued Eurocentric perspective contributed toward rendering Mexican Americans and Puerto Ricans, Asian Americans and native Americans invisible from the narratives of the period.[1] Yet during the civil rights era, Mexican Americans/Chicanos and Puerto Ricans joined other racial minority groups in the struggle to affirm their presence as citizens with "the right to have rights"[2] and to redefine the boundaries of political inclusion in the national community. Their movements responded to a long legacy of political and cultural exclusion, emphasizing their respective communities' histories in the United States. In the process of demanding their rights, they both reaffirmed and redefined in various ways the cultural and linguistic traditions, values, symbols, and myths that for decades had ensured their communities' survival.

Thus, although the history of the period is well beyond the scope of this book, it is important to examine the impact of what Maria Celia Paoli, in a different context, has called "the central role of the notion of rights in shaping new forms of thought and actions."[3] This chapter explores the dynamics and effects of movements based on cultural affirmation (including but not limited to the channeling of political demands in cultural nationalist terms.)[4] Participation served to unify Puerto Ricans and Mexican Americans/Chicanos and Chicanas within their respective movements and served to establish their respective collective and individual identities within the nation. At the same time, however, the emphasis on cultural affirmation deemphasized both internal ideological differences as well as the very real racial, class, and gendered diversity among each group's participants, contributing toward the eventual fragmentation of many of the movements. I argue that the necessary albeit varied emphasis each movement placed on nationalist and cultural heritage served to affirm the political presence of Mexican Americans/Chicanos and Puerto Ricans as two distinct groups within the "national community" even while simultaneously contributing toward shaping the context within which the homogenizing label Hispanic was to emerge by the early 1970s.

Prelude to the Movements: The Postwar Period

In the years following World War II, Mexican-American organizations and leaders, largely drawn from the ranks of returning war veterans, actively adopted integrationist strategies and emphasized their Americanism and patriotism as a means of fighting the continued racial prejudice, harassment, violence, and discrimination against their communities. As Mario Barrera notes, they often emphasized the search for equality at the expense of strengthening the collective values of their communities and were strongly supportive of the anticommunist, individualist, and conformist liberalism of the times.[5] Many organizations turned to the courts to end legal segregation and discriminatory practices in schools and at the workplace. New reformist organizations, such as the American G.I. Forum, the Mexican American Political Association (MAPA), and the Community Service Organization, joined older ones, such as the League of Latin American Citizens, in continuing the effort to achieve equal citizenship rights in California, Texas, and other southwestern states.[6] At the same time, many Mexican-American leaders were particularly active in the "Viva Kennedy" clubs of the late 1950s and initiated voter registration campaigns in their respective communities.

As they had in the past, Spanish-speaking community organizations continued to provide the new generations with cultural and linguistic affirmation, organizing social and cultural events and parades and, in some cases, facilitating individual youth access to higher education.[7] Yet racial prejudice and discrimination against Mexican Americans and the Spanish language persisted in the Southwest, Chicago, and California. Texas-born Rosa Guerrero, for example, vividly recalls her school days in the forties and fifties when teachers would "hit us on the head, but good, or they'd paddles us with what they called the board of education for speaking Spanish."[8]

Organizations in Chicago, for example, were largely ineffective in terms of providing the community with ethnic consciousness and solidarity and in addressing the conflicting needs of the more established Mexican-American community and the newer immigrants arriving through the bracero program.[9] The largely middle-class, liberal, professional organizations embraced both the ideals of American pluralism and the 1940 census reclassification of Spanish-surnamed people as white "and therefore worthy of equality." This, as Edward Escobar has noted, led Mexican Americans to "reject any classification system that equated them with blacks." Although individuals were to support and/or participate in the early civil rights mobilizations, voter registration drives, and sit-ins,[10] "by the mid-sixties," Escobar concludes, "Mexican Americans had defined themselves out of the civil rights agenda and found they were ignored by or even excluded from many of the War on Poverty programs intended to ameliorate the effects of racial discrimination."[11]

Puerto Ricans were to be similarly excluded, at least partially as a result of their lack of political power and their internal strife and fragmentation.[12] Like their Mexican-American counterparts to the west, early Puerto Rican organizations provided their communities with defense against the hostilities of a profoundly racist society. Moreover, as Bernardo Vega noted, as early as the nineteenth century Puerto Ricans had interacted with other Latin Americans in New York City, particularly Cubans, joining with them in the struggle for independence of their respective islands. He notes that by the end of the first decade of this century, there was in New York a strong supportive community of Puerto Ricans and other Latin Americans whose members self identified as Hispanos. Nevertheless, Vega makes a strong class-based distinction in describing who "would try to pass for 'Spaniards' so as to minimize the prejudice against them." In contrast, workers, he says, "were not afraid of being called 'spiks.' They did not deny their origin." Vega describes the active participation of Puerto Ricans in the early-century riots protesting the violence and brutality against the community and in labor unrest, and documents the prejudices and difficulties confronted by these early Puerto Ricans in New York. He documents the early nationalist movement struggles for independence of the island and shows that the political activism of Puerto Ricans, like that of other Hispanos living in the city at that time, included participation in both local and Latin American politics.[13] Numerous community organizations, both formal and informal, served to strengthen the cultural, linguistic, and political affiliations between Puerto Ricans in New York and on the island.

While the community may have been somewhat divided in class terms, nevertheless, Virginia Sánchez Korrol has also documented a variety of ways in which Latinismo among the Spanish-speaking populations of New York was fostered through newspapers, films, journals, magazines, and music. Mutual aid associations, political clubs, and local political organizations were very much a part of the Puerto Rican community life, and invariably were also open to the participation of other Latin Americans living in New York at that time.[14]

At the same time, the colonial status of the island and the political history of the Puerto Rican community in the United States differentiated their formal organizations from those of the Mexican Americans further west. As Roberto Rodríguez-Morazzani argues, these were not organized to directly access resources for the community, for they were tied to the Office of Migration and by extension to the colonial government of Puerto Rico, and hence of the United States. In the late fifties and early sixties a new generation successfully challenged the old leadership, determined to ensure the mainland community's political autonomy and control of the organizations. The new leaders provided services to the community and simultaneously developed cultural awareness and pride and an appreciation for education and community service among the Puerto Rican youth. Yet, strongly reaffirming the liberal pluralism of the period, their modernized service organizations were soon to become accountable to foundation funding sources outside of their community.[15]

As in the Mexican-American communities, racial and linguistic prejudice and discrimination against Puerto Ricans were overtly manifested in the labor market, the schools, and city streets.[16] At the same time, the postwar generations affirmed their Puerto Rican cultural heritage, which included the island's social, cultural, and racial values. As in the rest of Latin America, these were based on the prevailing gradated system of racial classification and clashed with the categorical black/white distinctions of U.S. society. Growing up as a black Puerto Rican in the 1950s exemplified the racial dynamics within the family and the community, minimally leading to exchanges such as the following between Piri Thomas and his brother, documented in Thomas's classic autobiographical novel, *Down These Mean Streets*:

"I'm a Negro."

"You ain't no nigger," José said.

"I ain't?"

"No. You're a Puerto Rican. . . . We're Puerto Ricans, and that's different from being *moyetos* [a black man]. . . . "

"That's what I've been wanting to believe all along, José," I said. "I've been hanging on to that idea even when I knew it wasn't so. But only pure white Puerto Ricans are white, and you wouldn't even believe that if you ever dug what the paddy said."[17]

Regardless of official citizenship status and their 1940 census reclassification as "white," in the postwar years of heightened nationalist and patriotic rhetoric, Mexican Americans and Puerto Ricans were confronted by the consequences of a daily experience of contradictory messages in their personal lives and respective communities: on the one hand, a constant hammering of patriotism and democratic ideals, whether through the emphasis on Americanization in the schools; in programs run by the YMCA; in local, primarily Protestant church–related, organizations; or in the Spanish-language media; and on the other, a persistent marginalization and exclusion from the justice, respect, dignity, and equality embedded in the ideology of Americanism and democracy.[18]

Excluded from the history of the "national community," both groups remained unacknowledged for their contributions to building the country's infrastructure, its defense in times of war and peace, and the continued expansion of the economy. Castigated for their differences in race and color, language and customs, their respective cultural legacies and sense of self were denigrated and consistently undermined in every area of their lives. Marginalized in segregated and neglected urban and rural ghettos, many had no access to adequate schooling, housing, plumbing, or electricity. Locked for the most part into low-paying menial jobs in canneries, factories, and fields, they were often limited to seasonal employment. Violently and indiscriminately harassed by the police and by a justice system established to protect all citizens under the law, they were denied access to political channels through which to voice their legitimate demands for equality and justice under the laws of their nation.[19] In short, even when allowing for variations based on the socioeconomic, regional, racial, and gender composition that diversified their daily lives and individual and community experiences, the lives of the majority of Mexican Americans and Puerto Ricans were permeated by what the Brazilian anthropologist Roberto Da Matta has in a different context called "the most profound experience of exploitation."[20]

This "profound experience of exploitation" both includes and transcends the material deprivation and poverty of their rural and urban communities, long documented in the country's historical imagination as a transitory experience of the ethnic-immigrant groups that peopled the nation in the past.[21] More specifically, however, and perhaps primarily, it also refers to the political, psychological, and social effects of unacknowledged citizenship rights. Their marginalization, exclusion, and/or persistent segregation was based on the interaction between the laws and customs that shaped the diverse historical experiences of all non–European-American minorities, the majority of whom had never been "the tired and poor" of other lands.[22]

Narrating "the images of . . . poverty," of a child's rumbling stomach, of his mother's joblessness and her struggle to get off the welfare she detested, of the insensitivity of humiliating welfare investigators who patronized the family in the privacy of its home, one Puerto Rican activist explained the survival mechanism he had had to develop growing up in Chicago during the 1950s and early 1960s:

> There's nothing extraordinary, you know, in my childhood—maybe just that I learned very early how to become accepted, how to rise above and beyond as they say. Even at that point we knew that to the extent that we became white—we would advance in school. To the extent that we spoke properly—we would get Satisfactory or Excellent on our report cards. To the extent that we conformed we were accepted.[23]

Many became responsible for their families early in their childhood, as Carmen, another young Puerto Rican activist, described:

> My father came to this country a very proud man, but he went to a factory to work—that's the only job he could get—and he was getting forty dollars a week. And here he started drinking. . . . At that time, I had to become the head of the family. Being the eldest, I had to handle all the situations going on in the house—and I was only ten, going on eleven, so I couldn't really do as good a job as I thought— but I was trying hard. I got part-time jobs in different small stores, I went to school, I took care of the family, I made sure they ate, I picked my father out of the hallways when he got drunk.[24]

The profound experience of exploitation was thus "a way of life."[25] Having been constructed historically, it was embedded in the material conditions of their respective communities. At the same time, it was reflected in each person's individual capacity to develop behavior patterns early in life, to counter the constant denigration of his or her racial, language, national, and class origins; in the inevitable process of developing strategies of accommodation, negotiation, rejection, and resistance to the ideological contradictions and material conditions of daily life; in short, in the process of forging a culture of everyday life through which to resist the conditions institutionalized in the denial by the "national community" of their citizenship rights, respect, and human dignity.

It is not surprising, then, that by the mid-1960s, sectors of the Mexican-American and Puerto Rican communities throughout the nation began to develop varied forms of protest and mobilization. Following the example of African-American civil rights movements, the various minority groups demanded recognition of their presence and their citizenship in the nation, often adopted and adapted their strategies, borrowed one another's organizational tactics, and certainly supported each others' mobilization efforts. As Elizabeth Martínez points out:

> In fact the 60s was an era of constant interconnection across both time and space. White radicals learned concepts and tactics from Blacks, who had learned some of their concepts from Asians (Ghandi) and adopted tactics from white workers of an earlier era. Asian youth were inspired by the Young Lords Party of Puerto Ricans. Native Americans took tactics from the Black struggle; young Chicanos were attracted to Native American values and also started breakfast programs like that of the Black Panther Party.[26]

Yet although individuals of all races participated in one another's movements, the Puerto Rican movements, like those of the Mexican Americans, remained largely distinct. Each increasingly adopted various nationalist strategies that affirmed their respective cultural and historical legacies. At the same time, the prejudices that divided them, as they did all of U.S. society, were at times also to contribute, albeit in subtle ways, to the separate paths forged by each movement.[27] As Pablo "Yoruba" Guzmán explained in discussing why the Puerto Rican Young Lords party decided not to join the Black Panthers on which it was initially modeled:

> At first many of us felt why have a Young Lords Party when there existed a Black Panther Party, and wouldn't it be to our advantage to try to consolidate our efforts into getting Third World people into something that already existed? It became apparent to us that that would be impractical, because we wouldn't be recognizing the national question. We felt we each had to organize where we were at—so that Chicanos were gonna have to organize Chicanos, Blacks were gonna have to organize Blacks, Puerto Ricans Puerto Ricans, etc.

until we came to that level where we could deal with one umbrella organization that could speak for everybody. But until we eliminate the racism that separates everybody, that will not be possible.[28]

Still, regardless of the strategy they adopted or the type of organizations that evolved, the movements generally aimed as much at improving the life chances of the racialized urban and rural populations as at redrawing the boundaries of the national community to force the recognition of their citizenship rights through political inclusion. Led largely by student activists who grew up in the postwar years, the character and nature of the varied Mexican-American and Puerto Rican movements reflected the specific regional and local histories and concerns of their participants and for the first time incorporated large numbers of working-class youths. Increasingly they were also to include the national concerns of a generation struggling against continued denial of their rights even while many were being drafted, often against their will, to fight in the Vietnam War.[29] These movements ultimately served to establish the respective identities of each national-origin group, particularly to themselves but also, at least temporarily, in the imagined "national community" of the United States. Let us turn first then, to the Puerto Rican movement.

Puerto Ricans in "the Sixties": The Young Lords Party

In civil rights hearings of the early seventies, leaders of largely reformist community organizations, as well as a number of social workers, teachers, workers, housewives, and other community members, protested the squalor and unsanitary conditions of the urban ghettos in which Puerto Ricans lived their lives, as well as the high levels of unemployment and lack of educational opportunities for their youth.[30] Although much research still needs to be done on the Puerto Rican communities during this period, Piri Thomas's description of those involved in the hearings would suggest that various sectors of the community as a whole were well represented and participated in various ways in the Puerto Rican population's efforts to achieve civil rights. At the same time, much of the early seventies activism of the Puerto Rican community was propelled by the various Puerto Rican student and youth organizations, which, like the Young Lords party, had emerged in New York in the mid-1960s.[31] Many were members of a generation who from very early on had been made acutely aware of the conditions of life of their communities. As Iris Morales, a Young Lords party member and community organizer, put it: "I was the one that was the go-between. This happens to a lot of older children in Puerto Rican families—they become the link between the Puerto Rican culture and the American culture and the Puerto Rican way of life and the American institutions. They become, in a sense, the ones that come up against oppression the most."[32]

Drawing its membership largely from former gang members and juvenile offenders and forbidding the use of drugs, the new generation's party insisted that members had to be Young Lords "twenty-five hours a day" and clearly stated its goal to achieve the political and economic self-determination and autonomy of the Puerto Rican community and its organizations.[33]

Many of those who later joined the party initially had to confront both the legacy of their island's colonialism, internalized in myths about Puerto Ricans' inherent passivity, and the effects of poverty and ghetto life on their sometimes limited understanding of even the city in which they lived.[34] As Felipe Luciano explained:

> You resign yourself to poverty—my mother did this. Your face is
> rubbed in shit so much that you begin to accept that shit as a reality.
> You've never seen anything else. Like the only thing we knew was
> that block. You never went out of that block. I didn't know there was
> a Museum of Modern Art. I didn't know that there were people who
> were living much, much better. I didn't know about racism. I mean
> we were just on that block—and that block was our home, it was all
> we knew.[35]

Iris Morales tells of her early sense of inferiority, and of the shame she had developed in her Upper West Side white public school toward her family "because they weren't what it was to be American." Describing the differences between her younger sister, who was sent to a Catholic school "so she could turn out better" than the older siblings, Morales concludes nevertheless that "all of us, you see, went through different kinds of things, and yet there's that common thing where we didn't fit for some reason or another, because we were labeled from the beginning, we were made tokens."[36]

On the streets, in new community-based movements, through the newly founded Young Lords party, in the literary and music scene of the late sixties and early seventies, Puerto Rican students and youth in Chicago and New York proclaimed the death of the docile Puerto Rican and the emergence of a new era of struggle for civil and social rights. The poet Pedro Pietri wrote of many Puerto Ricans who, having been denied recognition of their rights, had lost their struggle for survival in the urban ghettos. In his "Puerto Rican Obituary," he paid tribute to their lives even as he simultaneously immortalized his community's past passivity.[37] Looking back on the period, Felipe Luciano, explained: "It was 1969 and we were being told that we were economically necessary as consumers, politically and socially unacceptable as participants. So being young and brave and left . . . we took to the streets."[38]

Clearly inspired by over a decade of African-American civil rights protest—and in the case of the Young Lords, specifically by the Black Panthers party—the political development of the new generation was also "overdetermined by the experience of imperialism and colonialism, mass migration and the insertion of the Puerto Rican working class into the international division of labor."[39]

As the movement gathered momentum, the radical leaders—primarily students—increasingly adopted a critical stance toward their island's colonial political and economic relations and the corresponding status of Puerto Ricans. They rearticulated the call and struggle for their island's independence first made by the early-century Puerto Rican nationalists.[40] In so doing, they rejected as conservative the liberal, individualist, assimilationist ideologies of the 1950s generations and their community organizations. David Perez, a member of the Young Lords in Chicago and later one of the cofounders of the New York affiliate, described his own process of politicization in his mid to late teens:

> I went in a very short time from having a certain attitude towards
> America, where all these wonderful things were going to happen to
> me, where there was all this opportunity to get an education, and I
> was going to be a fireman, or a detective, or do construction work, to
> becoming conscious that it was an illusion. . . . I started to see that
> while democracy did exist, it was for the rich; the people who were
> poor weren't getting democracy.[41]

Yet the process of involving the community in the Young Lords' particular actions also included overcoming individualized fears and oppression, through mobilizing it to participate in collective actions that directly touched on their lives.[42] In referring to the early period of the Young Lords party in New York, Pablo Guzmán pointed out:

> The problem has been to tap that potential and to organize it into a
> disciplined force that's gonna really move on this government. Puerto
> Ricans had been psyched into believing this myth about being docile.

A lot of Puerto Ricans were afraid to move, a lot of Puerto Ricans really thought that the man in blue was the baddest thing going.[43]

Young Puerto Rican organizers initiated numerous self-help projects to get the support of the people in their barrios.[44] They were aware, for example, that the Sanitation Department did not provide services to neighborhoods like East Harlem and the lower East Side equal to services they provided to higher income areas. Thus, in the summer of 1969, the Young Lords began to clean the streets of their neighborhood themselves, bringing college students and community people together. Guzmán tells of the confused and suspicious reactions of sectors of the community—ranging from those who believed they were from Lindsey's Urban Action Task Force, to others who thought they were gang members "trying to be a social club," to still others who associated them with the Black Panthers—"and to that, we got a bad reaction, 'cause they were afraid of us. But some people just came out and looked."[45]

But when the Young Lords went to the Sanitation Department and were refused brooms and a truck to pick up the garbage, as David Perez describes, the party members

agitated in the neighborhood and got the support of the people to throw all of their garbage in the middle of Third Avenue. When that happened we got a response from both the police and the garbage men and they picked up what we had collected. After we made our point about sanitation, we started free breakfast programs.

The breakfast programs were begun in December 1969, following many unsuccessful meetings with officials of the neighborhood's First Spanish Methodist Church. The Young Lords took over its premises for eleven days, renaming it the People's Church and conducting free breakfast programs, health clinics, and a day care center. At the same time, party members such as Gloria Gonzales organized patients and workers in the hospitals serving the community to demand cleaner facilities and improved medical attention. They educated the community in health issues, initiating several door-to-door testing programs for tuberculosis, lead poisoning, and anemia.[46] These actions, like the garbage offensive, in effect were a response to the evident unsanitary and grim conditions of their neighborhoods and the lack of effective political channels through which to make their demands heard.

Within the party itself, the role of women and gender relations as a whole appear to have been subjects of much debate and discussion. Although women made up almost 40 percent of the party's membership, as Denise Oliver describes, "when the Party got started, there were very few sisters. It was mostly brothers, and those sisters that were in the Party got vamped on constantly. . . . We were not in leadership positions at all. We were relegated to doing office work, typing, taking care of whatever kids were around, being sex objects." The women argued that most of the people that would be affected by the free breakfast, clothing drive, and health care programs were women. Thus, after a difficult struggle early in the party's history, women were admitted into the central committee and also held significant leadership positions in organizing the party's various community actions.[47]

Members also organized both a women's caucus and a men's caucus in which each group discussed sexism, homophobia, and machismo in their lives and relationships. Pablo Guzmán writes of the party's acceptance of the notion of "women's oppression" put forth by the women's movement but adds: "Since I'm talking about sexism, the second thing that made perhaps a greater impact on us was when we first heard about Gay Liberation. That's a whole other trip, because we found out it's a lot quicker for people to accept the fact that sisters should be in the front of the struggle, than saying that we're gonna have gay people in the party." He goes on to explain that "from the time you were a kid your folks told you the worst thing you could be was gay." In his family, he was told that if he were to "turn out gay," he would be "disinherited, beat up, kicked out—and my father was *big*, you know, and fear . . . kept me from being gay. . . . When you think about fear keeping you from being anything, you realize there must be something wrong with it." Noting that he did not "turn out gay," Guzmán nevertheless emphasized that "the Gay Liberation struggle has shown us how to complete ourselves, so we've been able to accept this, and understand this."[48]

The party supported the goals of the women's liberation movement, and in particular of those within it who advocated a radical restructuring of the society. As Iris Morales explained, "There used to be only four choices for the Puerto Rican woman—housewife, prostitute, or drug addict, and then when the society needed more labor for its sweatshops, she would become a worker. . . . Now there's a new choice open to her that threatens the existence of the family and the state itself: the Revolution."[49] Nevertheless, party women were also clear in their awareness that "we do have some different views" from those of white middle-class women, largely stemming from the specific racial and class dynamics that differentiated their daily experiences.

As they struggled to position themselves on issues affecting all women's lives, the colonized status of their island also clarified the nationalist-based differences in Puerto Rican women's experience. They were torn, for example, by the issues surrounding abortion, insofar as women on the island had been victims of questionable birth control policies as well as of the practices of U.S. pharmaceutical companies. "We are very much aware of how genocide is practiced on Puerto Rican people and all Third World people through birth control programs, population control programs, and abortion programs," wrote Denise Oliver. She goes on to note the effects of the island's colonial experience manifested in women's lives in general and specifically in the number of miscarriages and deformed births both on the island and in their New York communities. As a result, the Young Lords women decided to support abortion only "under a system where abortion is not forced, under a system where there is community control of abortions, of health services of all institutions."[50]

The young activists refused both the passivity and conformism of the past and the fear of difference. They rejected the dominant society's images of Puerto Rican culture as "dysfunctional," of families as "demoralized," of youth as knife-wielding ghetto gang members who deny their homeland—all of which, as Richie Perez describes, had long prevailed in Hollywood films and Broadway plays, among which *West Side Story* is perhaps the best known.[51] In so doing, they urged their community to rethink and reassert their collective national and individual pride in Puerto Ricans' history, culture, and values.

Part of this history included the nineteenth-century ties between Cubans and Puerto Ricans in their struggle for independence. It is not surprising, then, that Castro's revolution was also a source of enormous inspiration. It politicized the young generation of Puerto Ricans both on the island and in the United States, as it did the Chicano students on the West Coast, and indeed the youth of all Latin America. Thousands of Puerto Ricans on the island were drafted during the Vietnam war, although their island's colonized status prevented them from voting for their president and commander-in-chief. This too led many Puerto Rican youth on the island and in New York to reject their treatment and status as a colonized population in the United States and to call for the immediate independence of the island.[52] In so doing, they continued the nationalist struggles of the past, following in the footsteps of previous generations of Puerto Rican militants like Pedro Albizu Campos and Lolita Lebrón.[53]

As Puerto Rican working-class youth and students became increasingly aware of the implications of their island's status, they renamed the island Borinquen, and many began to self-identify as Boricuas in an effort to return to its pre-Columbian indigenous Taino roots. Much like the Chicano Movement's adoption of Aztlán (to be discussed later), they reimagined the history of their community in largely mythical and poetic terms and increasingly adopted a strong cultural nationalist rationale in their actions. Nevertheless, the political nationalism of the Puerto Rican generation of the sixties was anchored in a different historical and political reality than that of the cultural nationalism affirmed by the Chicano Movement in the West. Indeed, unlike "Aztlán," the reality of the existence of Puerto Rico was never in question, for as Jorge Klor de Alva rightly reminds us, Puerto Rico "is an island where all national questions are reduced to *the* national question: is Puerto Rico a nation?" The effort to search and affirm their identity, together with a renewed sense of cultural nationalist pride, led many young activists to make the return voyage to Puerto Rico—although most were invariably disappointed when their mythical version of Borinquen was confronted with the harsh reality of the majority of Puerto Ricans' daily life on the island. At the same time, as "Nuyoricans" whose English language skills placed them in competition with the local labor force, they confronted the discrimination and rejection of the island populations.

For many, this clash was to mark their shift from the more cultural forms of organizing to more directly class-based strategies.[54] Sectors of the Young Lords became increasingly radical in their critique of the repressive violence of their society. At times they took up arms in self-defense, such as during the second takeover of the First Spanish Methodist Church, this time in protest of the police-related death of a popular community organizer and member of the party, Julio Roldán. Puerto Rican youth also protested the arrest of Juan Ortiz, the Young Lords' finance minister, and rioted and looted to protest the island's status and continuous police brutality within their communities.[55]

Nevertheless, the status of the island maintained the nationalist underpinnings of the new generation's activism and the cultural affirmation both within the party and among the radical youth in the communities. As Klor de Alva has noted, "Although it soon began to represent a practically impossible goal for the near future, the pro-independence movement continued to be in the 1960s and 70s an important *symbol* for uniting the nationalist elements in the U.S. And it was a superb tool for political organization on behalf of local barrio concerns."[56]

Throughout the Young Lords' years of activism, sectors within the Puerto Rican community remained ambivalent toward them, some opposing their actions either because of their strategies or because the party was unable to clearly formulate a direction that would mobilize more consistent grassroots support. "We knew somehow we would take them through some kind of struggle," wrote Guzmán, adding, "We didn't know where the hell we were going."[57]

The exacerbation of differences of strategy, ideology, and factionalism concerning the status question eventually led to purges within the party. Those who became more convinced of the need to focus on achieving the island's independence clashed with others who increasingly maintained that their struggle should be limited to their barrios in the United States. At the same time, many young activists began to leave the movement in favor of more institutionalized forms of effecting social change.[58] Yet despite their movement's decline, the cultural nationalist symbol of Borinquen and many youths' self-identification as Boricuas are still common among sectors of New York's Puerto Rican community, even today. Indeed, Blanca Vasquez perhaps best expressed the issues that confronted the postwar generation and the impact of sixties activism on both the participants and on the next generations of Puerto Ricans:

> As Puerto Ricans, we grew up with contradictions and in
> contradictions. Are we Americans? Well, not really. Are we Puerto
> Rican? Well, we may never have been to Puerto Rico. . . . There are
> parts of *here* that are us and parts of there that are not us. So we grow
> up with ambivalence, a sense of belonging to neither place until we
> begin a more conscious process of finding out who we are, where we
> come from, why we are here, and what we choose to be, until we
> begin to struggle it out and name ourselves. It was only through
> social movements that sought to *rescatar* (recover and reclaim) our
> history, honor our culture and ancestors, and to organize collectively
> to change the historical matrix of societal constraints imposed on us,
> that we found pleasure and joy and gloried in being Puerto Ricans.[59]

The Mexican-American and Chicano Movements

Like their Puerto Rican counterparts further east, leaders of the Mexican-American communities and the largely student-organized Chicano movements in California and the Southwest also rearticulated their struggles against the various forms of discrimination they had endured since the mid-nineteenth-century conquest of Mexico's territory.[60] Although all Spanish-speaking people of Latin American descent were homogenized as foreign to the style in which the "national community" had been imagined since the nineteenth century, the goals and strategies of Puerto Ricans necessarily differed in important ways from those of the Mexican-American and Chicano/Chicana movements. While sectors of the former could organize their struggle largely around their very real status as colonized citizens of the United States, the much larger Mexican-American population was more regionally diverse by the postwar period, and their conditions of daily life were more heterogeneous. Hence the rural and urban contexts within which the latter developed their movements were different from the more localized and strictly urban barrio organizing actions of the Puerto Rican movements. Still, like the Puerto Ricans, Mexican Americans and Chicanos were also to reaffirm and redefine their national heritage and cultural roots through their varied political movements in the pursuit of rights.

Rooted in the legacy of the conquest of the Southwest, the various Mexican-American and Chicano movements addressed at least two different, although deeply related, realities: the first was largely rural and included, on the one hand, César Chávez's movement to end the pervasive poverty and castelike status of Mexican Americans in rural areas and the discriminatory policies against Mexican immigrant labor in the fields, and on the other, Reies López Tijerina's Alianza de las Mercedes movement aimed at reappropriating lands taken from Mexican individuals and small farming communities following the Mexican-American War.[61]

The second was the urban reality of socioeconomic deprivation and persistent racism that continued to exclude Mexican Americans from first-class citizenship, rights, and equal protection under the law. Again, this was addressed by at least two different forms of political mobilization, organized largely by Chicano students and other working-class members of the new generations of the postwar period: one was the Chicano Power movement, led by Rodolfo Corky Gonzáles; the other, La Raza Unida party, founded by José A. Gutiérrez.

All four leaders were to incorporate and redefine the meaning of many of the cultural values, traditions, and legacies of their communities—albeit, as will become evident, some more overtly and self-consciously than others. Still, their political ideologies and the need to address the varied concerns of their respective constituencies led them to forge very different movements and strategies.[62] As Carlos Muñoz has rightly emphasized, they are all *not*, strictly speaking, representative of the Chicano Movement, which was characterized largely by its student youth constituency. Yet it is important to note that precisely because all four leaders (like the Chicana movement and the antiwar moratoriums) *did* address the diversity of Mexican-American/Chicano realities in the United States, all in one way or another contributed toward establishing the identity and presence of Mexican-Americans/Chicanos *as a distinct group* in the "national community."

The farmworkers movement organized by César Chávez and the early years of the United Farm Workers (UFW) are perhaps the clearest examples of the heterogeneity of political goals, the specificity of each leader's constituency, and the consequent type of movements that emerged. From his beginnings as a voter registration organizer in the 1950s Community Service Organization, César Chávez moved on to cofound the National Farm Workers Association with Dolores Huerta in 1962, later to become the United Farm Workers of America. Along with Helen Chávez, among others, he and Huerta organized farmworkers movements first in California and then throughout the Southwest, with the specific aim of improving the lives of migrant farmworkers and the labor conditions in the fields.[63] In his words, "The thing we are trying to accomplish here is the recognition of the union . . . and of the worth of the human being.[64] A few years later, Chávez elaborated on these reasons, explaining:

> We have adapted ourselves, as human beings will, to working conditions that few other Americans would accept. We work in open-air factories where temperatures rise to 115 degrees. We have had to accept the big humiliations of labor camps and being looked down upon as "dumb Mexicans." We have had to accept the little humiliations of no toilets, no mobile sanitary units in the fields.[65]

Together with Huerta, he organized workers to strike, walked endless miles in nationally publicized pilgrimages, and went on hunger strikes, insisting on labor contracts from the growers and demanding an end to the exploitative and divisive bracero program, which pitted Mexican Americans against newly arrived Mexican immigrants in the fields. Through his actions and rallying call—"Huelga!" (Strike!)—the UFW did achieve many victories. But also key to Chávez's strategy of nonviolence were the well-publicized national consumer boycotts he mobilized in support of the largely, but not exclusively, Mexican farmworkers—through which both the conditions of the farmworkers and the UFW (and Mexican Americans and Chicanos as a whole) achieved national visibility.

Although not primarily recognized in these terms today, Chávez, like other movement leaders, rearticulated both historical memory and the culture of Mexican Americans' everyday life in forging the growth of their respective movements. One of his strongest supporters, Luis Valdez, founder of the Teatro Campesino, wrote plays documenting the farmworkers' conditions, which were performed on the road, reinforcing Chávez's message.[66] Describing the three-week pilgrimage organized by the UFW in 1966 from Delano to the state capitol in Sacramento, Valdez explained the failure of traditional AFL-CIO methods of organizing Mexican-American farmworkers in Delano. He drew attention to Chávez's inclusion instead of the "triple magnetism of *raza, patria*, and the Virgin of Guadalupe" as part of his organizing efforts.[67] Similarly, Chávez's mobilizing strategies continuously pointed to the importance of recognizing the cultural strengths and daily life customs that had for so long ensured the survival, however precarious, of the migrant worker communities. Thus, as Valdez noted at that time:

> Chávez was not a traditional bombastic Mexican revolutionary; nor was he a *gavacho*, a gringo, a white social worker type. Both types had tried to organize the raza in America and failed. Here was César, burning with patient fire, poor like us, dark like us, talking quietly, moving people to talk about their problems, attacking the little problems first, and suggesting always suggesting—never more than that—solutions that seemed unattainable. . . . Chávez is our first real Mexican American leader.[68]

Chávez redefined the meaning of Mexican symbols such as the black Aztec eagle and the Virgin of Guadalupe.[69] Through door-to-door grassroots mobilizing of farmworkers' participation, he reaffirmed both the strong labor and union history of Mexican and Mexican-American workers and their right to "la huelga." In this way, the farmworkers' sense of the personal and collective humanistic values, deeply rooted in Mexican Americans' unwavering pride in their culture and communities' histories, was gradually restored and strongly reaffirmed.

Like César Chávez, Reies López Tijerina also focused on a particular aspect of Mexican Americans' history in the United States and drew on their cultural legacy to mobilize a particular constituency around it. Tijerina, a traveling Pentacostal preacher and once a migrant worker himself, spent years doing research and data collection in Mexico on the Spanish and Mexican land grants in the Southwest. The Alianza Federal de Mercedes (Federated Alliance of Land Grants) he founded was the first movement in U.S. history to take on the plight of New Mexico's small farmers left landless as a result of the 1846-48 War. Its stated aim was to restore ownership to Mexican Americans of the common-use lands (*ejidos*) taken from Mexicans in the war's aftermath.[70]

Tijerina continuously strived to make alliances with both the Native American and the black civil rights leaders and movements, although increasingly voicing a nationalist ideology with a strong emphasis on Mexican-American cultural affirmation. As he stated in an interview with a newspaper in Seville, Spain, "The Anglo absentee landlords are not content to just steal the Spanish-American lands, but wish to wipe out their culture and language." Along with his commitment to mobilizing rural Mexican Americans to fight for the restoration of their lands, he made it clear that his aim was also "to reinstitute the Spanish culture and language": "Americans want nothing to do with anything Spanish and hope to keep Spanish-Americans in a second-class category of citizenship worse than that of the Negroes, for at least the Negro problems are talked of while the Spanish-Americans are regarded only as potential soldiers to be sent to fight in other countries."[71]

Seeking redress from New Mexico's then governor Campbell, Tijerina organized a march from Albuquerque to Santa Fe on July 4, 1966, which, although unsuccessful, affirmed the identity of the participants as "a new breed"—La Raza, "people of New World Hispanic culture with its many increments from indigenous sources."[72] Thus, overtly rejecting the invisibility of "Spanish Americans" or Hispanos, he increasingly affirmed their identity as members of La Raza in cultural nationalist terms, making his movement's motto "The Land Is Our Inheritance, Justice Is Our Creed." The Alianza's *grito* or shout gradually spread throughout the Southwest and California, mobilizing thousands of Hispanos and Texan Mexican Americans who laid claim to Mexico's stolen lands, including middle-class Californians whose families had been affected by the economic restructuring of the previous century. Still, for many years, both Tijerina and the Alianza remained largely ridiculed or ignored by the nation's media—although, after 1964, not by the FBI, who again and again arrested, harrassed, and infiltrated the Alianza's membership. National recognition of the Alianza came on June 5, 1967, when Reies López Tijerina, along with twenty other Alianza members (and, according to Gardner, apparently supported by at least 80 percent of the town, if not more), raided the Rio Arriba county courthouse at Tierra Amarilla, to make a "citizen's arrest" of the district attorney, Alfonso Sánchez.[73]

Widely recognized among progressive leaders in various movements around the country, Tijerina's raid had a profound effect on La Raza throughout the United States, and he was soon recognized as one of its prominent leaders. Mexican-American progressive and radical leaders such as Luis Valdez voiced their open approval of the raid, as did Rodolfo Corky Gonzáles, who was emerging as the leader of the Chicano student and youth movement. Even middle-class and more moderate reformist professionals gave the raid some support. Some, like New Mexico's Senator Joseph Montoya, did it silently, limiting themselves only to general comments against the use of violence; others voiced more open support, although again distancing themselves from the violence it entailed. Addressing the national convention of the League of United Latin American Citizens (LULAC), a largely moderate Hispano organization, soon after the raid, Ralph Guzmán compared it to the violence in Watts, indirectly referring to the raid and the Alianza: "If we cannot condone their organization, we can plead the facts of poverty. If we cannot offer them congratulations on their methods, we can offer them our empathy—our understanding—and our support." César Chávez himself voiced his support of the Alianza, although again emphasizing his nonviolent stance. Moreover, as Gardner reports, many *corridos* were written about Tijerina, some disapproving but all nevertheless commemorating the raid, and villagers in northern New Mexico and throughout the border region discussed both its details and its historical significance.[74]

Several national leaders from other movements also acknowledged the raid in various ways, recognizing Tijerina's organizing strategies and mass mobilizing actions, including Martin Luther King, who with other civil rights leaders invited him to participate in the Poor People's Campaign in 1968. Although supportive of one another, relations between Tijerina's movement and those other groups were not completely free of tension, particularly between the Alianza members and African Americans. Tijerina was very aware of the self-concept of the majority of his followers as Hispanos de "raza pura," although as Gardner notes, this was "despite the fact that at least 80 percent of them had Indian blood." Thus, when he announced that he had invited Martin Luther King to the Alianza's National Convention in 1967, Tijerina ambivalently "assured his listeners, 'Of course we are only going to admit the Negroes when Martin Luther King speaks. After that they have to get out, because the convention belongs to our *raza*.'" Reflecting the increasingly cultural nationalist stance, he concluded by saying, "I want, when he speaks, for there to be more *raza* than Negroes." On the other hand, according to Acuña, at one point in his participation in the Poor People's campaign in 1968, Tijerina "threatened to pull the Chicano contingent out if Black organizers did not treat them as equals." Thus racial tensions at times also surfaced on both sides, even within movements deeply committed to the liberation of all oppressed groups. These, too, exemplify the various kinds of divisive political realities that perhaps inevitably were also shaped as a result of a legacy of prejudice and exclusion from the "national community."[75]

Nevertheless, although differing in the extent and reasoning behind their support or condemnation, there is no doubt that Tijerina's action resonated strongly among both civil rights leaders and various sectors of the Mexican-American and Chicano/Chicana communities throughout the United States, bringing home their historical and cultural legacy in the United States in overtly nationalist terms. Yet focused on rural and land-related issues, rather than on the urban barrios where the majority of Mexican Americans lived, as Carlos Muñoz points out, neither of the movements led by Tijerina or by Chávez directly addressed many of the concerns of urban Mexican-American communities in general and the issues that urban youth in particular confronted in the postwar years. Muñoz suggests that this may have contributed to the perpetuation of the stereotype of Mexican Americans as a primarily rural rather than urban community. Although both leaders certainly served as sources of inspiration and as role models for the students and working-class youth of the urban areas, the new generation of Chicanos turned for leadership to Rodolfo Corky Gonzáles, who had left his position as director of the War on Poverty program in Denver to organize the Crusade for Justice movement.[76]

Unlike the other two movements, the Chicano student movement, like the Chicano Power movement was, as Muñoz has rightly emphasized, a movement propelled specifically by Mexican-American youth in the "quest for a new identity and for political power."[77] In the late sixties, Corky Gonzáles's Crusade for Justice Organization brought Mexican-American students and youth from various states together for the first time. Through a series of Youth Conferences, the young generation of Chicanos organized to articulate their demands for better educational and social opportunities for their communities and their generation. As one of the participants, María Varela, described following the first Chicano Youth Conference in Denver:

> "Conference" is a poor word to describe those five days. . . . It was in reality a fiesta: days of celebrating what sings in the blood of a people

who, taught to believe they are ugly, discover the true beauty in their souls during the years of occupation and intimidation. . . . Coca Cola, Doris Day, Breck Shampoo, the Playboy Bunny, the Arrow Shirt man, the Marlboro heroes, are lies. "We are beautiful. . . . " This affirmation grew into a *grito*, a roar, among the people gathered in the auditorium of the Crusade's Center.[78]

The significance of the call for Chicano Power, for self-determination and self-liberation, must be seen in the domestic context initiated by the African-American struggle for rights. The latter movement was itself shaped by both the domestic and the international context of national liberation struggles in process in various countries of Africa, Asia, and Latin America.[79] It was a decade of protests, urban insurrections, and mobilization by racial minorities, women, sectors of the white middle class, students, and workers. It was a decade in which various domestic mobilizations and third world national liberation movements from colonial regimes were reflected—and indeed, the international context often distorted—in the demands for their communities' political and economic autonomy and self-determination. Whether in the United States or in other parts of the world, they mobilized to demand equality, to insist on justice, to reject the oppressive and human indignities of poverty—in short to refuse to conform to a way of life to which they could no longer adhere.[80]

Emphasizing the individual and collective empowerment of Mexican Americans in highly nationalist and at times separatist terms, Chicano students and youth rejected the assimilationist ideology of past Mexican-American leaders. Instead, they drew inspiration from third world countries' national liberation struggles and, hence, a new understanding of the history of their communities as "internal colonies" of the United States. The call for Chicano Power, like the institutionalization of Chicano studies, became a significant goal of the movement, as students recognized the need to struggle against the institutions that for so long had made their communities and their histories invisible.[81]

Their political commitment and movement participation was spread through newly created umbrella organizations such as Movimiento Estudiantil Chicano de Aztlán (MEChA). At the second youth conference in Santa Barbara, students adopted the term Chicano as their new form of self-identification, signifying their affirmation of their Latin American heritage, particularly their indigenous roots. "Choosing a name," as Richard King has explained, referring to the various names adopted by African Americans in different periods, is "an act of profound personal, social, and political significance. It is a way of rejecting an imposed role or identity and making a claim on a new one." A new cultural awareness and developing nationalism became an essential part of the new generation's strategy to articulate their identities and histories *as Chicanos* both to themselves and to the society at large.[82]

The 1969 *Plan Espiritual de Aztlan* reinforced the cultural nationalism underlying their movement. It openly rejected the government's official classification of Mexican Americans as "white" in favor of the students' new self-identification as members of La Raza. Breaking with the insistence on the traditional adherence to a "European only" legacy by previous Mexican-American generations (and indeed by Latin America as a whole), Chicanos grounded their version of Mexican Americans' "colonized" history in the mythical space and time of "Aztlán." Aztlán was the name for the legendary northern Mexican lands to which all Chicanos would one day return, both free and empowered. The students thus rooted their movement in nationalist narratives of a return to what Ramón Gutiérrez has described as a legendary and heroic Aztec past, peopled with strong and powerful warrior men who stressed virility and "the exercise of brute force." Emphasizing the need to construct a "moral community," Gutiérrez notes that the "imagined community" of Aztlán in effect excluded women. Indeed, like the men in the Young Lords party early in its history, Chicanos actively discriminated against them throughout the history of their movement: "Women were denied leadership roles and were asked to perform only the most traditional stereotypic roles—cleaning up, making coffee, executing the orders men gave, and servicing their needs. Women who did manage to assume leadership positions were ridiculed as unfeminine, sexually perverse, promiscuous, and all too often, taunted as lesbians."[83]

Although a largely mythical and ahistorical concept, the return to Aztlán, as Klor de Alva has argued, was "associated with the issues of poverty, land, sovereignty and political organization." Rooted in both the material expectations and political idealism of a generation committed to forging a better life for itself and for its communities, Chicanos and Chicanas insisted on their right to inclusion in the social and economic prosperity of their nation. As students participated in grassroots movements, organized political self-education through study groups, and began to attend classes in newly formed Chicano studies programs, sectors of the new generation also began to recover for themselves the conquered legacy in the United States of Mexico's early republican history. Through it, they, like their Puerto Rican counterparts in the East, gained a new knowledge of the histories of their communities' struggles as working people in the United States. Strongly influenced by the Cuban Revolution and rejecting liberal ideology of capitalism, they organized protests, rallies, marches, "blowouts," and demonstrations in schools, campuses, communities, and city streets, fighting for citizenship rights and demanding improved access to educational resources and facilities and better health facilities and higher standards of living for their communities.

Thousands of Chicanos, their families, and members of their communities increasingly attended yearly Chicano Moratoriums against the high numbers of Mexican Americans drafted to fight in Vietnam. Ricardo Pérez noted in 1971 that, although the Chicano population was 6 percent of the United States, it was 20 percent of the dead in Vietnam. These numbers, along with incidents such as the police murder of the *Los Angeles Times* journalist Rubén Salazar at the Moratorium of August 29, 1970, heightened the new generation's awareness of its exclusion from citizenship rights and the imagined community. They reinforced their belief that only a return to Aztlán would guarantee the economic and political control and autonomy of their communities.[84]

In adopting the term Chicano in Santa Barbara, then, the students and other youth had correctly identified it as also revealing "a growing solidarity and the development of pride and confidence."[85] According to Pina, the nationalism of sectors of the new generation was rooted in myths old and new, and nevertheless acted as a "myth of historical renovation." In the words of Anthony Smith:

> Rediscovering in the depths of the communal past a pristine state of true collective individuality, the nationalist strives to realize in strange and oppressive conditions the spirits and values of a Golden Age. The roots of the individual are buried in the history and ethos of his group, in its culture and institutions; and from these, and these alone, he can draw purpose and strength for the heroic deeds of the future.[86]

The style in which Chicano and Chicana cultural nationalists sought to reimagine their nation's boundaries also responded to "the material conditions of the time," through a plan that "although not class based . . . articulated a program for the liberation of a national minority."[87]

The attempt to institutionalize Chicano students' demands in nationalist political terms and on a nationwide basis led to the creation of *La Raza Unida* party, founded by José Angel Gutiérrez, a young Chicano nationalist from Texas, and his wife, Luz, in January 1970.[88] The party was initially built through mobilizing the Mexican-American community to challenge the state Democratic party in Crystal City,

Texas. Largely shunning the specific demands of Chicanas and relying instead on the cultural symbols and values of family and community, the party won control of the city council. Although its electoral losses two years later made this victory short-lived, it was the first time that Mexican-American men and women had political control of their community's schools since the Mexican-American War.[89]

Like the other movements, the campaign and election process also exposed the heterogeneity of the Mexican-American population. Referring to the April 4, 1970, vote, which brought four out of seven Mexicanos into the school board (Gutiérrez among them), an article on La Raza Unida party, summarized Gutiérrez's analysis of the election:

> The election neutralized two elements in the area. . . . It neutralized the intellectual Mexicano vote, the guy who thinks and feels it is un-American to vote anything other than Republican or Democrat. Some of these same Mexicanos had been very helpful in keeping our Chicanos in the same condition by not taking a stronger stand on such issues as bilingual education, debates relevant to local issues or the Vietnam War. They had constantly refused to go along with some of the Chicano student demands. . . . "The election also neutralized the Texas Ranger," Gutiérrez said. "They are nothing but a bunch of thugs with guns."[90]

The party spread to other states, including California, and was initially able to override the skepticism of both the Anglo and the Mexican-American sectors of the population in Texas. But by 1972, internal divisions—based on divergent interests, ideologies, strategies, and interpretations of nationalism—combined with the strong personalities and the ideological clashes among the four recognized Chicano leaders seriously undermined its effectiveness. This, together with the political inexperience of its largely student-based constituency (particularly in California) and lack of strong grassroots community support, was eventually to lead to its demise.[91]

In many ways, the cultural nationalism of the Chicano students contributed toward the affirmation of Chicano identities of an entire generation. Yet at the same time, it also hindered rather than propagated meaningful change for the Mexican population as a whole. The adoption of Aztlán, for example, meant that the everyday reality of Mexican Americans—and certainly of Mexico's rigid social and racial hierarchy—was not fully addressed and remained largely unacknowledged. The student movements emphasized a cultural nationalism grounded in the myths of Aztlán. As such, issues of citizenship rights, of exclusion from the national community, of equality and freedom, as Richard A. García suggests (although referring specifically to Gutiérrez), were ultimately resolved in an imaginary territory rather than within the boundaries of the United States.[92] Noting the continued poverty in which most urban Chicanos and Chicanas live today, Ramón Gutiérrez points out that curricular changes and Chicano studies departments and programs are "perhaps the most significant and enduring legacy" of the youth movement. In contrast, although both Chávez and Tijerina reaffirmed and redefined Mexican Americans' cultural heritages in political terms, albeit in different ways, there is no doubt that, unlike the legacy of the Chicano students, "the impact of the struggles that both of these men led are still felt in labor relations and land rights litigation."[93]

In this sense it is important to consider the diverse historical, regional, and social contexts that both shaped the Mexican-American/Chicano experience in communities and led thousands to take part in these varied movements. As seen above, the Chicano student and youth movement was largely urban-based and focused on the participants' identities and rights as second- and later-generation United States–born citizens. It was removed from the culture of Mexico's daily life, and its goals were in stark contrast to those, for example, of the migrant farmworkers movement. The latter included mitigating the effects of its constituencies' immigrant status and the constant threat of deportation—thus continuously bringing home the reality of the proximity of the border and reinforcing their own identity as Mexican nationals. Moreover, notwithstanding the emphasis on cultural nationalist strategies of mobilization, Tijerina's demands and constituency also differed from those of the Chicano and farmworkers movements. His Alianza de las Mercedes was grounded in very specific and legitimate historical claims to the land. This was to reinforce, rather than to create anew, the identities of the Hispanos as longtime residents and citizens of the Southwest.

There is little doubt, as even this brief overview suggests, that throughout "the sixties" and particularly between 1965 and the mid-1970s large sectors of Chicanos and Puerto Ricans mobilized in different ways, in response to the specific local and regional needs of their communities. In the process, their organizations and their cultures were rearticulated according to the variety of ways that class, race, gender, and generation shaped their experience of everyday life. Throughout the decade, for example, the older, more traditional organizations such as LULAC or the G.I. Forum, led by middle-class liberal professionals, continued to pursue Mexican Americans' civil rights through court actions and government institutions. But as Manning Marable has noted, like the NAACP and other African-American organizations, even they were forced by the later and more progressive movements to take a more aggressive stance in making their demands. In addition, new calls for "Brown Capitalism" were increasingly heard among the small nationalist entrepreneurial sectors, who demanded federal programs to support and enhance their interests. Similarly, the more traditional Puerto Rican organizations, too, continued the efforts to integrate Puerto Ricans into the agenda of the national community, some redefining their nationalist struggle in New York, and new organizations such as Aspira and the Puerto Rican Forum, among others, were created to reinforce their demands.[94]

But new forms of mobilization also emerged in both the Mexican-American/Chicano and the Puerto Rican communities, with a new emphasis on collective values and cultures. These were to help participants in the grassroots movements to establish their respective identities in ethnic-national terms, even as they adopted a wide range of liberal, reformist, radical, and separatist strategies in their varied struggles for citizenship rights.

Las Mujeres: Redefining the Experience of Exclusion

A key aspect of the growth of the Mexican-American/Chicano and Puerto Rican social movements of the 1960s and 1970s was the acknowledgment of the *experience of exclusion* as a significant factor in shaping the diverse communities and the individual lives of movement participants, as well as in the consequent varied perspectives, approaches, and strategies they developed in their organizations. It is true that regardless of the ideological and organizational differences, they did not escape, for example, the mutual exchange of accusations of opportunism; the envy and "ego fights"; the discord, mistakes, disappointments, and frustrations that are characteristic of many movements and perhaps inherent to the process of change. Still, in one way or another, participants expressed their determination to name, to voice, to recognize and acknowledge both their individual experience and the collective historical and social experience of their communities. This included affirming primarily to themselves, to one another, to their group, and, ultimately, to the society as a whole the moral and political imperative of participation in the struggle to redefine the way the United States was imagined as a nation.

Put in different terms, along with economic and political demands, a defining element of the Mexican-American and Puerto Rican movements for civil rights in the late sixties and the seventies was "the central role of the notion of rights in shaping new forms of thoughts and action." In this sense, the recognition on the part of Mexican Americans, Chicanos, Chicanas, and Puerto Ricans of the need to "establish an identity" also involved the struggle for their own collective affirmation as both individuals and citizens with "the right to have rights" in the national community of the United States.[95]

Many of the cultural values and traditions, the symbols and myths both old and new, that had sustained and reinforced their marginalized communities for so long were rearticulated in new ways to shape the growth and direction of the grassroots movements. Dolores Huerta, cofounder with César Chávez of the United Farm Workers Union, for example, describes the union as a "communal family," adding that the idea was neither "new" nor "progressive":

> It's really kind of old fashioned. Remember when you were little you had always had your uncles, your aunts, your grandmother and your comadres around. As a child in the Mexican culture you identified with a lot of people, not just your mother and father like they do in the middle class homes. When people are poor their main interest is family relationships. A baptism or a wedding are a big thing. In middle class homes you start getting away from that and people become more materialistic. When you have relatives come to visit it's a nuisance instead of a great big occasion.[96]

Similarly, as seen above, an essential prerequisite for Chávez to forge the terms of a new institutional relationship among the nation's farmworkers, the Democratic party, and organized labor was the reaffirmation of cultural pride and the collective values that had sustained Mexican-American communities for so long. In this sense, it was a relationship based as much on the acknowledgment of traditional power relations as it was on the emphasis he and the UFW placed on their organization's autonomy and on Mexicans' collective values of honor, dignity, and self-respect. In the words of Paul Jacobs, a member of the Citizens for Farm Labor, "It was a new kind of farm strike, a new kind of farm labor movement, which put the *campesinos* in the driver's seat and the "dignitaries' quite firmly in their place."[97]

Still, in seeking to understand their respective movements' impact on mainstream society and on the participants themselves, it is important to keep in mind the entrenched customary behaviors and traditional beliefs of significant sectors of the white populations in the post-war period. The latter were long accustomed to full and exclusive participation in the "national community." Thus their values conflicted, often violently, with the new civil rights laws, with their real and imagined fears of their implementation, and with the consequent implications of the changes for their daily lives. In this sense, it is not surprising that although the *Brown v. Board of Education* decision of May 1954, the 1964 Civil Rights Act, or the Voting Rights Act of 1965 were of momentous significance for the achievement of civil rights for minorities and women, opposition both to desegregation as well as to the now legally based demands for civil rights and political inclusion grew more violent as the decade progressed and the various movements developed.[98]

Violence certainly played a significant role in racial minorities' experience of the sixties—police harassment, FBI infiltration of their organizations, innumerable arrests, and brutal, often unexplained deaths were increasingly common as the nation felt the impact of the struggle for political inclusion. But escalating violence was also to strengthen collective ethnic group identification among Puerto Ricans and among Chicanos. As Escobar argues, the Los Angeles Police Department's increased repression and brutality in effect strengthened Chicano organizers' efforts to politicize large numbers of Mexican Americans who might otherwise not have joined the movement, thus reinforcing their communities' collective resolve to struggle *as Mexican Americans* for citizenship rights.[99]

At the same time, the culture of fear, repression, and exploitation that for so long had organized people's sense of self, as well as the lives of their families and communities,[100] cannot be underestimated in exploring the meaning and diverse forms of participation adopted by various groups in the civil rights period. The experience of women in both the Puerto Rican and the Chicano movements is particularly illuminating in this respect. Beyond reversing some of the effects of overcoming the "profound experience of exploitation" alluded to above, their participation in the various movements points to the contradictions in people's personal and collective lives as the movements adopted strategies that reinforced cultural traditions and simultaneously rearticulated them in political terms. The blunt words of Chicana scholar and activist Martha Cotera perhaps best summarize the gender issues women confronted early on in their movements: "When women speak, the community listens. But they seldom speak."[101]

Indeed, the human contradictions inherent in confronting long-held customary beliefs and actual daily life survival practices made themselves manifest in the discourse and relationships of both men and women. Although César Chávez was always quick to point out the importance of women in the movement, he once noted that "if you haven't got your wife behind you, you can't do many things. There's got to be peace at home. So I did, I think, a fairly good job of organizing her."[102] Yet as Margaret Rose has shown, from the early days of the farmworkers movement, Helen Chávez quietly acted as the UFW's credit union manager, an essential component of the UFW's development and of its successful growth particularly in its early years. As Dolores Huerta has emphasized, "You should see her books. We have been investigated a hundred times and they never find a mistake."[103] Due to lack of coverage by the mainstream press and perhaps to her own reticence, Helen Chávez, like many other women, remains largely unrecognized to this day for the long and significant role she played in developing the UFW.

As people gradually began to join together in movements for social justice, for equality and change, women's varied involvement reflected their determination to change the conditions in their communities and in their own lives. Puerto Rican activists confronted the sexism of men in the Young Lords early on in their party's history, and they along with other women also fought it within their communities. Chicanas fought for equality and justice within their own organizations and communities, participating in different ways according to their generation, their class, and their particular experience with oppression, racism, poverty, and unemployment.

The movements variously welcomed their participation, some more equally than others. Frances Swadish notes, for example, that women in the Alianza movement became active leaders, particularly following their experiences with arrests, their struggles while their husbands were jailed, their encounters with the FBI, the repression of local and state police, and the violent opposition of the national community to their collective struggle for recognition of their rights.[104]

While gender inequalities and sexism were rampant in the Chicano student movement, many women were in leadership roles in several local community efforts. When she addressed the Texas Women's Political Caucus in 1973, Cotera remarked that in grassroots movements, "a woman who thinks and acts on community issues is respected and does assume posts of responsibility. In Crystal City, for example, we have Chicanas as City Commission members, and in all administrative boards which make local decisions."[105] And similarly, speaking of the Puerto Rican women, Antonia Pantoja explained: "The reason women were in leadership was not that we sat and planned that we were going to have women's leadership. It is that because of the conditions of our community and the migration at that moment in the history of our community, it was women who took leadership.[106] Regardless of the form it took, movement participation, even in subordinate terms, was to help many women redefine the meaning of their historical roles in ensuring the survival and livelihood of their families and communities. Explaining how she became an organizer, Jessie López de la Cruz, once a housewife largely confined to the home and childcare, recalls the arrival of César Chávez at her home near Fresno one night in late 1962: "Then César said: 'The women have to be involved. They're the ones working out in the fields with their husbands. If you can take the women out to the fields, you can certainly take them to meetings.' So I sat up straight and said to myself, 'That's what I want!'"[107]

As the decade of the sixties progressed, the meaning of liberation, of the need to organize people so that they are "self-sufficient rather than . . . dependent upon the charismatic leader, or the Moses-type leader," as Ella Baker, founder of Student Nonviolent Coordinating Committee (SNCC) put it,[108] found new expression in the movements of blacks, of women, of other minority groups. The call to recognize "women's oppression" and to articulate personal and political issues in the collective struggle for rights resonated among Mexican-American and Puerto Rican women, many of whom were already actively participating in their respective communities and in the movements' organizations. Both among the Puerto Rican Young Lords women and particularly within the Chicana movement, "male concerns over job discrimination, access to political power, entry into educational institutions, and community autonomy and self-determination, gave way to female demands for birth control, and against forced sterilizations, for welfare rights, for prison rights for *pintas*, for protection against male violence, and most importantly for sexual pleasure both in marriage and outside it."[109]

They began to recognize the personal and collective issues that were specific to their lives as women and that hindered their visibility and full and equal participation as citizens in their respective movements and in the society as a whole. As Esperanza Martell, cofounder of the Latin Women's Collective (1975-78), explained:

We identified that what stopped women from taking leadership was that we had emotional blocks created by our oppression. The conditioning of Puerto Rican and Latina women is not to talk, not to open your mouth. The issue is respect, respect your mother, your brother, your father, respect anybody older than you in authority. You look down when spoken to, you do not ask questions, you just do. So we had women who were very dynamic who just did what was expected of them and never said anything.

In the process of participating in movements for social justice and for finding collective solutions to the conditions of their communities, they encouraged and supported one another as leaders of their own newly forming groups; they learned to speak in public, to hear their own voices, to shape their political identity, and to affirm themselves: "It was a [collective] process of talking through tears, of listening to each other, of identifying that we weren't alone, that we had the same problems and coming to the realization that we could change, that we could move forward and that we could do it collectively."[110]

As women came together they gradually created a culture organized not around fear or machismo, but around the recognition of each other's experience—and in the process, they discovered their own diversity: "Every time I begin to write something about a general group of people such as Chicanas," Isabelle Navar noted in 1975, "I am struck by the reality of our diversities, our heterogeneity." This recognition of the variety of women's experience went hand in hand with their acknowledgment of their continued historical role in their communities: "To speak of Chicanas is to speak of a multitude of experiences, of histories and of realities. As more of us begin to speak and write, the truth of the variety of our people emerges, something that was submerged and not understood as long as we were a forgotten and unrepresented people in the public eye."[111]

In the process of the collective struggles for their rights to equality, respect, justice, and recognition for the Mexican-American and Puerto Rican communities, women gradually learned to affirm themselves in the public sphere and to establish their respective identities as Chicanas or as Puerto Rican women. They acquired a renewed sense of self-respect, for as Richard King has suggested:

Self-respect is not only concerned with establishing moral and psychological equality but also with asserting difference. It is not just that I/we are as good as you; but also that I am/we are in some sense unique and acknowledged as such, whether by a transcendent power, another person or oneself. . . . Thus to assert a right, whether moral or legal, is a way of pointing to and asserting equality in difference.

Most discussions of self-respect fail to pay sufficient attention to "otherness," not just as that which helps constitute what we are, but also as the source of constitutive acknowledgment (the ideal form of which King called *agape*) from an "other."[112]

As the 1970s progressed, Chicanas increasingly affirmed themselves in various ways in their families and communities and as citizens with equal rights in the public sphere: "The American system also has its appeal in its romantic myths of equality and freedom—and perhaps it is not only by chance that our Mestizo culture, in our reality of yet another Mestizo American and Mexican mesh, is call for a making of those myths real," wrote Isabelle Navar, a Chicana psychologist in 1975. And she goes on to say that

across our own prejudices and differences, we are beginning to see our general links. A few of us are rich, and many of us are poor. Many are young and some are old. We live in cities and farms and we come in all different colors. But we are linked because we have not deadened the emotion in us that recognizes itself in another member of La Raza—the cultural bond and love that is hard to describe in ordinary American terms. Because we have not lost that ability to recognize ourselves in each other, I believe that we have a chance for a particular awareness of our present, a clear vision that we are here.[113]

Nevertheless, whether in the diverse Puerto Rican communities or in the various Mexican-American communities and Chicano movements, women were met by men's resistance. Many men tried to silence them in various ways: "There have been numerous attempts, on the part of women in general organizations to express themselves as a group," one woman wrote. "However, men have been mildly interested and amused by their efforts."[114] Chicanos in both the leadership and the grassroots levels accused the women of being divisive, of disrupting their respective movements, of being traitors to La Causa. They rejected them as imitators of white middle-class women, and appealed to class-based cultural nationalist ideologies, denouncing them in sexist terms as betrayers of their race and ethnic identity. In 1970, for example, one well-known leader interrupted his discussion of the newly created La Raza Unida party to say:

We understand and realize after having been involved in many kinds of movements, what the strength of a woman is, and what her strength is to the movement. . . . I want only to say this: That one of the problems that I see, as one of the grass roots people that came out of the *barrios* as someone who worked in the fields, is that I recognize too much of an influence of white European thinking in the discussion. I hope that our Chicana sisters can understand that they can be front runners in the revolution, they can be in the leadership of any social movement, but I pray to God that they do not lose their *Chicanisma* or their womanhood and become a frigid *gringa*. So I'm for equality, but still want to see some sex in our women.[115]

Indeed, aware of their very real class, community, and racially de-fined differences from the white middle-class women's movement and recognizing the importance of unity in the Chicano movement's struggle for rights and recognition, many Chicanas initially held back from voicing their demands. As Leticia Hernández put it in 1971: "If La Chicana tries to initiate a new role for herself in a Chicano organiza-tion, she receives an undercurrent that her activities are threatening the unity of the organization. Many Chicanas then begin to limit and select their activities."[116] And at an early Youth Conference workshop, women were led to report on their reticence in the following terms: "It was the consensus of the group that the Chicana woman does not want to be liberated," although as Denise Segura and Beatríz Pesquera have pointed out, this statement clearly obscured the intense debates in which women were engaged both at that conference and throughout the period.[117]

If the ideologies of the Puerto Rican and the Mexican-American/ Chicano movements forced women to choose between nationalism and feminism in embracing La Raza, many often neglected the racial and class dimensions within their own ranks that underscored their struggle for civil rights and the movements for inclusion in the "na-tional community." The realities of political movements such as Tijer-ina's in New Mexico or Gutiérrez's in Texas and the Southwest, for example, had sometimes forced the leadership to acknowledge the pervasive racial and class prejudices within their own constituencies. Still, sectors of the Mexican-American and Chicano movements never-theless emphasized their miscegenated roots in what José Vasconcelos first theorized as "La Raza Cósmica" of the New World, often in sepa-ratist terms;[118] many were perhaps even unaware of the ideologically assimilationist "whitening" roots that originally underpinned the phrase. The exaltation of their Latin American and indigenous roots, like their nationalist pride, often precluded the full and open recogni-tion of the very real and pervasive power relations between upper-class mestizos or whites and indigenous peoples, or of the castelike condition of blacks throughout the Southern Hemisphere.

Indeed, to a certain extent, nationalist affirmation of the respective cultures of Chicanos and Puerto Ricans downplayed the groups' internal racial, social, gendered, and generational experiences, which paradoxically had for so long marked Mexican Americans and Puerto Ricans as "Other" and ensured their exclusion from the national community in the first place. While both Puerto Rican and Chicana women emphasized the largely racial and class-based oppression of their communities ("the political context," as Esperanza Martell termed it) in explaining some of their very real differences from the white, largely middle-class, women's movement,[119] black Puerto Rican feminists tried to bring the specificity of their own experience as members of "three minorities in one" to the attention of their own movements. In a 1976 speech entitled "The Black Puerto Rican Woman in Contemporary American Society," delivered at a Symposium on the Hispanic American Woman, Angela Jorge noted that "for many the title . . . will be unacceptable, since it will be perceived of as divisive precisely at a time when the Puerto Rican people need to be united." She goes on to discuss the inherent divisiveness of unacknowledged racial differences and prejudices in Puerto Rico and in the United States, noting that being black, Puerto Rican, and woman was "in and of itself, a tremendous psychological burden which must be understood."[120]

Still although the recognition of difference was not encouraged by the movements as a whole, early in the 1970s many, usually women, already pointed to the diversity within their communities and movements. They hailed it as a strength, while some also recognized the importance of confronting the potential divisiveness of difference in forging the growth of political movements and alliances as a whole.

Internal differences notwithstanding, the various movements of the period reexamined their histories and roots and embraced in different forms and to different extents the cultural nationalist values, symbols, myths, and traditions of their respective communities. In so doing, by the mid-1970s there was no doubt that Mexican Americans/Chicanos and Puerto Ricans had established their respective identities— certainly to themselves—as citizens with "the right to have rights," and their presence was now at least acknowledged in the "national community."[121] Yet, as the following chapter discusses, it was precisely at this point that the term "Hispanic" began to be heard. Once again, the racial, class, and gender heterogeneity and the very real ideological differences within their respective communities were to be deemphasized. At the same time, it served to obscure the specific historical roots of each group's respective experiences in the United States. In other words, both in a sense were once again thrown into invisibility, although this time under an umbrella term ostensibly aimed at strengthening awareness of "ethnic diversity" within the "national community."

Chapter 4

Hispanic Ethnicity, the Ethnic Revival, and Its Critique

The Mainstream Response: Creating a "Hispanic Ethnicity"

The experiences of Puerto Ricans and Mexican Americans in the United States were long excluded from popular historical knowledge, ensuring that until the mid-1960s, neither group received national attention and their respective histories in this country remained largely invisible and unknown to the public at large. In fact, despite their repeated efforts to make their demands for political inclusion heard, when the mainstream media of the late 1960s did cover their mobilizations, they were often portrayed as groups that were organizing for full citizenship rights for the first time:

> Tio Taco—or Uncle Taco, the stereotype Mexican-American sapped of energy and ambition, sulking in the shadow of an Anglo culture—is dead. . . . From the ghettos of Los Angeles, through the wastelands of New Mexico and Colorado, into the fertile reaches of the Rio Grande valley in Texas, a new Mexican-American militancy is emerging. . . . Given the plight of the Mexican-Americans, the only surprising thing about the *movimiento chicano* is that it took so long to get started.[1]

Thus proclaimed the June 29, 1970, issue of *Newsweek*, for example, noting the regional diversity of Mexican Americans' experiences in the western and southwestern states, even as it emphasized the historical and widely accepted stereotyped version of them as passive victims of their own lack of ambition. While the magazine's article recognized that the forms of their militancy of the 1960s did give credence to the assertion that the "death" was irreversible, *Newsweek*'s description of the "new" Chicano militancy nevertheless ignored their long history of protest, revolt, and political organization throughout the Southwest and California. Thus, if one were to believe *Newsweek*'s portrayal of the "newness" of the 1960s Chicano movement, the stereotypes of Mexican Americans' passivity and lack of ambition of the past could easily be reinterpreted as historical "facts."[2]

In view of each group's specific forms of protest stemming from its particular demands and respective historical ties to the United States, it is not surprising that initially, when each group did receive national media attention, it was not as "Hispanics," but as Puerto Ricans and as Chicanos or Mexican Americans. But in the context of an emerging awareness of the two largest Spanish-speaking minorities on the national scene, one cannot help but remark on a curious, tiny article related to "Hispanics" published on September 13, 1969, in a major national newspaper. Almost hidden in the middle of column 5 on page 17 of section 1 of the *New York Times*, the title words—"Hispanic Heritage Week Set"—like the one-square-inch article itself, are almost lost in the midst of the pronounced headlines and photographs announcing the day's socialite "nuptials" and engagements. The article is so short that it is worth quoting in its entirety:

> Washington, Sept. 12 (UPI). President Nixon today designated next week as National Hispanic Heritage Week in tribute to the Spanish-speaking Americans and to promote ties with Latin American neighbors. In a proclamation, Mr. Nixon said that this particular week was set aside because it included the dates of September 15 and 16, when five Central American nations—Guatemala, Honduras, El Salvador, Nicaragua, Costa Rica and Mexico—celebrate independence days.[3]

Although the Presidential Proclamation 3930 of September 12 explains that the recognition of Hispanic culture had been requested by Congress the year before,[4] the question of why the very different historical and cultural legacies and experiences of the Mexican Americans and the Puerto Ricans were now to be homogenized precisely when their movements were emphasizing their indigenous Latin American roots, rather than Spanish European legacies, was never addressed. Why, one cannot help but ask, in this period of national emergence of Chicanos and Puerto Ricans and in view of their specific divergent demands and cultural affirmation *as two distinct groups*, would the president of the United States designate a "Hispanic Heritage" week? Unfortunately, the article limits its explanation to noting that the choice of the week coincided with the independence days not only of Mexico but also of

Central American nations whose populations at that time were numerically among the least represented in the United States.

In fact there were very few representatives of other Latin American nationalities in the United States at the time of the proclamation.[5] Political refugees from the Cuban Revolution after 1960 constituted a recent and numerical exception. Like most of the South Americans and Central Americans in the United States at the time, the Cubans were racially and socially homogeneous representatives of the Latin American elite—white, middle- and upper-class bankers and professionals, often highly educated and literate in English. Many of them had previously visited the United States, owned real estate properties, had long established business and financial ties in Florida, and were familiar with American cultural values and norms.[6] Still, compared with the Puerto Ricans and Mexican Americans, their numbers, like those of the Dominicans and of the Central and South Americans in the country at the time, were also not significant.

To a certain extent, the federal government's decision to proclaim a Hispanic Heritage Week must have been influenced by the new presence of Puerto Rican and Mexican-American leaders in Washington.[7] Indeed, one plausible explanation for the proclamation is that recognition of a Spanish-speaking "ethnic group" was in keeping with the emergence of a new way of defining U.S. society, one based on the recognition of "ethnic groups" and the concomitant reevaluation of the theory of the melting pot. Moreover, as I suggested in chapter 2, people of Latin American descent—regardless of their country of origin, race, or class—had never been differentiated in terms of their individual nationalities; rather, following the rise of the ideological superiority of the "new breed" of American, they had been lumped together as "Mexicans" and non-Anglos as early as the period of the Conquest of the Southwest. In this respect, the use of a term such as "Hispanic" in the late 1960s and early 1970s to homogenize the experiences of people with ties to Latin America in the United States was not new. But it did serve to blur the distinctions between the newly affirmed national and cultural identities emphasizing indigenous and third world legacies and the concomitant and respective demands made by Mexican Americans/Chicanos and Puerto Ricans.

The proclamation made no mention of the largely mestizo, indigenous, and/or black populations that make up the majority of the Central American nations whose independence the proclamation celebrates, nor of the indigenous and mestizo cultural roots that both the Chicanos and the Puerto Ricans emphasized in their movements. Instead, it focused on the Spanish European legacy of "Hispanics" in the New World, excluding from its definition any consideration of indigenous and black populations.[8] This emphasis cannot be underestimated, for a few years later in the mid-1970s, the federal government's guidelines for "racial and ethnic" categories were to emphasize that the designation "native American" was to be exclusively used for North American indigenous populations in the United States, drawing the line at the U.S.-Mexican border. As a result, as Jack Forbes has cogently argued, the ethnic and racial categories issued by federal agencies have meant that Native Americans from Latin America (regardless of their lack of Spanish language and culture) are considered, along with black Latin Americans, to be subgroups of the "Hispanic" category. One of the results of these categories, overtly adhering to political and bureaucratic criteria, has been in effect to obscure awareness of the indigenous and black roots of many Latin American immigrants in the United States, while simultaneously preventing indigenous refugee populations fleeing repression and discrimination by Latin American governments, or guerrilla actions on their villages, from seeking political asylum in the United States. Thus Nixon's proclamation, renewed every year and reinforced by later census definitions of Hispanics, paved the way for what Forbes called "a conscious effort . . . to build a *historically European Spanish-based and Spanish dominated group rather than a regional 'Latin' group or a regional 'American' group*"—known today as Hispanics in the United States.[9]

The struggle to raise the national community's awareness of the long historical and cultural legacies of Chicanos and Puerto Ricans during the specific period in which the term Hispanic began to be disseminated was thus largely dissipated by the fusion of the two groups into a newly created "ethnic group" with a new notion of its heritage and identity in the United States.

It is true that the post-1960s *public* awareness—*at the federal and national levels*—of the existence of populations of Latin American descent was unprecedented in the history of the United States. At the same time, it is important to note that the traditions, history, and experience of "the Hispanics" have since been in the process of being "invented" and affirmed by politicians, mainstream social scientists, the media, advertising sectors, and the public at large.[10] Referring to the establishment of Hispanic Heritage Week, Edna Acosta-Belén has correctly noted that "this proclamation was a symbolic recognition of the major role played by Hispanic groups in the past and present of this nation, from the early days of exploration, conquest and colonization of the Americas to the modern technological world of today."[11]

But while on one level the proclamation of Hispanic Heritage Week may indeed have acknowledged the presence of Spanish-speaking populations in the United States, it did so at the expense of publicly acknowledging the respective histories and demands of the two distinct national-origin groups, as well as the distinct political status of Puerto Rico. Thus, rather than signifying a new national and public recognition of these populations' "major role" in this country's history, the proclamation of Hispanic Heritage Week can instead be better understood, as the following pages suggest, as yet another sign of the significant shift in the mainstream perception of U.S. society as a "melting pot" and a consequent new approach to the way the "American community" would be imagined in the post-1960s period.

Reimagining the American Community: The Debate on the Melting Pot

Throughout much of the twentieth century, the image of the melting pot—whether in its "Anglo-conformity," "assimilation," or "cultural pluralism" versions—served to encapsulate the way the American community was imagined.[12] Coined by the playwright Israel Zangwill in 1909, the term *melting pot* embodied the idea that the cultures of immigrants arriving in the United States would mix with one another to create a new "American" population. But by World War I, Zangwill's original vision had been "drastically" narrowed down to the belief that "to be 100 percent American . . . was to be Anglo-American."[13] Even today, some scholars and sectors of the U.S. population still perceive the melting pot as "the dominant metaphor guiding our understanding of ethnic relations."[14]

But in the early 1960s, a few scholars began to refute the image of the melting pot, focusing on the enduring impact of ethnicity to suggest instead that U.S. society should be perceived as a plurality of ethnic groups with competing interests.[15] As racial minorities' diverse movements increasingly gained national attention, references to "new" culturally and politically homogeneous ethnic groups of "Hispanics," "Native Americans," "Blacks," and "Asians" began to appear in scholarly works and the national media of the post-1960s. The rejection of the melting pot definition of American culture was explained in terms of the emergence of a new notion of equality: an equality of difference, rather than of opportunities. Hence, Stephen Thernstrom's description of the 1960s celebration of ethnicity:

In the 1960s and 1970s, the United States experienced a cultural earthquake. Or so it seemed from reading the press or watching the tube. The "unmeltable ethnics" were on the rise, and the WASPs—revealingly, the only remaining ethnic slur permissible in enlightened circles—were on the run.

At congressional hearings on the bilingual education act, a congressman from New York announced that "we have discarded the philosophy of the melting pot. We have a new concept of the value of enhancing, fortifying, and protecting differences, the very differences that make our country such a great country."[16]

Thus, previously hierarchized at the symbolic level according to their origins and racial composition, ethnic groups, both old and "new," were now socially and culturally perceived horizontally by both scholars and public opinion makers.

Nevertheless, in spite of the 1960s celebration of ethnicity and the subsequent emphasis on ethnic studies and theories, the image of the melting pot continues to appear in some studies on ethnicity and race to this day, leading one study to note that the metaphor is "yet to be replaced."[17] Some scholars continue to argue that the "melting pot really did happen," particularly in terms of past white European groups. At the same time, pointing to the "rapidity and thoroughness with which [old immigrant groups] assimilated," Thernstrom, for example, has argued that "channels of opportunity like those open to earlier immigrants have at long last opened to [blacks and various other American racial minorities]." The problems confronting the latter, he suggests, stem from the emphasis placed on securing *group* rights, which in his view are "likely to be ineffectual and probably counter-productive." As a result, the extent to which opportunities are actually open and made available to all persons within these groups is blurred. Arguing that "equality of persons and equality of groups . . . are two very different things" and recognizing the difficulty of coalition building between poor blacks and whites, Thernstrom suggests that rather than continuing to support affirmative action, which benefits more affluent and educated minorities, new measures should be devised aimed at achieving "greater equality of persons," measures that would "redistribute income toward the poor of all races."[18]

Other scholars, however, have insisted that the lack of rights and recognition of nondominant ethnic *groups* in U.S. society has historically been determined by the dynamics of race and class. Non-white-European people and those of low-class status have long been citizens in this country and have experienced neither the assimilation nor the cultural pluralism predicted by either the melting pot hypothesis or later mainstream ethnic assimilation theories. Thus, rooting their analysis in the historical context of exclusion, as a result of which Chicanos and Puerto Ricans, like other minorities during the 1960s, mobilized for rights and group recognition, these analysts reject the concept of the melting pot as an explanation of various groups' experiences in the United States. They strongly suggest the need for a continued emphasis on group rights and affirmative action programs in the struggle to improve all minority persons' access to full citizenship, social justice, and rights.[19]

Within the context of this debate, the case of the Hispanics is particularly interesting to explore, given that this "ethnic group" includes both Mexican Americans and Puerto Ricans—historically present as racialized national minority groups in the United States—as well as the large numbers of post-1960s Latin American immigrants who have now also been officially designated as Hispanics in the United States. As I argue in the following sections, the 1960s focus on ethnicity as an approach to understanding the current processes of incorporation of diverse groups with ties to Latin America obscures the class and racial dynamics of the interaction both within each group and between them and the society at large. In spite of the differences in their time of arrival, as well as their unique class and racial heterogeneity, the automatic incorporation of Latin American immigrants as "instant Hispanic ethnics," members of the "Hispanic" group *as it is defined in the U.S. context*, is at best reinforcing Latin American cultural traditions and language and at worst once again rewriting the respective histories of the Chicano and Puerto Rican populations. Indeed, as the issues raised by the bilingual education debate and the English Only movement exemplify, both the past invisibility of these groups as citizens of the United States and the concomitant historical stereotypes stemming from their foreignness to the style in which the "national community" is imagined continue to be solidified by the reemergence of these issues in increasingly nativist terms.

Ethnicity as an Explanation of Immigrant Integration

A series of scholarly reinterpretations of American history and contemporary society focusing on the political, social, cultural, and linguistic aspects of ethnicity in the United States appeared in the period from 1960 to the 1980s.[20] Although these works continue to support the idea of the eventual assimilation of particular groups, their purpose was to document the ways in which each group's ethnic cultures and identities affected their assimilation trajectory and continued to persist in American society.

In 1963, for example, Nathan Glazer and Daniel Moynihan sought to explain the persistence of different ethnic groups in American society by arguing that they represented interest groups that established ties to the broader society in those terms.[21] A year later, Milton Gordon developed a paradigmatic model that was to substantiate this approach to ethnic groups. Noting the extent of acculturation following the first generation, Gordon argued that the study of immigrants should distinguish between assimilation in terms of their cultural behavior, which had been "massive and decisive," and the effects of race and religion, which hindered their structural assimilation.[22]

Others soon began to use Gordon's cultural/structural ethnic assimilation framework to present historical, cultural, linguistic, and sociological accounts of the experiences of past immigrant groups. Leonard Dinnerstein and David Reimers, for example, used it to present the history of U.S. immigration, providing a chronological account of the incorporation of the successive waves of immigrant "ethnics" into U.S. life.[23] Joshua Fishman focused on specific aspects of cultural integration, studying the dynamics of language maintenance as indicative of the continued cultural "authenticity" of specific ethnic groups.[24] While some have applied quantitative methods to the reconstruction of the experiences of Jews and Italians of the past, others have verified the process of assimilation of past Jewish immigrants using qualitative research among the second generation.[25] Thus, as Silvia Pedraza-Bailey has pointed out, Gordon's study on various forms of assimilation has served as the basis for much of the research on ethnicity since the 1960s, whether to emphasize "ethnic identification" or to examine "tangible outcomes, such as occupation, education and income."[26]

The framework has also been used in some studies about the populations who arrived in the post-1960s period from third world countries to analyze their progress in becoming "new ethnics." Joseph Fitzpatrick, for example, studied later waves of Puerto Ricans, focusing on the cultural differences underlying the assimilation process of this group, while Shih-Shan Henry Tsai explored the variations in the types of assimilation within the Chinese community. Both viewed the integration of these groups as continuing the patterns of previous waves of immigrant-ethnic groups. Speaking of the Chinese, for example, Tsai explains:

The newcomers have demonstrated during the past two decades that they, like the eighteenth-century French Huguenots, nineteenth-century German forty-eighters, and the twentieth-century Russian Jews, have adapted to American culture and therefore have succeeded in their diaspora experience.[27]

But since the 1980s, other studies on the more recent third world immigrant populations have increasingly criticized the ethnic assimilation paradigm, pointing to its inadequacy for understanding the experience of nonwhite immigrant groups arriving today in the United States. In his study of the Haitian population in New York, for example, Michel Laguerre concluded that it is "the racist structure of American society" rather than Haitians' own decision to adopt the U.S. ethnic categorizations "which compels them to use ethnicity in their adaptation process." As a result, he argues for "refining" the theory of ethnicity, to include generational, class, and racial dimensions in the process of studying the adaptation of nonwhite European immigrants to the United States—a point also raised by Clara Rodríguez in her study on Puerto Ricans.[28]

Moreover, scholars have increasingly recognized the importance of accounting for the effects of transnationalism as new immigrant populations continuously interact across borders and between the home country and the host society, constructing in the process what one scholar has called a "transnational socio-cultural system."[29] Shaping new identities, lives, and views on integration in the United States, the emphasis of this approach is on the effects of the restructured global economic context in shaping new immigrant flows, a context in which "the comforting modern imagery of nation-states and national languages, of coherent communities and consistent subjectivities, of dominant centers and distant margins no longer seems adequate."[30]

Indeed, the transnational perspective has clarified that several factors contribute to the inadequacy of the 1960s ethnic assimilation paradigm for understanding the more recent experience of nonwhite immigrants—among them the historical elusiveness of the definition of ethnicity and ethnic identity, the lack of a clear theoretical framework that incorporates the shifting nature of the historical and economic conjunctures in which immigrants arrive in this country, and the neglect of the impact of the racial and class dimensions in assessing immigrants' experiences and life chances in U.S. society.

Ethnic Assimilation: A Critique

A review of the vast body of literature on ethnic groups of the period from 1960 to 1980 leaves little doubt as to the elusiveness of the definitions of ethnicity and ethnic identity. H. J. Abramson provided a brief history of the term *ethnicity* within the context of assimilation/pluralism versions of American society, noting that although the usage of the concept of ethnicity is recent, "the idea is old." Although Abramson suggests that this idea was conveyed in the past through terms like "immigrant group, foreign stock, language group, race and national background,"[31] other scholars have noted that the definition of ethnicity in the United States has always been historically contingent and cannot be separated from the class position of immigrants and minorities in this country. As Stephen Greer has noted, "ethnic" has been used to refer to poor white immigrants (at the turn of the century), then to black Americans (who were "yet to be included in the mainstream"), and finally, during the 1960s Great Society and civil rights era, no longer representing arriving newcomers but rather "a record of an alternative, a more truly American style."[32]

Indeed, lacking in most studies on ethnicity is contextualization about the definition and uses of both the very notion of ethnicity itself and a recognition of the shifting meaning and historical nature of labels in society. If, as noted in chapter 3, naming oneself is, in Richard King's words, "an act of profound personal, social, and political significance," then of equal importance is recognizing the detrimental effects of focusing on identifying *which* particular fixed, subjective cultural traits underly "ethnic solidarity" for developing our understanding of both the historical contingency and continuous complex process of social life.

While not denying the importance of individual self-definitions or of group pride, some scholars have noted the recurrent lack of a contextual framework and of specific "objective" criteria in the study of ethnic groups leading to studies that emphasize instead the need to define ethnicity in terms of the society's economic processes. Criticizing "academic intellectuals" who suggest that ethnicity today is increasingly symbolic, David Muga, for example, discusses the relationship between ethnic attribution and economic opportunity. He points to the nativist backlash, racism, and discrimination and concludes that those who view ethnicity as symbolic only "speak for a middle strata and all those who have achieved material 'success' within a capitalist society while remaining blind to how ethnicity has been most authentically preserved among the economically and politically pressed."[33]

Other authors have criticized ethnicity theorists for their neglect of class and racial considerations. Attributing this neglect to the tendency to conflate the 1960s racial and ethnic forms of organization, Joan Moore argues that "the idea of caste and the ethnic-assimilationist model continues to suit a large group of social scientists who find the ferment of the 1960s repugnant. The ethnic-assimilationist model fits extremely well with the neoconservative emphasis on 'pure' market factors as an explanation of status mobility and on cultural factors as an explanation of failure."[34]

Thus, precisely because the dynamics of race and class are rarely seen as significant in ethnicity theorists' perceptions of past immigrants' integration into American society, the focus on ethnic assimilation has meant that the *power differences* in ethnic and minority status attributions are often neglected in the analysis of a particular group's social mobility and usually obscure within-group variations.

Approaching this discussion from a different perspective, Michael Omi and Howard Winant focus on the shifting meaning of race in this country's history to construct a framework from which to conceptualize race. They underline the implications of the genocide of native Americans, the enslavement of African Americans, the invasion and colonization of Mexican Americans, and the exclusion of Asian Americans in the nation's history. The key to their analysis is the recognition of the significance of race and the need to specify the "racial formation" of a specific historical period—the political, economic, and social forces that shape both the content and significance of racial categories and meanings at each historical conjuncture.[35]

These critics of "ethnicity" theorists argue against what they call the "immigrant analogy"—the idea that "blacks" and other "nonwhite minorities" could or should be analyzed in terms of their adherence to the patterns of assimilation of previous white immigrants. While they agree that in the 1960s "white-ethnics" returned to their roots and celebrated their advances from their *racially white* immigrant forebearers, they suggest that nonwhite, racial minority groups—long excluded from the immigrant advancement version of the melting pot by legally sanctioned discriminatory practices—organized not as "ethnic groups" but rather in racial terms. As the respective sixties movements of African Americans, Chicanos, Puerto Ricans, and other minority groups exemplify, this form of organization was a political device in their confrontation with the state and their struggle for social equality and full-citizenship rights before the law. Thus Omi and Winant suggest that rather than agree to "become" ethnics and accept the equal opportunity legislation that would allow African Americans, for example, to follow the "example" of previous white immigrant ethnics, "many blacks (and later, many Latinos, Indians and Asian Americans as well) rejected *ethnic* identity in favor of a more radical *racial* identity which demanded group rights and recognition."[36] As I suggested in chapter 2, the historical acknowledgment of the presence of African Americans in the United States did not necessarily mean that they were perceived as equal members of the nation. As Ronald Takaki has argued, the citizenship and suffrage guaranteed by the 1790 naturalization laws to all men of white European ethnic origins arriving in the United States was historically denied to all men of color—establishing a "sharp distinction between ethnicity and race."[37] Thus Omi and Winant argue that the important distinction between racial and ethnic forms of organization, long neglected in the literature on ethnicity, re-emerged yet again during the 1960s and was at odds with the aims and goals of the various minority movements.[38]

In fact, the strongest challenge to ethnicity approaches has come from analysts who critique the ways that the distinction made between race and ethnicity has shaped American history. Ideologically, the use of the term *melting pot* had contained an implicit idea of equality, at least at the level of the equality of rights and opportunities of all the citizens it embraced. Yet the very history of the United States bears witness to the existence of legally supported racial discrimination and widespread prejudice. As E. San Juan Jr. has argued, "From its inception, the United States has been structured as a racial order," and thus, as seen in chapter 2, race has historically been the basis for the construction of a social hierarchy according to which members of different ethnic groups were granted or denied citizenship rights and responsibilities.[39]

The importance attributed to ethnicity in the political and social events of the 1960s to 1980s is indicative of the extent to which the social modes of clarifying the national identity of the United States cannot be separated from the historical forms that racism has taken. One has only to recall the black liberation movement's emphasis, during the years of the 1960s, on black pride, identity, and cultural heritage as an example of how social and political issues had to be raised and channeled within cultural referents in order to be heard in a now "ethnically awakened" multicultural society.[40]

That sectors of the black liberation movement, like those of the Chicano and Puerto Rican movements, were to channel their demands within cultural referrents is actually not surprising. For as seen above, the testimony to the power of cultural classifications is recorded most clearly in the history of race relations and their legislation in the United States. The 1896 *Plessy v. Ferguson* Supreme Court ruling in favor of segregation on the curious grounds that "legislation is powerless to eradicate racial instincts" is itself a telling example of the state's overt differentiation between prejudice and discrimination in terms of the power of these classifications. At the time of its enactment, this ruling contributed to the social recognition that blacks' lower socioeconomic position was in fact *illegitimate* in a social structure that "measured" status not only socioeconomically but also culturally and educationally.[41] The use of segregation as a lived manifestation of status measurements contributed to the development of the "separate but equal" rationalization of a class society in which race has been the motive force underlying the social formation throughout most of U.S. history. Hence the distinction between race and ethnicity, as noted in chapter 2, stems at least in part from the historical distinctions made by the law itself between prejudice and discrimination. Not surprisingly, "minority" intellectuals and activists have increasingly played a significant role in exploring the implications of distinguishing race from ethnicity. Insofar as the minority movements and riots of the sixties showed the extent to which race had historically played a pivotal role in preserving and reproducing the social order, it is perhaps not surprising that many mainstream analyses of the 1960-80 "ethnic revival" period are being challenged specifically on racial grounds today.[42]

The distinction between ethnicity theory and minority demands and practices during the 1960s is particularly interesting to explore in the light of the historically contingent definition of the term *ethnic* and the way its meaning has continuously been renegotiated in the context of the ongoing social and power *repositioning* of assimilated "acceptable Americans." While the latter are defined as those in a position to have the "benefit of social and political inclusion," their opposites, "unacceptable Americans," are perhaps not so easily defined.[43] As seen in chapter 2, the very ideological definition of American national identity has historically been largely based on an "act of choice" by both the individual and the society.

Indeed, the struggle for "social and political inclusion" of minorities is exemplified through the battle to establish the (legal) right to bilingual education and its implementation in the schools. As Arnold Liebowitz has argued, "Official acceptance or rejection of bilingualism in American schools is dependent upon whether the group involved is considered politically and socially acceptable."[44] This struggle in turn clarifies the role of the state in both protecting minorities and reinforcing through law the relationship between race, class, and language.

The Dynamics of Ethnicity, Language, Race, and Class: The Bilingual Education Debate and the English Only Movements

Key to understanding the ongoing social and power *repositioning* of who might be considered an "acceptable American" is the fact that, unlike the present time, earlier immigrants did not "need advanced English language skills to get jobs and survive in the less complex economic order of the time. Whatever problems such groups had, they were not as critical to economic survival as such language skills are now."[45]

Indeed, particularly since the 1960s, there has been what might be called a significant increase in linguistic discrimination through the gradual politicization of language (whether English or not). This is visible in the discussions on ethnicity and the significance attributed to "de-ethnization" as the basis for assimilation and integration into U.S. society. Seen in these terms, language is an integral part of these ethnicity debates on what it means to be American, what it means for a new American national identity, an *American ethnic-nationalism* in a now-awakened "multiethnic" society.[46]

According to Joshua Fishman, indifference to ethnicity among assimilated Americans matches their indifference to the English language: people speak English because it is the language used to communicate in this country, "rather than because it is beautiful, divine or indivisible from American tradition."[47] Publications of the English Only movement, represented by such groups as U.S. English and English First, agree with this assessment of Americans' relationship to the English language, although they draw a different political conclusion. The aim of these interest groups is to achieve a constitutional amendment that would declare English the official language of the United States. In a 1983 justification of their support for the English Language Amendment, or ELA, U.S. English wrote, "We hold no special brief for English. If Dutch (or French, or Spanish, or German) had become our national language, we would now be enthusiastically defending Dutch."

The stated indifference of "assimilated Americans" to the language per se is particularly interesting to explore in view of the historical battles to ensure the prevalence of English among arriving immigrants today. The battle over language policy and usage has been most apparent in the educational system itself, long recognized as the principal site for immigrant socialization and Americanization processes.[48] Yet, it is important to consider that historically, non-English and bilingual instruction were actually quite common in the United States. For this raises the question not of why bilingual education "emerged" in the 1960s but rather why it was not federally recognized by formal legislation before.

As Maria Matute-Bianchi noted, the recent history of language legislation and bilingual-bicultural education describing federal intervention in public schools was an "intervention that was unknown prior to the passage of the Elementary and Secondary Education Act of 1965."[49] In this sense, history thus points to the increasing political relevance, for the state, of language policy and its effects on the socialization and Americanization of non-English-speaking minorities and immigrants alike.

The language-related policies and debates that have emerged since the passing of the Bilingual Education Act in 1968 are perhaps the clearest indication of this process. For when the sixty-five-year-old "separate-but-equal" justification for school segregation was challenged and revoked by the Supreme Court's 1954 *Brown* decision, a new period of legislative debates and court cases did begin. But, with them, the issue of the ability of legislative action to effectively "eradicate racial instincts" was once again the underlying motif of the legal battles that have since been waged. Like the 1896 *Plessy* case, the court decisions over the past thirty years have centered on the issue of racial discrimination in education. Today, however, the protagonists of these more recent cases are not only, or primarily, African Americans. Rather, they are sectors of the "Hispanic" population who, together with other minority and immigrant groups and their children, are formally challenging not only the racial prejudice of yesteryear but also the deeply embedded myth of the melting pot.

The trajectory of this challenge is most visible in the political impact that the court cases by minorities concerning the right to bilingual-bicultural education have had (or have failed to have) on the ideological belief of the melting pot image of the national community. Furthermore, the results of their challenge to the existing social hierarchy can be partially summed up in its "unanticipated historical consequences" on the power of legislation to deal with racial and ethnic tensions since the late 1960s.[50]

The 1968 Bilingual Education Act is "often hailed as a masterpiece of ambiguity" for failing both to define "bilingual education" and to specify its goals. In this sense, it was a linguistic "side effect," so to speak, of the antidiscrimination provision stipulated by Title VI of the 1964 Civil Rights Act.[51] Indeed, the passing of the Bilingual Education Act seems to have been more the result of the prevailing liberal mood rhetorically proclaiming the "equality of difference" than of a well-thought-out project aimed at addressing the issues specifically related to providing equal educational opportunity to each child. The definition of what constituted an American education (that is, the question of nationality in a pluralistic society with an increasingly heard ethnic-minority voice) was more important than the recognition that even within minority groups, there were significant distinctions concerning their social and educational needs and cultural heritages.[52]

It took five years, for example, for the Supreme Court decision in *Keynes v. School District no. 1* to begin specifying the existence of various and diverse ethnic groups within the category of "minority." This 1973 decision stated that Spanish-speaking students could not be sent to schools with primarily African American student populations as a means of circumventing the 1954 *Brown v. Topeka Board of Education* decision against segregation.[53] Similarly, the practical implications of implementing "equality of opportunity" in the American educational setting were raised only after the *Lau v. Nichols* decision of 1974, which ruled that "access to educational facilities and resources alone cannot be the sole determinants of a child's educational rights."[54] In spite of the *Lau* decision's recognition of the need for "affirmative action," the type of action and its practical application and punitive fines for noncompliance remained unspecified by the courts, and thus the decision was not pursued by most school districts until the *Lau* remedies were stipulated the following year. The issue of what would constitute an appropriate plan was theoretically resolved in the 1973 *Serna v. Portales Municipal School* in New Mexico. This court had "established bilingual education programs as viable solutions in language-related issues."[55]

However, the lack of specification of both the quality of instruction and the means to determine need and eligibility for such programs led to further confusion. Court case decisions such as *Otero v. Mesa County Valley School District no. 51* (1975) were successful in dismissing bilingual programs on the grounds that "few students in the district experienced any real language difficulties. Therefore, the lack of evidence to substantiate a violation of Title VI or the Fourteenth Amendment and the lack of numbers resulted in the dismissal of the claimed right to bilingual education."[56]

But, while there were successful attempts against bilingual programs, some advances were made through other court cases, such as the *Rios v. Reed* case. This court ruling recognized not only the importance of bilingual education and the 1974 Bilingual Education Act, but also that

> it is not enough simply to provide a program for disadvantaged children or even to staff the program with bilingual teachers; rather the critical question is whether the program is designed to assure as much as is reasonably possible the language-deficient child's growth in the English language. An inadequate program is as harmful to a child who does not speak English as no program at all.[57]

In spite of renewed federal support for bilingual education in 1978 and during the 1980s, the resistance of school districts to implementing adequate programs and their lack of concern as to their effectiveness—like the society's own growing antipathy, if not prejudice, against immigrants and minority children and adults alike—has continued unabated from the bill's enactment to the present day.[58]

While many within the bilingual education community would hope that their efforts ensure English language proficiency as much as they guarantee that children do not forget their native language skills, there is no doubt as to the transitional nature of most language programs in the United States.[59] Nevertheless, during the 1980s, numerous attempts were made to deny the validity of bilingual education. Cases such as the 1972 *Aspira of New York City Inc. v. Board of Education of the City of New York* had successfully argued for defining criteria to assess and evaluate language proficiency as a means for determining students' needs for bilingual programs. Yet faulty studies in the late 1970s and in the 1980s soon purported to measure their effectiveness. Together with support from individuals within the federal government, such as former U.S. secretary of education William J. Bennett, these studies bolstered groups such as the English Only movement who used nationalist discourse to lobby against ethnolinguistic diversity and in favor of declaring English the official language of the United States.[60] Their movement's agenda appears to be to move from "English-only in government to English-only in society."[61] In so doing they consistently negate the founding principles, which included tolerance for language differences and in fact receive consistent support from the courts, which at various points have upheld the unrestricted right to use foreign languages in the United States.[62]

The Bilingual Education Act of 1968 evolved from a bill sponsored by Senator Ralph Yarborough of Texas, which initially sought to address the psychological trauma resulting from linguistic discrimination and the consequent high dropout rates from schools among Mexican Americans and Puerto Ricans.[63] Although later extended to include all students with limited English-speaking proficiency, "Hispanics" have remained a primary target of the anti–bilingual education groups as well as of the English Only movements. Yet for obvious reasons, such as social class and the time of arrival of different individuals and groups, there are mixed levels of language proficiency within the Hispanic community. For English is the first language of second and later generations of Chicanos and Puerto Ricans, as well as of the children of other Latin American immigrants, all of whom have been raised and socialized in the U.S. school system. More recent immigrants and their children, particularly if they have working-class origins, on the other hand, usually only encounter the English language for the first time when they arrive in the United States. Although this disparity in language proficiency within the Hispanic community seems self-evident, nevertheless the focus of both the detractors of bilingual education and the lobbyists of the English Only movements is primarily on the lack of English language abilities (and hence on the new immigrants) rather than on long-established English dominant groups within the Hispanic community, such as the Mexican Americans/Chicanos and Puerto Ricans. Similarly, these movements ignore the scientifically established fact that by the second or at most third generation, non-English-speaking immigrants (including "Hispanics") have become fluent English speakers.[64]

Thus, the real issue for the detractors of bilingual education and the adherents of the English Only movement is not equal educational opportunity for each child but rather their persistent refusal to acknowledge or tolerate difference, or as Ana Celia Zentella has bluntly stated, "The root of the problem lies in an inability to accept an expanded definition of an American."[65] Indeed, in the present context of the declining leverage and economic performance of the United States in the global context, as Fishman has suggested, recent nativist attacks on racial minorities and immigrants are increasingly fueled largely by the insecurity of the power classes—like that of those Anglos and non-Anglos alike who aspire to their ranks—about their leadership role and power in the United States. Movements to make English the official language of the United States "boil down to the 'who's in control here anyway; we who deserve to be or those riff-raff and upstarts?' " As a result, the politicization of the English language of the 1980s represented a "patriotic 'purification' campaign against 'foreign elements,' akin today to the anti-Catholic, anti-immigrant, anti-Black, and anti-hyphenated-American campaigns of past eras in American history."[66]

Hispanics: Ethnics or Minorities?

The above case study of the dynamics of ethnicity, race, and class in shaping the current national identity and image of the United States and the history of bilingual education legislation and the English Only movements points to the complexity of disentangling prejudices and discrimination against individuals within a group, in this case the Hispanic community. While it is difficult to disagree with Stephan Thernstrom that group rights and rights of persons are two very different things, language discrimination and the concomitant racial underpinnings are indiscriminately directed at now officially established ethnic groups such as Hispanics, with no regard for individuals' language skills, U.S. citizenship, or time of arrival in the United States. Besides going against the minimum principles of respect for individual rights, this in effect lays bare the extent to which today, as in the past, persistent discrimination against *groups* based on long-held stereotypes about "foreign Others," rather than any serious consideration about the reality of the persons involved, continues to shape the "channels of opportunity" actually open to all individuals identified as its members. Thus, insofar as the political struggles against equality of opportunity are established in group terms, affirmative action policies aimed at improving the conditions of *groups* must be reinforced to ensure equality of opportunity and citizenship rights to all individuals.

At the same time, while the continued struggle for full citizenship, equal rights, and social and cultural inclusion in the "national community" requires that Latinos and other minorities affirm group rights and interests in political terms when confronted by nativist attacks, the complexity of the dynamics of "ethnic" and "minority" status in U.S. society stemming from the heterogeneity of race, class, and language within the Latino community in the United States cannot be overlooked in seeking to understand the meaning and social value of the label Hispanic in individual lives.

Arguing that it is important to distinguish between ethnic and minority group status, Joan Vincent identifies the differences between "ethnic groups" and "minority groups" as stemming from their differential positions of power and status in society:

> For individuals, ethnicity must consistently be placed in the context of alternative status articulation: the essence of minority status is that it cannot. Ethnicity may be seen to lose out in competition with economic status opportunities, whereas the maintenance of economic discrimination is the bedrock of majority-minority domination.[67]

Thus, an ethnic group *chooses* to articulate its collective common cultural norms, values, identities, behaviors, and self-recognition in particular situations. But members of a "minority" group have to contend instead with the common experience of prejudice and discrimination "imposed from above."

Vincent's use of status and power as the basis for distinguishing between the social experiences of ethnic and minority groups is particularly important to bear in mind in analyzing the case of Latin American immigrants in the United States. For, unlike previous immigrant groups, the populations with ties to Latin America are characterized not only by national, linguistic, and religious differences but also, and perhaps more important in the U.S. context, by racial and class heterogeneity. Indeed, following Vincent, while white, middle- and upper-class Hispanics might be able to attribute an *ethnic* status to themselves, others would assign to many "non-white Hispanics" a *minority* status based on class and racial considerations. This distinction in turn raises questions about the effects of race and class in determining the types of insertion that different sectors within the Hispanic populations achieve in U.S. society.

Crucial for exploring the differentiated experiences in the United States of the populations with ties to Latin America is the fact that the understanding of the social hierarchy in Latin American countries has traditionally been based on a continuum rather than on division among the races. This does not necessarily mean that ethnicity, nationality, race, and language are not socially and culturally significant in Latin America, nor that class is secondary in establishing relationships and communications here in the United States (see chapter 2). Yet it does point to two different ways of stratifying and classifying groups, which in effect differentially organize people's sense of self, feelings, and ways of belonging, participating, and positioning themselves in society, while simultaneously defining and legitimizing their political rights and social obligations—and hence their national and cultural identities both at home and abroad.

Indeed, the perceived prevalence of class over race in organizing the social hierarchies of Latin American societies is a Latin American cultural truism that can serve as a barrier against intragroup or ethnic solidarity for many Hispanics once in the United States. As the sociologist Martha Giménez poignantly stated: "Nationality is not as important in determining patterns of association and participation in the host society as social class. . . . *Middle and upper-middle class immigrants are more likely to share the values of the dominant classes including class, racial and ethnic prejudices.*"[68]

The shift from a social hierarchy with representations based on class relations and differences to one in which race assumes a "legitimate" status in explanatory models of social and cultural differences thus raises the issue of how class distinctions are articulated with racial (as distinct from ethnic) practices within and among recently arrived groups from Latin America. The indiscriminate use of a homogenizing ethnic label such as Hispanic obscures both their respective experiences in this country and the power and status differences within the Hispanic population, while minimizing these distinctions in relation to the larger U.S. society. Given the unique heterogeneity of the population identified as Hispanic, it is important to address the neglect of the racial, class, and language dimensions that structure their daily lives and experiences as "ethnics" *and* "minorities" in U.S. society. The following chapters, presenting qualitative research data drawn from interviews with diverse individuals encompassed by the label Hispanic, are thus an attempt to explore the impact of race and class in shaping the diversity of experiences of a group of people with ties to Latin America currently living and working in the United States.

Chapter 5

Hispanics and the Dynamics of Race and Class: The Fieldwork Data

The question that motivated the research for this study centered on how the specific label *Hispanic* resonated in the lives and self-perceptions of a group of first-generation immigrants from various Latin American countries in the United States. The term, after all, brings them together as a group, even as their own national experiences and social class and certainly their lack of experience in the American racial and ethnic hierarchy might in itself differentiate them from Latino populations born in the United States. As I suggested in the Introduction, I began the study with the assumption that arriving Latin American immigrants categorized as Hispanics by mainstream U.S. institutions would not always choose to identify themselves primarily as Hispanic, since they do not necessarily share common national, social, or historical backgrounds. Moreover, they would not all automatically adhere to the notion that they must share a common identity with people of other nationalities who are labeled Hispanic. I wanted to explore the ways that the shared commonality of the label and its connotations both unites a group of individuals in terms of distinguishing them from non-Hispanics and simultaneously separates them as they struggle to affirm their sense of self, grounded in their own particular experience and shaped by their national origins and history, as well as their social class and racial backgrounds.

In fact, insofar as *Hispanic* is an English-language term coined in the United States and disseminated primarily by mainstream government institutions, it could be argued that a label such as Hispanic identifies and groups a particular population regardless of whether the individuals involved are themselves aware of the label or whether it coincides with their own forms of identification in society. Indeed, which labels are actually used in society and by individuals, the positive and negative connotations these acquire in people's lives, and hence their consequent political effectiveness were the ongoing concerns underlying this study. I sought to address them indirectly by bringing to the fore the notion of *process* in reconstructing individuals' personal, social, gendered racial, ethnic, and political identities in their daily lives.[1]

This chapter suggests that even when considering a small group of twenty-one Latin American immigrants and one U.S.-born Puerto Rican, the label does not do justice to the variety of backgrounds and experiences of the immigrant populations who, like the more historically established communities of Chicanos and Puerto Ricans, are called Hispanic in the United States. It describes the institutional context in which this study took place and profiles the demographic characteristics, educational and work backgrounds, and reasons for immigration of the people I interviewed. I also present data on the ways this particular group of immigrants with ties to Latin America perceive the significance of racial, ethnic, and class belonging in shaping their social identity in the United States. This provides the background for the subsequent analysis in chapter 6 of the impact of race, class, language, and national origins in shaping the dynamics of identity construction in the United States and the meaning and social value that this particular group of people with ties to Latin America attributed to the label Hispanic in their lives.

The Study: Research Procedures and Local and Institutional Context

Between September 1988 and July 1990 I interviewed nine men and thirteen women who worked in the New York garment industry. When I decided to use interviews for this study, I was conscious of the difficulty of capturing the meanings and social values that people might attribute to the term Hispanic in terms of their daily lives. I knew, of course, that there are contexts in which, as Félix Padilla's pioneering work has exemplified, the group connotations of an ethnically derived term are undoubtedly politically advantageous in specific local struggles for social justice and equality, or in encouraging support and adherence to grassroots mobilizations.[2] But I was interested in the meaning of the term more specifically as it was perceived by individuals as part of their self-identification and as they felt that it affected their experience of daily life.

It is important to recognize that self-identification with and use of a particular term also depends on the alternatives available in each context. For example, observing a group's voting patterns or behavior in particular contexts, while certainly informative in general quantitative terms, does not *necessarily* capture an individual's use of the term as self-referential, since one cannot always be sure, for example, that if a Latino or Latina votes for a Latina politician or participates in a neighborhood parade, this alone would establish the individual participant's *conscious adherence* to the term. Alternatively, for example, he or she may instead be adhering to the politician's campaign promise or ideology or may have decided to participate in the parade simply because she likes parades or because he wants to march with friends through the neighborhood. Thus Latinos' formal or informal identification with the term will also be contingent on the other, wider social and political alternatives available in each specific context and situation.

Indeed, one of the aspects I found interesting in the responses by the people in my study was that the men and women were willing to consider or reject the label for purposes of self-identification *at all*— whether in a formal situation such as an interview or in casual conversation about the label Hispanic documented below. Thus, while some might suggest that the self-reported use of a term as a self-identifier can provide a "more general" understanding of the meanings and value attributed to the label, it seems to me that it is also a very *basic* level of the term's meaning. As such, it can contribute toward understanding the impact, on both people's sense of self and on their lives, of the post-1960s decision to emphasize ethnic classifications in identifying various population groups in United States society.

I was also very conscious that narratives of one's past life and experiences such as those I collected through this study's interviews will invariably be mediated by memory and hindsight, as well as by an awareness of both the listener's identity and the relationship established between the people involved in the interview context. My relationship with the people I interviewed, like the timing and content of the interviews, was shaped and greatly facilitated by the work I did in the Education Program in which I conducted this study in New York City. The program was originally begun as a degree program in conjunction with a local college, as part of a larger effort by some of New York City's unions to provide workers in various industries with the opportunity to get a college education. It soon became evident, however, that many union workers had not had the chance to complete their high school education in their own countries or lacked the necessary English skills to enter an American college. As a result, the education programs were expanded to include both G.E.D. (high school equivalency) and English as a Second Language classes. The twenty-two men and women I interviewed made up approximately one-third of the Spanish-speaking garment workers enrolled in English as a Second Language (ESL) classes in one such program at the time of my research.

I was hired in 1988 to coordinate and develop all aspects of this program, including setting up more classes, student recruitment, teacher hiring and evaluation, curriculum development, and academic counseling. As on-site coordinator, I also spent several hours a week talking to students, tutoring individuals, initiating, and generally being involved in all the on-site and outside social and educational events of the school.

When I first began working in the program, the worker-students perceived me primarily as the authority figure in the school—"The Director," or "La Directora." Perhaps conditioned by their past educational background and experience, some of the students were initially deferential, considering the figure of La Directora to be distant from them and their individual learning difficulties. The fact that I am myself from Peru and a native Spanish speaker was very positive in developing a relationship of trust with the worker-students. Many were clearly aware that I did not share their social and educational background in Latin America and, with the obvious exception of the Peruvians in the program, they also knew I came from a country with a different national experience from their own. At the same time, they recognized that as someone who like themselves was not born and raised in this country, I was sensitive to the cross-cultural issues and problems that the different social and cultural context of the United States raised for them.

It is important to note that these adults' educational experiences had taken place in Latin American countries. For the majority of them, the ESL program represented their first attempt to return to a classroom in many years. Thus one of my first tasks was to create an atmosphere in the school that could break down the strong and more rigid barriers of formality and hierarchy that have traditionally prevailed in Latin America's educational settings. In this respect, the fact that I was aware of the cultural differences embedded in the educational context itself and that I acknowledged the student-workers' backgrounds and spoke Spanish with them in the English school context greatly contributed toward helping them to feel more comfortable in a school environment.

Like many returning students and adult learners, a large number of the workers in the program were insecure about their learning abilities.[3] In fact, for a variety of reasons, most of the workers enrolled in the program had left school in their own countries before the tenth grade. The following narratives of two of the people who participated in this study perhaps best exemplify this point. María is a forty-four-year-old single mother, born and raised in a small town in the Dominican Republic. Her father was a soldier, "but he never took care of us," she told me. So her mother, herself an orphan who never had the opportunity to go to school, worked as a tobacco sorter and brought her two daughters up by herself. "History has repeated itself," María commented, referring to her own situation as a single mother today, bringing up her two girls in the United States. "Sometimes I think it has to do with fate." In the Dominican Republic, she lived on the outskirts of a small town:

> It was only a little wooden shack, but at least we paid no rent. I went to school and finished up to the first year in high school. I wanted to go on studying but because of my mother's financial situation, she couldn't afford it. She says she tried but it couldn't be done because she couldn't buy me the books, the uniform, or anything and so that's as far as I got. So then I tried to put myself through typing school . . . but I only lasted there three or four months. I couldn't go on paying for it so I quit. (María, Dominican Republic)

Alicia's reasons for dropping out of school were quite different. A year after she was born in Colombia, her mother died, leaving her father alone to raise Alicia and her two brothers. The strain was too much for him and he soon became an alcoholic. "After my mother died," she recalled, "he lost everything they had ever owned," including his small wholesale pots and pans business and "even the old sewing machine." Alicia also had an older half-sister, whom "he had had on the street somewhere." When she got married, the older sister came to her father's house and took Alicia and her brothers to live with her:

> I hated school. I was eleven, but I didn't want to study. I lived with my step-sister and her husband used to shut me up in my room until I did all the homework. I would cry and scream and I know the neighbors would hear me. But they assumed it was because I was an orphan. Then my sister died, when I was about 13. So I moved out and quit going to school altogether. (Alicia, Colombia)

From the beginning, I made a conscious effort to get to know each worker-student and to ensure that all the people enrolled in the program knew that my position as "La Directora" meant that I both recognized and was willing and able to discuss their specific concerns and educational problems. By the end of my first year, I had gained the students' confidence sufficiently for them to begin to tell me their reactions and responses to the classes and teachers, as well as to make suggestions about ways of improving the program. Many soon began to take control of their own educational process and to participate actively in shaping the events in the school. They often stopped by my office to talk about their lives, their families, their own educational progress, the successes and shortcomings of the program, the teachers, and their books. The "old-timers," like María, Alicia, and others, in particular liked to discuss the pros and cons of the size of their classes; compare their past and present teachers' styles, methods, and techniques; and suggest ways of expanding the types of classes and the program's social and educational activities. Moreover, in the course of the first two years, my job had also unofficially evolved to include a substantial amount of nonacademic counseling and support outside of the program's schedule and beyond the students' educational difficulties, involving personal or family problems ranging from health and child-care issues to wife battering and alcoholism in the family, and including problems related to individual workers' immigration status.

Perhaps as a result of the ongoing dialogues I had established with the worker-students over the two years, by the time I began this study, they perceived the in-depth interviews more as a continuation of our other conversations.[4] This attests to the genuine curiosity on the part of many of the Latin American workers I interviewed as they struggled to make sense of the changes that the process of immigration had made on their sense of self, as well as of the discrepancy between the ways they identified themselves in their own countries and the identity imposed on them by U.S. society.

The process of gathering data for this study thus went hand in hand with the development of both my role in the school and in the worker-students' lives and the concomitant relationship that grew between us. Although the program itself collected general demographic information on the students, approximately one year after I began working there I interviewed twenty-two men and women using a partially open-ended questionnaire to obtain a more specific demographic overview of the Latin American workers in the program, including their backgrounds and reasons for immigration, as well as preliminary information about their perceptions of U.S. society, of "Americans," and of the term Hispanic.

I then conducted additional more extensive and open-ended interviews with eight of the men and women about the meanings and values—if any—that they attributed to being called Hispanics in the United States. I chose this open-ended interview format as a follow-up to the questionnaires because I wanted to explore the impact of the category of Hispanics as it emerged in their own words through the telling of their lives. Specifically, I asked the men and women I interviewed to narrate their immigration experience—including their lives in their respective countries of origin prior to their decision to emigrate from their homelands, their reasons for coming to the United States, their expectations upon arrival, and their actual experiences as immigrants and residents in the United States, making sure that the following issues were covered in the interviews: the extent to which they were aware of the term Hispanic as a label used both as a way of identifying people with ties to Latin America and as a self-referential concept; their perception of their nationality in relation to their self-identification as Hispanics in this country; the relationship they had to people of their own nationality in the United States, to people of other Latin American nationalities, and to non-Hispanic Americans; their views on Hispanics as American citizens and the use of Spanish and English as it relates to their self-concept and national identity; and their actual or perceived experience of discrimination as Hispanics in the United States.

Finally, the fact that my study on this ethnic label coincided with the federal government's data collection for the 1990 census allowed me to collect data from yet another source: a two-hour, open-ended conversation about "being Hispanic" in the United States that evolved informally among four of the women who were participating in my study: Milagros (Peru), Verónica (Dominican Republic), Dolores (Guatemala), and Soledad (Colombia). The bulk of the interviews were conducted primarily although not entirely in Spanish at the high school where the classes were held, and some were then continued in people's homes. Each person was interviewed at least twice, and, with their permission, I tape recorded all but two of the people in this study. The data from the first transcriptions thus served to guide the subsequent interviews, which I deemed to be completed when the information became repetitive.

A Note on Interview Methodology: The Use of Narrative Techniques

The question of what constitutes an "interview" is an often-discussed theoretical and methodological concern among social scientists. In this respect, Elliot Mishler's review of researchers' manuals and practices notes the lack or, at best, the inadequacy of definitions of the term itself; this inadequacy consequently serves as the point of departure for his critique of "standard" research practices.[5]

Mishler's point of departure for his approach to research issues is his critique of the positivist "stimulus-response" behaviorist framework informing the way researchers frame their questions in quantitative research methodologies. He argues, instead, in favor of the need to recognize the individual informants' social backgrounds and cultural differences to support his claim that not all people respond to question stimuli in the same way. The alternative methodological approach Mishler offers is thus instead firmly grounded in his emphasis on qualitative in-depth interviews, on recognizing the contextual dimensions of meaning and its interpretation—based on his argument that the meaning of both the questions and the answers is jointly constructed by the interviewer and the informant. His discussion of research methods and analyses thus centers on developing a theoretical framework for the relationship between discourse and meaning in the interview context. Mishler defines interviews as "speech events or speech activities, particular types of discourse regulated and guided by norms of appropriateness and relevance that are part of speakers' shared linguistic competencies as members of a community."[6]

In spite of his enthusiastic support of in-depth interviewing methods, however, Mishler does not neglect the potential limitations inherent in this qualitative approach. Key to studies such as this one, which are based on what Mishler calls "interviews as narratives," is the role played by the relationship between the researcher and the informants as it affects the issue of "objectivity" both during the interview and in the data's interpretation. It is important, for example, to ensure that the questions themselves do not lead the informant either to assume a normative position in the interview or to be concerned with "giving the right answer" to the interviewer.[7] In this respect, A. M. Rodrigues coincides with Mishler in her solution to this problem, suggesting that the informant be allowed to narrate his or her experience through open, in-depth interviews, focusing on the study's main themes. This allows the interviewer to gather narrated data containing the representations and explanational resources used by the informant in his or her sociocultural experience. Although the interviewer does suggest the theme of the interview, "biasing" the responses can be kept to a minimum through the interviewer's minimal interference in the informant's narrative.

Once the data have been collected, however, the complex relationship between the interview narratives and their interpretation comes to the fore. Indeed, this too has been the source of much debate in the social sciences, in terms of researchers' difficulties in "objectively" approaching not only their sources but also their data analyses and interpretations.[8] Echoing Mishler's assumption concerning the joint construction of meaning, scholars in the fields of sociolinguistics, anthropology, literature and communication studies, and social history increasingly agree on the need to acknowledge, in the analyses of narratives, the "positioning" of the participants not only in the society's hierarchy but also in the process of communication itself.[9]

Communication is seen in this perspective as an inherently ongoing and, therefore, unfinished process between two (or more) individuals or groups who act interchangeably as producers and consumers of cultural meanings.[10] The individuals involved in this process are constantly negotiating and redefining their understanding of their culture's meanings and identities according to the various social and power positions they occupy both in their society and in the communication context.

Stuart Hall notes that these differentiated positions point to the specifically *social* nature inherent in a seemingly "selective" understanding of the particular message being communicated. For, as he and others have suggested, the latter is grounded in the multiple "discursive domains" interacting in the communication process.[11] Hence the importance, stressed by Mishler, of narrative analyses taking into account the sociocultural, contextual elements involved in this process, and of understanding how these elements are related to the subjective understanding of social experience. This understanding is based on the underlying desires and interests that individuals or groups express through their struggles for survival and power in the society.[12] The diversity of conflicting interests involved points, in turn, to the need for a method that would incorporate the resulting varied interpretations of the social order. In this respect, Van Velsen notes that a researcher's fieldwork is not "to look for the *correct* interpretation or story. Rather, it is to obtain different stories and interpretations of conflicts or of other specific events, provided by various people." This entails presenting the total context of the cases, "focusing on the situation and specifying the actors."[13] It also involves recognizing, as Victor Turner suggests, that the narrative component of these differentiated versions of events are in fact "attempts to rearticulate opposing values and goals in a meaningful structure, the plot of which makes cultural sense."[14]

Indeed, insofar as the aim of my study was to examine the meanings and values that people assign to a particular social force—the label Hispanic—specifically in shaping their respective senses of self and lives, I assumed from the beginning that the process of arriving at a "meaningful structure" whose plot might make "cultural sense" of human identity and experience was both inherently complex and often contradictory, given the multiple national, social, and cultural identities involved. Thus, my aim in this study was by no means to interview a "representative sample" of "Hispanics" in the United States, nor to assume that the ultimate conclusions I would draw from this study could be generalized to other people currently identified under this umbrella term. Instead I chose this particular group of workers precisely because they represented individuals who quite by chance and unlike others in their respective workplaces chose to attend the English as a Second Language classes in the same program provided by their union during the two years in which this study was conducted. Following accepted racial and ethnic categories used to group people in the United States, these individuals were perceived by the teachers; by worker-students from Eastern Europe, Italy, Greece, and other non–Latin American countries; and by themselves as "Hispanics" in relation to the other non-Hispanics in the program.

In this particular context, the people who participated in my study constituted a heterogeneous group of Latinos, originating in Mexico and El Salvador, Guatemala, Honduras, and Nicaragua in Central America; Colombia, Ecuador, and Peru in South America; and the Dominican Republic in the Caribbean. In addition, because of the political and neocolonial relations between Puerto Rico and the United States and its consequent ambiguous national status and cultural position in relation to Latin America, I decided to include Puerto Ricans born both on the island and in the United States. Unfortunately, because of the lack of Cubans in the program, this group could not be represented at all in this study.

The workers also represented different races, genders, and generations. At the same time, they shared a continuous experience (year-long English classes in the education program) and an institutional affiliation (they were all members of the same union). Moreover, the fact that they shared traditional working-class immigrant occupations in the garment industry meant that I could explore the meaning of the label Hispanic in their lives without the added complexities of professional or interclass differentiations in the U.S. context. But class, years of schooling, and occupational heterogeneity in their own countries prior to immigration were taken into consideration in the analysis of the interviews, insofar as these factors might influence different perceptions of the meaning of the label Hispanic in their lives in the United States.

Age, Marital Status, and Years in the United States

The characteristics of the group of workers I interviewed varied in some respects from the demographics of the Hispanic population statistically portrayed in the United States.[15] For example, the years of schooling among the women I interviewed was in keeping with the census figures, according to which "more than half of Latino women over the age of 25 lack . . . a high school diploma and less than 8 percent graduated from college."[16] However, the same cannot be said of their economic situation. The income of the group of workers in my study averaged $10,000—almost 50 percent less than the median provided for all Hispanic ethnic and racial groups, with the exception of Puerto Ricans. Similarly, given the worker-education context of the study, the age range of this group was not at all representative of the overall Hispanic population in the United States, which according to Davis, Haub, and Willette is actually much younger: "In 1980, the median age of the Hispanic population was 23, compared with 30 for the total U.S. population and 25 for the black population. . . . Nearly one-third (32 percent) of Hispanics were younger than 15 and only 5 percent were 65 or older."[17]

Moreover, while many Hispanics, regardless of country of origin (and again, with the exception of Puerto Ricans), are "married-couple families" living in the United States, most of those in this study's group of twenty-two were either not married or were currently not living with their spouse—whether due to divorce or widowhood or because their spouse was in Latin America. In this respect, as Klor de Alva has noted, although "most Hispanic women over the age of 15 are married and have dependent children (under 18 years), [they] are more than twice as likely as white women to be heads of households with no husband present. Seven out of ten in this position have dependent children."[18]

Their profile was, however, characteristic of the people who were members of the union sponsoring these English classes. Although the membership's ages ranged from people in their early twenties to those who were in their sixties, the majority of the workers in this union were primarily older-generation immigrant women, who outnumbered the men by a ratio of two to one. Most of the members came primarily from Spanish-speaking countries of Latin America, although there were also immigrants from Haiti, Guyana, Greece, and Italy, as well as Eastern Europe (primarily Poland, and Romania) and Asia (especially China and Vietnam). All of the English as a Second Language students in the program were first-generation immigrants in the United States. While the length of time these worker-students had been in the United States ranged from six months to thirty years, the majority of the union's members had been in the country for many years. On the whole, then, it was not a union of very recent immigrants. In fact, although a few of the workers in the education program were newly arrived, most had resident status, and still others had become citizens of the United States. Thus, of the twenty-two people who ended up participating in the study, all were U.S. residents and only eight had been in this country for less than ten years. Because of their relatively long periods of residence in the United States, I had initially assumed that those who participated in this study would be familiar with the practice of ethnic and racial categorizations that prevails in United States society. As it turned out, they were eager to discuss this subject, and their confusion about it became apparent in the interviews, which raised issues of great concern for them as they struggled to make sense of their identity in terms of the racial and ethnic categories prevailing in U.S. society. The following tables present a profile of the twenty-two people who participated in either one or both phases of the study:

Table 1. Profile of the women informants: Age, country of origin, marital status, and years in the United States (N = 13)

Name	Age	Country of origin	Marital status	Years in U.S.
Ofelia	45	Colombia	M	19
Alicia*	59	Colombia	S	11
Soledad*	34	Colombia	W	7
María*	44	Dominican Republic	D	16
Verónica	24	Dominican Republic	S	3
Mónica	44	Dominican Republic	D	16
Irene	52	Ecuador	S	20
Rosa*	42	El Salvador	S	20
Dolores	52	Guatemala	M	16
Julieta	53	Mexico	M	18
Gloria	40	Nicaragua	S	6
Milagros*	42	Peru	M	9
Teresa	59	Puerto Rico (born in P.R.)	M	25

*Interviewed in depth.

Table 2. Profile of the men informants: Age, country of origin, marital status, and years in the United States (N = 9)

Name	Age	Country of origin	Marital status	Years in U.S.
Francisco*	58	Colombia	D	12
Arturo	32	El Salvador	M	12
Charles*	28	Honduras	S	7
Jaime	63	Honduras	M	15
Paulo	32	Nicaragua	S	4
Angelo	21	Nicaragua	S	2
Julián	45	Peru	M	5
Jorge	46	Puerto Rico (born in P.R.)	M	18
Juan*	34	Puerto Rico (born in U.S.)	D	34

*Interviewed in depth.

As Tables 1 and 2 show, the Colombians and Dominicans in this study outnumbered other nationalities, corresponding to the fact that these two national groups have the largest representation of all Latin American foreign nationalities in the union education classes and are also numerically among the largest Latin American populations in New York City.[19] The average age of the group of workers I interviewed was 42 years and 7 months. The women averaged 45 years and 4 months while the men were considerably younger, averaging 39 years and 2 months. Thus the women came to school to learn English at a later age than the men, whether because they had been busy making ends meet, raising children or grandchildren on their own, or were in the process of bringing the rest of their families to the United States.

Although all the people I interviewed expressed concern about their family's well-being, in some ways the men's family and marital situations contrasted sharply with those of the women. Five of the nine men I interviewed had no children and were either single or divorced; only two of those who were or had been married were living with and helping to raise their children in the United States. The other three married men had left their children with their wives or relatives in their country of origin and were sending money home for their upbringing. As Julián explained:

> I'm only here [in the U.S.A.] because they are there. I couldn't support them working in Peru. Now I can't see them grow up, but at least I can support them while they are doing it. (Julián, Peru)

As Table 2 shows, the men had been here for less time than the women and were attending English classes at an earlier period in their immigration experience. For many of the women on the other hand, regardless of their marital status, raising children—their own or those of others or both—was initially a major obstacle preventing them from attending English classes earlier in their lives as immigrants. As one of the five single mothers I interviewed noted, coming to school at an earlier period of their lives in the United States was not an option:

> If I could have, I would have gone to school to learn English
> before. But I was all alone with two children, and I was working.
> I brought my entire family to the United States. When was I
> going to find the time to learn it? I know I should have come to
> class when I was younger, but I couldn't. (María, Dominican
> Republic)

Later, however, as their children reached school age, the children's schooling became a significant motivating force for these working mothers to continue their own education:

> I'm learning English so that I can better myself and leave the factory. I
> want my children and myself to finally see that I *can* do it. I want to
> show them that if you know English you can make more money.
> (Milagros, Peru, 42 years old)

Comments such as "I want my children to see that I *can* do it" point not only to the women's concern for the well-being of their family and children, but also to some of the emotional difficulties experienced by these working adults as they return to a classroom. Many of the men and women in this study lacked a full high school education in their countries of origin (see Table 3).

As Tables 3 and 4 show, of the twenty-two people I interviewed, one had no formal schooling prior to the ESL classes in the program, and only two had completed college. Six had finished high school. Not surprisingly, four of the six are men and three of the six are from South America—part of a migration that until very recently has been largely composed of middle- and upper-middle-class professionals. The rest of the people I interviewed had completed only a junior high school education.

Tables 3 and 4 also show that the men in this study tended for the most part to have had higher-status and higher-paying jobs than the women in their home country. Even the two women who *had* com-

**Table 3. Women informants' schooling and profession
in home country (N = 13)**

Name	Country	Years of schooling	Profession in home country
Dolores	Guatemala	0	Housewife
Julieta	Mexico	6	Garment worker
Teresa	Puerto Rico	8	Student
Alicia	Colombia	8	Garment worker
Rosa	El Salvador	8	Secretary
María	Dominican Republic	9	Garment worker
Ofelia	Colombia	9	Garment worker
Milagros	Peru	9	Office clerk
Irene	Ecuador	10	Garment worker
Gloria	Nicaragua	10	Garment worker
Mónica	Dominican Republic	10	Typist
Verónica	Dominican Republic	12	Secretary
Soledad	Colombia	16	Teacher

**Table 4. Men informants' schooling and profession
in home country (N = 9)**

Name	Country	Years of schooling	Profession in home country
Jaime	Honduras	5	Tailor
Charles	Honduras	7	Policeman
Arturo	El Salvador	7	Machinist
Jorge	Puerto Rico	9	Sugar inspector
Angelo	Nicaragua	11	Student
Juan	Puerto Rico	12	U.S. Army
Paulo	Nicaragua	12	Technician
Julián	Peru	12	Accountant
Francisco	Colombia	16	Hearing specialist

pleted a university and a high school education, respectively, in their countries had only achieved low-paying, white-collar professions traditionally allotted to women—teaching and secretary, respectively.

The Significance of Gender

Gender ideologies throughout the globe have traditionally privileged men with better employment possibilities, and Latin American societies have been no exception to this rule.[20] Indeed, in spite of the economic realities on the continent, Latin American societies continue to uphold the idea that a respectable woman's place is in the home.[21] Discussing women and work in the United States, Rubin has pointed out that "historically, it has been a source of status in working-class communities for a woman to be able to say 'I don't *have* to work.' "[22] This observation is applicable to Latin America, although status considerations there are not limited to working-class communities. As Francisco, whose social status in his home country was middle class, explained:

> I had to work for so many people in the family that it got very difficult for me because in Colombia, the wife [*la señora*] doesn't work. When one reaches a certain position, *la señora* becomes the gracious hostess. She's the one who takes care of the children, she's the person who collaborates, but she doesn't really produce any money through work. . . . My wife got used to living off her husband; that lifestyle is the problem of our countries, you know? Because the social side has to be kept up. There are those who say, "How can so-and-so's wife go to work! It's unheard of!" (Francisco, Colombia)

In fact Francisco's declining fortunes in Colombia began with bad business decisions followed by a robbery of his office and equipment, which led him to other problems:

> I was doing very well—although I worked long hours as a hearing therapist. For a while, I was also working at night, teaching human relations and foreign commerce which was my degree. So I began to acquire some properties and then came the problems. I started having difficulties with the banks.
>
> You, see, unfortunately, when you start out, you want to make sure that your children will be better off than you are; that they'll have everything they need, bicycles, social clubs, everything people have in the United States. But then I couldn't keep up that level, I couldn't really put that money back. And then I started having other kinds of problems. I used to think that money didn't have that much value. But it has so much value that it weighs on the moral, sentimental, affective aspects of life, it weighs on one's internal organization, doesn't it? And so then other problems began—*la señora* couldn't adapt to that tighter lifestyle. But it was all my fault, I was the one that got her into those bad habits. And then came the separation. . . . I wouldn't do it the same again. (Francisco, Colombia)

Coming from this male-privileged employment context, the opinions that the people I interviewed had about men and women in the work force once in the United States are revealing. For the most part, these depended on their particular backgrounds and the issues that the new social and employment context in this country raised for each of them.

The interviews indicate that immigration had directly affected men's perceptions of women's traditional roles. It was the women, however, who provided the best interpretations of the types of cultural adjustments men have to make when women enter the work force here in the United States. Mónica, for example, described it this way:

> Men in my country are more home-oriented, while here they become less responsible. . . . He takes the money he makes during the week and spends it with friends when he's not out with another woman. Sometimes they form another family. (Mónica, Dominican Republic)

According to Soledad (Columbia), "It's harder for men because they have to forget their *machismo* and depend on themselves here." Indeed, most of the women echoed Soledad's comment concerning the change in men's sense of self and in their roles and relationship to the household as a result of immigration. They reported, for example, that many men begin to help with the household chores, which sometimes leads some to feel that their masculinity and pride is undermined in the immigration process—a finding confirmed in Patricia Pessar's study of Dominican households in the United States.[23] Indeed, comments such as "they [men] do things here which I would never ask or expect them to do back home—it's different there" were common among the women as they described the participation of men in their households in the United States. The changes in men's behavior once in the United States can be seen as a shift away from the adherence to what Pessar has explained as a "cultural model [which] ascribes men 'by nature' to the 'public sphere' and women to the 'domestic sphere.' "[24]

Although both the men and the women I interviewed agreed that men had better job opportunities here in the United States, only the women expressed negative feelings about men's working lives:

> He's got to pay the rent, the big bills. They have to have two jobs here. It's easier to buy a house there than it is here. Come to think of it, he hasn't gone up in life like I have. (Milagros, Peru)

> Men here can't give their families as much time as they do there. Most of them work six or seven days and don't take time out for their children and wives. (Verónica, Dominican)

Immigration to the United States has reinforced women's sense of self and confidence, particularly in relation to working outside the home and traditional Latin American ideologies about single motherhood. Rosa's story of her early years in the United States exemplifies this. Although she was scared to leave her small northern town in El

Salvador, she emphasized that "things here [in New York] were very nice, very different" when she arrived in the United States in 1971. "You could find work easily—any work: domestic work in people's home, or in a factory." Her first job was at a sock factory, but she left it to go work for her boss as a domestic worker. "It was better for me. I earned too little, about $45 a week." As a live-in domestic worker, she earned $50 a month and had food and lodging guaranteed. She had the names and numbers of other Salvadoreans from her village, and eventually left the job to live with her boyfriend in a small furnished room. She recalled:

> I began to walk and walk around the streets of Lower Manhattan . . . and then I started to work in a doll factory. But I couldn't work much there because I was pregnant by then and the chemicals were bad for me and made me sick. We used to paint the faces on the dolls, or put eyes on them. The foreman was a Columbian. But the old man fired me, because you had to keep up with the work and I couldn't. . . . I felt horrible. So I spent a month at home, I had some savings.

Then Rosa told her child's father that she was pregnant:

> He started asking me who was going to support me, and things like that. I got so desperate! I had a return ticket and every day I would look at it and I would say, one day I'm going to leave. And one day, I took the ticket and said to him "Look. I am not going to be a burden on you. I'm leaving." And he said, "Then leave." So I did. (Rosa, El Salvador)

She went back to El Salvador, where her father was the village postman and her mother worked as a domestic worker. Three years later, she returned to the United States, leaving her child behind.

"But this time," she said, "I came back with a different mentality: I wasn't so scared. This time I had a new way of thinking. I could help to raise my child from here. . . . I knew I could find a job and survive."

Interestingly, many also tied their responses to women's opportunities to get an education here. The only woman who was a housewife in her own country felt that because "women can work" in the United States, life here is generally better for women than it was in her own country. Still, one cannot help but note the way she carefully constructed her statement to include her awareness of the way the inequities between men and women in her country are continued in the United States:

> Life is better here, first because a woman can work even though she

doesn't have a profession and because she has *almost the same* rights as men. She's not just a subjugated wife. And also she can study. (Dolores, Guatemala; my emphasis)

Thus, the women incorporated the changes in men's positions and gender roles into their own sense of self as people with "the right to have rights," challenging the stereotypes of women's roles within themselves.[25] As a result of immigration, a woman's sense of self begins to shift from her previous "othered" socialization and values to the "new self" constructed in a daily life of active participation in the work force—a process that often, as Pessar and Grasmuck have noted, results in her becoming the primary, or at least an equal, contributing member of the household.[26]

Comparing their juggling of work and household chores here and in their own countries, some recalled the difficulties of housework there to explain why life for them was easier here:

It's better because you don't have to wash all day long, and you can get clothes that don't have to be ironed. You can study. Back home, I wouldn't be able to do what I do here. I pay for electricity, gas, telephone, the kids' clothes. I've gone up in life. I can just go out to work. There, it was like I was locked up. (Milagros, Peru)

Although she had worked in Peru as an office clerk, Milagros primarily identified her life in Peru as a housewife "locked up" in the home. The ability to pay some of the bills that gave Milagros a new sense of freedom and of self also provided her with a concomitant sense that she had bettered herself, or to use her words, "gone up in life." But for some of the women, life here raised other issues:

It's not better here because here mothers have to leave their children with someone outside of her circle of family and friends to go to work. (María, Dominican Republic)

For María, then, the need to rely on people other than "her circle of family and friends" clearly makes life for women here more difficult and is a forced departure from the traditional cultural patterns of the Latin American extended family. Dealing with this break—and with the struggle not only for daily survival but also to recognize oneself and adapt to changes in gender roles, values, and expectations—is thus at the heart of immigrants' lives, both men's and women's, in the United States.

Latin American gender ideologies notwithstanding, only one of the women I interviewed had not worked outside the home in her country of origin, attesting both to the difficult economic crises of the Latin American countries and to the increasing incorporation of third world women in the development process as a result of the structural changes in the world economy.[27] As some scholars have noted, the truly poor of Latin America and the Caribbean are excluded from the migration process[28] and thus, in contrast to the widely discredited yet persistent images of immigrants as poverty-stricken, uprooted "huddled masses," the people I interviewed for this study were not, for the most part, from the poorest strata of their own societies, but rather had been employed in blue- and white-collar jobs in their own countries and had had some schooling before they immigrated to the United States.

Reasons For Immigration

The economic and/or political turmoil of many of the Latin American countries together with the hopes and expectations about the United States as a golden land of opportunity underlie some of the reasons why the people in this study immigrated. In this sense, their motives seem to reinforce traditional and popular explanations in the U.S. media as well as early immigration typologies, which classically focused on the "push-pull" factors affecting the individual to explain people's desire or need to leave their homelands.[29] Indeed, insofar as the individual immigrant interprets his or her migration in personal rather than broader socioeconomic terms, reasons for emigrating appear at first sight to be in keeping with the individual push-pull framework of interpretation. Some of my informants said they decided to leave their country and come to the United States "to search for better opportunities" (Jaime, Honduras) or "to change my lifestyle and help my family" (Ofelia, Colombia). Others gave the following reasons:

> I decided to come to this country because I left my husband and I didn't want to burden my family. (Mónica, Dominican Republic)

> I had the chance to come because my father brought me and since I'm young I decided to see what it was like. I wanted to see different things than I can find in my own country or in any other country. (Verónica, Dominican Republic)

> Something attracts one to this country, like it attracted me. It wasn't the economics. It was something else. It's as if this country had a magnet. Because sometimes it gets boring, and you want to leave. But then, when you get back home, you want to come back here again. I really came to get my husband off my back and I came to see what it

was like. I didn't have to come. I have my own house back home in Colombia. (Alicia, Colombia)

Yet more recently, scholars have noted that earlier explanations of immigration did not pay sufficient attention to the ways in which these factors were interrelated with the larger structural aspects of the international economy.[30] It is important to recall that the increasing internationalization of the economic order and the changing relationship between the developed and developing nations over the past twenty-five years have been instrumental in making emigration a commonplace option in many parts of the world today. Indeed, as a transnational experience, emigration can be seen increasingly as an integral part of an emerging global culture, whereby a growing number of people in the world can refer to relatives or friends who have migrated to other countries.[31]

Particularly in the past decade, individual push-pull interpretations of immigration have been abandoned in favor of analyses of immigration patterns that focus on the structural and social effects of global labor flows on sending and receiving countries. Some have also explored immigrants' strategies to find economic solutions not only for themselves but also for those that stay behind.[32] Others, like Pedraza-Bailey, have noted, however, that "the danger of the structural emphasis . . . lies in its tendencies to obliterate people, to lose sight of the individual migrants who do make decisions. The theoretical and empirical challenge immigration research now faces lies in its capacity to capture both individuals and social structure."[33] Indeed, some of the men and women I interviewed seemed to be aware of the need to explain their personal motivations for leaving their homeland in terms of the larger structural context of the international economy, which visibly intruded in their lives and homelands in the form of U.S. company recruiters. Alicia, who used to work in a factory of one of Colombia's largest garment manufacturers, is an example. Asked why she decided to come, she flatly stated:

> I didn't have to come here. But I wanted to. When they [U.S. textile entrepreneurs] came looking for us from here, a lot of people in the factory where I worked [in Colombia] came with them. . . . That was in '67 or '68. They offered us everything. They were looking for skilled labor, for textile workers, in Rhode Island, and they offered us work papers, residence papers, everything. But I wanted to have some security in my own country. So I didn't come at that time. . . . I came later, in '73. (Alicia, Colombia)

Thus, while many Latin Americans were forced to leave their countries throughout the 1980s because of the deep crises of their national economies,[34] understanding the development of the migration process also entails bearing in mind, as Piori points out, that it is often employers rather than workers, and jobs rather than incomes, that are the more crucial elements in determining the initial course of immigration. Thus, while conditions in the home country cannot be underestimated, "the active agent seems to be the evolution of the developed country and the forces emanating from it. This is almost impossible to see once a migration flow has become well established because by then it is almost completely self-sustaining."[35]

The initial immigration experience of the people in this study does reflect the extent to which emigration from Latin America had become self-sustaining by the early 1970s. Leaving aside the U.S.-born Puerto Rican, all of the men and women—regardless of their year of immigration—had either relatives (thirteen), friends (four), or both (four) who urged them to come and greeted them when they arrived in the United States:

> I worked as the accountant's secretary in an electrical appliance store. I was about twenty at the time. My brother came to this country and he wanted me to come to learn English. He was twenty-five, older than I was. He talked me into coming: he was very enthusiastic about it! (Rosa, El Salvador)

> I tried to go to typing school, but I only lasted three or four months. I couldn't go on paying for it so I quit. I married, had a daughter. But I always had the wish to better myself, to go forward. . . . I left my husband. There was no future with him. I decided to separate. . . . I met a friend and told her how bad the situation was. I had a small child and I needed money for milk. I'd sold almost all the clothes I had to buy milk for my little girl. She told me she knew where they needed someone to make collars, and me, with no experience! I really didn't know how, but you know, need can help you learn more than anything. . . . Then one of my first cousins who lived in Santo Domingo told her mother about my troubles. Her mother sent me the papers from here. They gave me a residence visa and I came. That was in 1974. (María, Dominican Republic)

While personal economic improvement was certainly present in all cases as a reason for their immigration, it was not always perceived by the individual as sufficient cause in itself for immigration, and in some cases it was not even the prevailing reason for leaving their countries of origin.

Unlike the other women in the study, for example, Soledad was brought up in a middle-class environment in Colombia. "My husband died in an accident. I was twenty-eight so I left. I had no expectations. It was almost like running away. It was like looking for new experiences." Until then, she had taught ceramic arts in an experimental school for mentally handicapped children. Soledad insisted that she did not have to come to the United States:

> My world did not include coming here, except as a tourist—I'd come here once for three months as a student and I'd come back on vacation. But I never had the urge to come here after that because I had my world all made there. But it went to pieces after my husband died. Coming here was never part of my life plan.

At one point before she left, one of her nieces, who had returned to Colombia after getting her degree in engineering here in the United States, tried to dissuade her from coming: "But I told her, 'No, I have to get away from my problems here.' But once I got here it wasn't difficult, I had family here and they helped me."

Still others considered the consequences of the political turmoil in their respective homelands in their decision to leave their homeland: "I left because of the political situation in my country over the past ten years, and the repression against me" (Paulo, Nicaragua).

But regardless of the reasons, leaving one's homeland to "begin again" in a new country is a complex decision, often motivated by more than one factor alone. Charles' decision to emigrate, for example, was a combination of factors. A Garifuna, or black Carib, Charles worked in several parts of Honduras, first as a policeman for five years and later, following a short stint in a banana company, as a night watchman. Charles wanted to begin a family of his own very much, but he could barely make enough money to support himself in any of the jobs he found. He also wanted to help his family, who was very poor, particularly after his sister died unexpectedly, leaving two young children behind. ("She was killed, I don't know how. Some people say her husband killed her—I'm not sure.") Thus, both economics and his desire to begin his own family and to help his parents by taking his sister's children into his home explain why he decided to head toward the United States: "Honduras is a poor country and if I left my country it's to look for a better life, but above all to find a good wife, to get married."

Moreover, beyond the political and structural economic causes of immigration, as well as each person's individual background, are the dreams and expectations that also, and perhaps ultimately, helped to trigger these men and women's decisions to immigrate to the United States:[36]

> Ever since I was little, I used to look at the post cards and the pictures of snow on the calendars and I would say to myself "if one day—if God helps me and I can—one day, I'd like to go to the United States." (María, Dominican Republic)

For some, however, their dreams and expectations did not necessarily coincide with the reality they experienced once living in U.S. society, leading to the search for varied solutions in keeping with their new assessment of their situation. For some, like Rosa, for example, this meant reluctantly modifying her expectations to accommodate herself to the reality she found:

> My dream was to learn English well and go back to my country. I used to say to myself: "I'm a secretary. If I have good English I could work anywhere as a bilingual secretary." Because, you see, in my country people work and also study and gradually you get a career that way. I have a friend who became an accountant like that: she worked in the day and in the evening she'd go to school. So I thought it was the same here. You could work and earn and go study afterwards. But what a mistake! Here is where they squeeze you the most! At the end of the day, you don't have any energy left to do anything. So now I'm just trying to learn a little English. (Rosa, El Salvador)

Others found that life here was better than in the countries they'd left. Milagros, for example, noted that she was definitely going to make this country her permanent home:

> It doesn't matter who wins the next election for president [in Peru]. You can't go out just like that. They [the Shining Path guerrillas] killed one of my friend's sons. There's a lot of deaths, no food, everything is so expensive. The electricity goes off or you suddenly don't have any water in the house because the Shining Path bombed something somewhere. . . .
> I'm very grateful to this country and I'm used to it now. . . . I want to become a citizen. There are a lot of advantages to that, of course, like getting Social Security and health benefits when you get old. If you're a citizen, the government takes better care of you here than in Peru. (Milagros, Peru)

Others had thoughts about returning to their country, a solution that, like the decision to leave, would also be determined by a variety of simultaneous considerations. In fact, with the exception of political or religious refugees (such as Eastern European Jews at the turn of the century), many people have immigrated to the United States throughout its history, only to return to their native lands—a practice that many continue to this day. As several authors have shown, personal family problems, inability to adapt to the new land, nostalgia, or more structural causes such as lack of jobs, insufficient income, or immigration laws are some of the varied reasons for return migrations.[37]

But immigrants themselves, of course, explain their reasons for both leaving and returning to their homelands in individual terms. Moreover, one researcher noted that "from interviews and narratives, it seems that the migrants usually accepted the idea that it is up to them to make it and that it is their fault if they don't succeed."[38] This may lead some returning immigrants to claim they have achieved their dreams, while others might return in recognition of their failure to do so.

But regardless of what action they ultimately take, this decision, like the one they made to immigrate, is also difficult, contradictory, and full of complex considerations. Soledad, for example, found herself weighing the reality she encountered here against the memory of the life she had left behind:

> I don't like to go to Colombia. It makes me feel bad. Too many memories. I went back four years ago and I didn't feel well there. I went back because I wanted to return but I said, no, no; the same streets, the same people and everyone comes and asks you how . . . and so I said no. I will go back to the United States where no one knows me, I am just me, here and that's it. (Soledad, Colombia)

Charles was caught between wanting to go back and his awareness of the economic difficulties in Honduras:

> I imagined that one could have a much better life here than in my country. But people here are bad: drugs, murders, that doesn't exist in my country like it does here. So I want to go back to my country. I just want to save a little money and go back. (Charles, Honduras)

Ultimately, it is the hopes—and, for many, their disenchantment—along with the specific economic and political reasons that underlay and motivated their immigration that will have some bearing on both their decision to stay and their assessment of their lives and positions within U.S. society. Although, for the most part, the men and women in this study articulated their hopes for a better life in broadly the same terms, their expectations and the ways they came to terms with the reality they encountered in the United States were also shaped differentially according to their particular age, gender, schooling, professional status, and social class background.

Chapter 6

Language, National Identity, and the Ethnic Label Hispanic

> I couldn't repudiate my past even if I wanted to, but what can I do with it here, where it doesn't exist?[1]

The Dynamics of Race, Ethnicity, and Social Class

It seems almost a truism to say that historically many of the European immigrants who stayed in the United States, whether by choice or by force, achieved some social mobility[2]—or at least, like some of the women in my study, the sense that they have indeed improved their life chances. Less fortunate others might have stayed on in this country, either permanently exiled from their lands or in some cases loath to give up their struggle or to recognize their failure, perhaps feeling that something would or must change, that their lives would somehow take a turn for the better.

Between these two extremes lie many other reasons why people might prolong their immigration experience or cut it short. A major consideration for Latin American immigrants when deciding whether to stay in the United States or return to their homelands is their understanding of their previous status in their respective Latin American countries and its comparative implications for their lives here and at home. For it is important to note the absence in many Latin American countries of the practice of a system of justice that recognizes the notion of equality under a universal and impartial law. As such, people's lives and social relations, like the forms of access to citizenship rights and social justice, are generally contingent on the social group to which they belong, the group's public standing, and the state's recognition of the groups' social and power status in society.[3]

As Roberto Da Matta has suggested in his provocative article "Do You Know Who You're Talking To?," an unspoken distinction between *persons* and *individuals* mediates daily life relations in Brazilian society. Persons, according to Da Matta, are those who have the power and status to make themselves known to others through affirming their social relations and position in society. Through the customary recognition and acknowledgment of status and power, the wife of Senator X, the brother of the president of Y newspaper, or even the chauffeur of Mr. Z, for example, have a certain social capital and thus can claim personal relationships and substantive social ties, which in effect allow the laws of the land to be bypassed or ignored.

Individuals, on the other hand, have no such social connections and relations, and are thus part of the anonymous masses. Unlike "persons," they are directly subject to the strict application of the laws of the land. As Da Matta puts it, restating a popular Brazilian dictum: "For individuals the law; for persons everything." Da Matta goes on to explain: "That is to say, we will give everything to those who are inserted in an important web of personal dependencies. The law is for those who are isolated, and confront society without personal mediations." Although Da Matta is referring specifically to Brazil, this emphasis on personal relations to varying extents seems also to organize the daily life of the social sectors in many Latin American societies.[4]

In this chapter I discuss the extent to which the past social positions and immigration experiences of the people I interviewed differentially affect their perceptions of themselves once in the United States. I also explore their views of "Americans" and of the treatment they encounter in this country. Both their acquired self-perceptions and their perceptions of Americans are relevant to their interpretation of the label Hispanic. Using this information as background data, the chapter then explores the meanings and values they attributed to the term Hispanic in their lives.

The self-assessment in the context of U.S. society of the people I interviewed points to the recognition of their previous social class backgrounds in shaping both their expectations and the ways they perceive how far they've come in this society. Statements along the lines of the following example were common in most of the interviews:

> I've always wanted to better myself, to get ahead. . . . It's been a lot of sacrifice and effort but when I decide to do something, I achieve it. Even if I have to go one or two days without food, I get what I want.

... You see, it's different. Everything back there is so expensive, you can't even buy any shoes. ...

I've gone up in life here. I can't complain about this country. It's helped me a lot. I've brought my whole family, I brought my mother, my sister, the daughters I've raised, the two of them. (María, Dominican Republic)

Yet, insofar as racial and ethnic distinctions in Latin America are not attributed the same significance as class, Latin Americans' "discovery" of the salience of race and ethnicity as a form of social classification in this country is particularly significant to explore. While the men and women in this study could easily describe their perceptions of their situation in relation to their own past, most of them—particularly those with a working-class background—found it more difficult to articulate their position in the hierarchy of racial and ethnic classification and distinctions that they encountered in the United States. While some of the Latin American immigrants I interviewed tried to understand its rationale, others viewed it as an unresolved given. The following exchange among four Latin American women is telling in this respect:

In the census you're not allowed to write down that you're white. It's so strange. I have a Colombian friend, he's really very white. He looked like an egg-white. He became an American citizen and when they asked him for his skin color, he wrote down "white." But they said to him: "You're not white," and they erased the color. "What color are you going to make me?" "Black," they said. Can you imagine that? A guy who's so white that he's virtually transparent! (Soledad, Colombia)

Sure I can. But you know, my passport *says* I'm white. (Verónica, Dominican Republic)

Well, it may say you're white, but you're not white here. (Milagros, Peru)

That's right. Here they won't say you're white for anything! The only whites here are Americans. They won't put you down as white. (Soledad, Colombia)

Why not? (Verónica, Dominican Republic)

I don't know. It's the way they do things here. (Soledad, Colombia)

It's because their race is white. So they think no one else can be white. (Dolores, Guatemala)

Yes. It's their source of pride. (Milagros, Peru)

These women are critical of the fact that Hispanics are differentiated from "whites." At the same time, this exchange points to the fact that Latin Americans filter the racial categories in this country through their own racial categorizations. In so doing, however, they implicitly acknowledge that perceptions in their societies do indeed adhere to the same type of racial criteria that prevails in the United States, although it is important to emphasize that these perceptions are interpreted in a different light in the dominant Latin American discourse. Hence, statements such as "They think no one else can be white" suggest the value that is attributed to "being white" in Latin America. So does their perception of "whiteness" as representing a "source of pride." Nevertheless, any similarities or comparisons should be drawn with caution, for in Latin America, race-related value judgments are publicly articulated in a different way than they are in U.S. society.

Indeed, every attempt is made to minimize the recognition of the effect of race in the organization of daily life in Latin America, to such an extent that the renowned Brazilian sociologist, Florestan Fernandes, once suggested that Brazilians' prejudice is rooted in their belief that they aren't prejudiced. This observation can be extended to represent, to varying degrees, the racial attitude present in Latin American countries.[5]

In this sense, one can say that although Latin Americans may find the emphasis on racial categorizations in the United States perplexing, this does not mean that awareness of racial differences are passed over in their perceptions:

> My language is Garifuna,[6] it's similar to English, and some of the words we use are identical to English words. I speak perfect Spanish because I wasn't brought up with my race. . . . Now, I don't get offended when they call me Hispanic, even though I'm not Hispanic. What bothers me is when they call me black, because I don't offend anyone, and I don't like it when anyone offends me. (Charles, Honduras)

Although Charles does recognize that the term Hispanic categorizes him in the context of this society, he does not necessarily see it as a denigrating term. Instead, given his awareness of the negative connotation of blackness in both Latin America and the United States, language clearly assumes a significant role in shaping his self-definition and cultural identity. Because he was also brought up among Spanish speakers, he explained, he both spoke their language and understood their culture. Thus he could accept being mistaken for a Hispanic. Unlike his reaction to the category of Hispanic, he is clearly disturbed, although he is black, by being called black, and unequivocally expresses that it is an offensive category in both this society and his own. At the same time, he made it clear that as a Garifuna, he perceived Spanish speakers regardless of race as "the other" whether in Honduras or in the United States.

Similarly, confusion about ethnic or racial classification doesn't mean that racial prejudices are absent from the ways that Latin Americans perceive African American people in the United States. Toward the end of a long conversation about her life as an immigrant and the experience of Latinos in the United States, María began to talk about African Americans:

> I don't think it should make any difference where we're from, because
> we're all humans and it doesn't matter what country we come from,
> what our origins are. For me, we are all the same and what we have
> to look at is the behavior of a person, how the person acts. For me
> when I see a black on the street, and I pass him I say "hi." I try to
> make him feel good, because they are people and they have their
> origins in their minds. It's their parents that are to blame, because
> they've told them everything, everything they went through during
> slavery and all that. And that's why they behave that way, they carry
> their complex in their blood. (María, Dominican Republic)

What comments such as this express is the veiled insistence that as Latin Americans we are indeed color-blind whether at home or abroad; that if black parents would not pass historical experience on to their children, they somehow would not "have their origins in their minds" or their "complex in their blood"—and thus the question of whether they were perceived as humans would be moot.

If traditional Spanish perceptions continue to be found in Latin Americans' discourse on racial differences, the nineteenth-century emphasis on the American national identity as "white Anglo-Saxon Protestant" is also alive and well today in Latin America, largely as a result of the (mis)representations about "Americans" in U.S. popular magazines sold abroad or in Hollywood's film exports:

> I was sure they [Americans] were all white people, with green eyes
> and blonde hair. My surprise was when I began to see blacks. You see,
> there are no blacks in El Salvador. There are *trigueños* [literally, wheat-
> color], people darker than me. But there are no blacks. And so, at first,
> I used to think, "They [American blacks] are so ugly." But then you
> get used to seeing them, more and more. And some of them are very
> nice people. (Rosa, El Salvador)

Rosa's surprise at her "discovery" of the existence of American blacks is gradually transcended as she gets "used to seeing them more and more" and establishes relationships with them. Prejudices are easily formed as defenses against new and different environments. At the same time, negative experiences can also sometimes reinforce prevailing prejudices about blacks, even as a sense of "group solidarity" may lead some to try to make distinctions about them in ethnic terms:

> I don't have anything against blacks. But black Latinos are not the
> same as the blacks here. I've seen gangs of blacks breaking phones.
> . . . My husband [also Peruvian], now he *is* prejudiced against
> American blacks. He's a cab driver and he was held up by them. . . . I
> don't like to hear people being talked about the way he talks about
> them. He's very racist. (Milagros, Peru)

Although the Latin Americans I interviewed come from a variety of racially diverse contexts, some discovered the prevalence of racial and ethnic forms of naming people and groups very early in their immigration experience: "When I first came, my friend said to me, 'Don't ever call them Negros, call them *morenos*.' Because she used to tell me, 'They don't like it when you call them Negros. They understand you, so be careful.' " (Milagros, Peru).

Nevertheless, to a large extent the meaning this group of immigrants attributed to the use of racial or ethnic forms of classification in this society was also influenced by the values stemming from their class positions in their own countries. These included not only class-based values but also the *culturally specific* racial prejudices that accompanied them in Latin America, given the close and gradated correlations between class and race there. Thus, for example, when asked to comment on whether his life had changed in the United States, Francisco, formerly a middle-class hearing specialist in his own country and now working in the garment industry, first established his class background, pointing out that there was considerable social distance between him and the other Latin Americans with whom he worked in the factory:

> They [Americans] exploit us with very low salaries, and they delude
> us into thinking that life is owning a car. Here it's common for people
> to have a car—you can get one dirt cheap; there's no status in it. You
> see, having an acceptable car, a good house does bring you status in
> any South American country. They delude people who could never
> have had a car in their own country. But the comforts of a good
> kitchen, of being able to wash your plates, of having a dishwasher, a

refrigerator, a good sound system, a television: none of that is really
life. *There is no pride in acquiring any of it for anyone who comes here with
an education.* (Francisco, Colombia; my emphasis)

In Latin America, having an "education" is one of the euphemisms for
being middle class, and thus Francisco's discourse echoes a point
raised by anthropologist Teófilo Altamirano in his study on the diversity of Peruvian immigrants in the United States:

> In concrete terms, the "American Dream" is associated with a
> comfortable lifestyle, with owning a house and car, with the benefits
> of the latest technology, with trips inside and out of the United States,
> with many dollars in the pocket and in the bank. In Peru, these
> aspirations are solely within the reach of the members of the upper
> and upper-middle classes.[7]

Having both distanced his aspirations and differentiated his (class-
based) definition of "real life" from that of his working-class colleagues, Francisco proceeded to speak of the shift in his social status
using the racial-ethnic hierarchy prevailing in the United States: that is,
he compared his position and aspirations to those of the Latin American working-class immigrants with whom he worked and *not to other
middle-class immigrants like himself*:

> The fact is that they've got *us* [Latin Americans] poorer here. . . . *Our
> people* are coming here and are really being taken in by material
> factors. (Francisco, Colombia; my emphasis)

Terms such as "us" and "our people" clearly refer to an assumed Latin
American "ethnic group"—regardless of the various nationalities and
class positions it encompasses. Thus, Francisco used the classification
based on ethnic grouping that prevails in U.S. society, rather than the
Latin American emphasis on class, to discuss his perception of the social issues affecting him in this country.

Indeed, although in our discussion Francisco constantly separated
himself socially from the other Latin Americans in the factory, he was
also very conscious of the ways in which racial and ethnic categories in
the United States obviate his own use of social class distinctions:

> My eyes have been opened in relation to Europeans here. I've found
> out that a lot of Europeans are illiterate. The problem is that we Latin
> Americans are not appreciated. We are considered the lowest race
> here. We are only here to work at the bottom. Because there's a bad
> policy here in the U.S. There are around 32 or 33 million of us and yet
> we are considered a minority. The percentage of Greeks, Germans,

Poles, is very low, yet they have special privileges which we don't
have. (Francisco, Colombia)

In the above statement, Francisco does not talk about the "special privileges" accorded to *all* Americans: Instead, he refers to "privileged"
white European ethnic groups, whom he perceives as sharing his social, racial, and educational background, and excludes African Americans and other nonwhite citizens. Thus he believes his own trajectory
in this country should emulate "Greeks, Germans, Poles," because in
his country, he shared what he perceives to be their white, middle-class
values. He does not take into account their national origins or the specific immigrant history of their respective groups in this country.[8]

Indeed a comparison between the ways that the previous class backgrounds of Francisco and María have shaped how they perceive their
position in this society are quite telling. María discusses her successful
position today in terms of a past situation that she identifies negatively:

"It's hard, life is really hard there [in the Dominican Republic]. . . .
I've gone up in life here. I can't complain about this country. It's
helped me a lot." (María, Dominican Republic)

Francisco, on the other hand, speaks of his past in glowing terms,
and does "complain about this country." Moreover, whereas María
looks to the past in assessing her current situation, Francisco projects
himself into the future, comparing his (low) status as a Latin American
with "Greeks, Germans, Poles"—that is, with Americans who, as he
states, "have special privileges which we don't have." In other words,
Francisco has adopted the ethnic-racial discourse prevailing in this society as a strategy that, on one hand, differentiates him from other
Latin American workers and, on the other, claims the same rights accorded to middle-class, assimilated Americans. In order to preserve his
previous (higher) class position, he adopts ethnic and racial categories
of discourse prevalent in the United States to articulate his position in
his new society.

Both María's satisfaction with what she has achieved here and Francisco's evaluation of his situation in this society are linked to their respective past lived experiences. Francisco's demand for equal and full
rights is in accordance with his class position in his old society and his
desire to attain it once again in his new society. María's discourse, on
the other hand, appears to be grounded more in her accommodation or
resignation to a particular social status, which she perceives more pos-

itively here in the United States. In her words, "After paying all the bills, it's almost the same here [as the Dominican Republic], but you are more comfortable here." In contrast to Francisco, María identifies and compares her current status in relation to her home country rather than to United States society. Indeed, María's discourse—which includes the bringing of her family to this country—contrasts with Francisco's in that it emphasizes her successes: her expectations in terms of achieving a better life for herself and her family at least appear to have been fulfilled. As she put it, "Everything I used to think about [coming to the United States] when I was a little girl has become a reality for me. I achieved it on the basis of sacrifice and effort."

Francisco's aspirations, on the other hand, are far from fulfilled. His references to the past serve primarily to point out how much better off he was in his old country. His discourse, unlike María's, includes a desire for incorporation into U.S. society, albeit projected into the future and defined by him in terms of equal access to the rights and privileges of the (white) middle classes in the United States.

Indeed, for poorer Latin Americans like María, accustomed as they are to perceive class belonging as the determinant of social mobility and status, social mobility in the United States may indeed be enhanced, at least potentially, whether or not they are "lumped" together with nonwhites and regardless of nationality. However, for those who, like Francisco, were better off before they immigrated, the road to incorporation into American society may be more costly, at least in terms of cultural perceptions. Once in the United States, all Latin Americans are "Hispanics," and thus all have to come to terms with this ethnic label assigned to them by the host society. At the same time, those like Francisco confront discrimination often for the first time and are further forced to recognize, through their own individual experience, the significance of racial and social prejudices, stereotypes, and labels that their own country's social organization historically allowed them to bypass, by virtue of their previous higher social status in their society's hierarchy.

Where the Personal Meets the Political: Issues of Latino Unity

These distinctions should by no means be interpreted as implying that all the men and women in this study, regardless of their class backgrounds, did not also acknowledge the cultural and particularly linguistic commonalities that emerge in the context of the presence of other ethnic groups and that might thus unify Latinos in particular situations. Discussing the various ethnic groups in the factory where she works, Soledad went to great lengths to emphasize the unity among her Latina coworkers:

> Where I work right now, almost everyone is either Greek or Yugoslav. There's only about a dozen of us, you know, who speak Spanish, who understand the language. We are only about a dozen at my workplace. And everyone is Salvadorean, Ecuadorian, Colombian, there's even one Peruvian woman there. We're all very sisterly, we celebrate our birthdays. . . . We have a block, we've united. So we have it all written down, like when the birthday of the *señora Cubana* is. She's the oldest of us, she's 62, but she works because she only came here seven years ago, and so she has to work. So for us the ol' lady is like everyone's mother. We celebrate her birthday and she celebrates ours. We make food and take it to work and we celebrate Christmas, Thanksgiving, we even have a party for Holy Week.
>
> It's like a block, we're like family. Very together. We go everywhere, and we invite each other over; if someone has a baby, we're all invited to the baptism. *We're a group—and we're not even from the same country or anything. We found ourselves. We looked for each other.* (Soledad, Colombia)

Soledad's comments in fact illustrate Edward Murguia's statement: "When one meets those who are Latino/Hispanic but not of the same national origin as oneself, the commonality of language and culture often results in a feeling of inter-personal comfort. . . . One source of this comfort is the Spanish . . . language and the way it structures reality, and a second source is Catholicism from Spain."[9]

Yet, as some authors have asserted,[10] these very real shared linguistic and cultural commonalities should not be confused with automatic adherence to political and ideological panethnicism. Alicia, for example, noted that not all Latinos, or even all people of the same national origins, agree on the strategies that Latinos might want to adopt in their relations with Americans in the United States:

> I think Americans should learn Spanish because since we are part of their country now, and of their culture, maybe that way we could understand each other better. There's a Colombian woman who doesn't agree with that, a friend of mine, who said no, because then they would have us even more enslaved. But I don't think so. . . .
>
> Let me give you an example from my own country. My first bosses were Italians. . . . It was an enormous factory. You couldn't see one building from the other. It had schools, it had everything. It had a day-care room that mothers could go to at certain times to breastfeed

their babies. And in case anything happened, there was a nurse right
there, or a doctor, one in the morning and the other at night. . . .
Then the Colombians came and took over. And it hurts me to say
this. But little by little, they took all those things away from us. . . .
The Colombian bosses thought we workers had too many privileges.
(Alicia, Colombia)

In this excerpt, Alicia begins by recognizing the different opinions
among Colombians concerning what kind of strategies to adopt in developing relations with non-Latinos in the United States. But equally
important, in using the example from her previous job in Colombia,
she acknowledges, albeit reluctantly, that class-based differences
within her national-origin group may be deeper than the possible differences between Latinos and non-Latinos in seeking ways of improving relations between them in this country.

Alicia's assumption of the possibility that Americans and Latinos
may at times have more in common than upper- and lower-class Latinos is noteworthy in itself and requires closer examination. As becomes clear in the following sections, the men and women of this study
as a whole often homogenized Americans in defining their Latino or
Latina self and culture in relation to the U.S. context. In this respect, it
is important to note that the extent to which people will emphasize
their perception of the differences of "the other" from themselves—
whether those differences are between Latinos and Americans or are
internal to the Latino community—may depend on how socially and
culturally distant "the other" is from the self. For many people of Latin
American descent, for example, "the American"—as the "external"
referential other—may be perceived as much more distant from the
cultural experience of a Latino than another Latin American national.
But closer distinctions (the internal boundaries) are also essential in
forging the cultural horizon of the Latino self within the group. Hence
many of the people in this study were prone to erase the differences
among those they designated as Americans while stressing the subtle
distinctions between self and other within the Latino population. In
specifying this strategic internal boundary, national differences and
prejudices like class, gender, and race variations and biases within each
national-origin group will also be easily identifiable, as Alicia's earlier
statement exemplifies.

Although he adopted the racial and ethnic forms of classification,
Francisco too strongly affirms the need for Latinos' unity in the interest
of the social mobility of the entire group. But in his interview he also
recognized that in spite of its political and economic potential, there are

issues within the Latino community that hinder collective action. Discussing the importance of unifying the millions of Latinos in the United States in order to forge a strong economic base, he commented:

> We don't do anything for ourselves here. If all 33 million of us were united here, we could form conglomerates through which we could create industries, generate jobs, have hospitals. But I don't know where it came from, or who inculcated into us the idea that each of us is very intelligent and that each person from each country thinks that he is more intelligent than the next: that cultural egoism and his status here makes him be different. (Francisco, Columbia)

Thus, on the one hand, he notes the tendency toward *personalismo:* the need for public acknowledgment of each individual's traits, but on the other, he recognizes that this shared cultural aspect also determines both social relations and the social distance that Latin American people establish in relation to one another in the United States. Francisco is also aware of the national differences that have long hindered the integration of the continent:

> I have even suggested meetings with the Cubans, the Dominicans, in the Puerto Rican cultural center, but each one is such a different world. You don't get friendship from those meetings—only a fantasy friendship of appearances, but in the end it's as if that truly Hispanic unity isn't there. The blood ties aren't here. One discriminates against the other, and on the job each doesn't allow the other to rise because of differences that go back to antiquity.

At the same time, like Alicia, he also recognizes the class differences that mark people's experiences and shape their personal, social, and political relations in their homeland and abroad:

> Or else, if someone arrives and makes the big mistake of saying that he has higher education, that he is a professional, the doors are automatically closed to him. We don't trust each other.

It is these distinctions of class and national origins that we need to consider in order to understand both the meaning and social value that Latin American immigrants attribute to the label Hispanic in their lives. This is what I discuss in the next section.

The Impact of Social Class in Defining the Label Hispanic

As seen above, for a middle-class, college-educated immigrant like Francisco, incorporation into U.S. society involves access to the same rights and privileges of the (white) middle-class citizens. Francisco measured the extent of his potential or actual incorporation into U.S. society in terms of those (whites) he perceives as belonging, like himself, to the category of "first-class" citizens in this country. In so doing he shifted his categories of interpretation to include the ethnic and racial classifications prevailing in this society, abandoning his past as a measure of comparison. Many of the working-class people in this study tended, on the other hand, to measure their progress in the United States specifically against their life chances in their past society. Since their point of comparison is their homeland rather than their new society, at first sight, they seemingly pay little attention to the categories used to measure progress in this society or to the extent of their incorporation into U.S. society. Instead, they perceive themselves more in terms of having achieved the greater material comfort promised to them by the American Dream, long exported to their countries, that motivated their immigration in the first place.[11] Unlike the middle-class immigrants, then, it seems reasonable to suggest that many of the working-class participants in this study tended to perceive the very act of their immigration as a significant step toward fulfilling their dream for social mobility and an achievement in itself.

The Middle-Class Response

> "They invented the word Hispanic to discriminate against us."

The culturally derived importance of establishing one's identity and position in social terms in Latin American society can lead middle-class immigrants to use U.S. categories about their origins to define their group's social position in the United States. In her interview, Soledad, the other middle-class, college-educated person in this study, insisted that each individual should be identified by her or his nationality. Nevertheless, like Francisco, she also immediately adopted the U.S. ethnic category, Hispanic, rather than that of her nationality to refer to Latin Americans in this country. Her perception of both its positive and negative value emerged in the following discussion among Soledad and three other Latin American women concerning the census questionnaire:

> I'm Colombian, but I wrote down that I was Hispanic. (Soledad, Colombian)

I think they wanted you to write it so that they know who speaks Spanish. (Verónica, Dominican Republic)

Yes. But it's also to send more help to the Hispanic communities, like for bilingual schools and things like that. (Soledad)

I remember that further down on that [census] form they had something about what race or tribe you belong to. (Verónica)

Yes, there was a part that said, Dominican, Puerto Rican. (Soledad)

Well, I know that they separate Puerto Ricans. (Dolores, Guatemala)

I didn't see that. Why do they do that? (Milagros, Peru)

I don't know why. (Dolores)

Oh, I do. It's because they're undecided about Puerto Ricans. They don't really know if they're American or if they're Puerto Rican. See, they have a problem with Puerto Ricans because they can't believe that they can be Americans and still speak Spanish. So they catalogue them as Americans for some things, but for others they're Puerto Ricans. When they count for something they're Americans, but when they don't need them to count for anything they're *boricuas*. But in different ways, they do that with all of us who speak Spanish. You know, if an American is running, he's just doing exercise; but if one of us is running, we've just committed a robbery. (Soledad)

In the above conversation, Soledad first identified herself as Colombian but insofar as she recognized the discussion was within the context of the U.S. census, she then immediately translated her identity into the U.S. terminology, Hispanic. ("I'm Colombian, but I wrote down that I was Hispanic.") Her discussion of the greater social benefit to be derived from grouping all Latin American nationalities together as Hispanics—in terms of resource allocations for services such as bilingual schools and so on—shows that she is aware of the government's policies and the relationship between formal ethnic identification and the distribution of resources. However, while Soledad recognizes the social value of the term Hispanic, she is also aware of the stereotypes associated with it: first by implicitly alluding to her understanding of its source—the unresolved political condition and ambivalent position of Puerto Ricans in the United States—and then by attributing to language much of their difficulties ("They can't believe that they can be Americans and still speak Spanish"). Soledad ends her statement by extending her allusions to the prejudice she perceives against Puerto Ricans to encompass "all of us who speak Spanish" and provides an example of her perception of the prejudice against Hispanics as committing crimes in the United States.

Like Soledad, Francisco did not hesitate to include himself in the category of Hispanic as he discussed his position *as a Hispanic* relative to the rest of the population in this society. According to him, "there are around 32 or 33 million of us and yet we are considered a minority. . . . They do not appreciate us. Hispanics' labor must be among the lowest here. We are doing jobs that Americans don't want." (Francisco, Colombia). Similarly, he too seems to be aware of the importance of ethnicity in the organization of U.S. society and discusses the term itself, referring primarily to its negative attributes in this context:

> They invented the word Hispanic to discriminate against us. It is used to separate us from a cultural point of view. It is used to separate us from a religious point of view. It is used to separate us from an economic point of view. It is used to separate us from an intellectual point of view. They do not recognize our merits. We have several Nobel prize winners. . . . But in this country, they don't acknowledge our achievements. (Francisco, Colombia)

Both Francisco and Soledad perceive the term Hispanic as signifying discrimination against Latin Americans and hence identify it as a term of segregation of "all of us" from mainstream U.S. society. Nevertheless, they use it to identify themselves within the U.S. context, thus accepting the ethnic and racial categories in the country. At the same time, they both discussed the position of all Hispanics in the United States in broader sociological rather than personal terms, commenting on the negative implications of the term and comparing the position of Hispanics to that of other groups in this society. This is in marked contrast with the response of the working-class men and women for whom the term's negative connotation is perceived to have directly personal implications. As the next section demonstrates, they seek to distance themselves from being considered Hispanics by emphasizing their national rather than ethnic identity.

The Working-Class Response

"Hispanic? That's what they call us"

Unlike either of the middle-class people discussed above, the rest of the men and women in this study were not as prone to identify themselves explicitly as Hispanics. Like that of their middle-class counterparts, the point of departure in establishing their identity in this country stemmed from their past social status and position in their country of origin. But unlike Francisco and Soledad, the working-class immigrants measured their progress in the United States in terms of their society of origin, where it is not unlikely that, given their social standing, many of them would be considered, in Gilberto Velho's terminology, second- and third-class citizens. In this sense, they would view themselves as better off in this country—as the case of María exemplifies—and hence would be applying the categories reserved for measuring incorporation into their previous society, rather than this one.

It is not surprising then that when asked about the meaning of the term Hispanic, many, unlike Soledad and Francisco, initially dismissed the term altogether. Two of them flatly stated that they hadn't heard the word before. One identified it by explaining that she had "heard on the radio that that's what they call us."

Pointing to the word Hispanic on the union's school registration form, María acknowledged that she would check it off rather than any of the other ethnic identifiers on the form, but added:

> I never even noticed that it had an "H" and an "I" in front of it. For some reason, I only saw the rest of the word "SPANIC." I assumed it referred to Spanish, to my language. That's why I'd mark that one. I think they use it because they want to know if you speak Spanish. (María, Dominican Republic)

Moreover, most of the comments and explanations about the usage of the term invariably contained qualifiers such as "I think," "I believe," "maybe"—attesting to their lack of familiarity with the subject of our discussion, the meaning of the term Hispanic in the U.S. context and, particularly, with "their" (namely, Americans') intentions in formulating the concept.

While several explained the term Hispanic as reflecting language use, others made statements whose meaning in one way or another reflected the following comment by one informant: "Hispanic? Oh, yes, that's what *they* call us" (Dolores, Guatemala). However, the majority were reluctant to self-identify as Hispanics and hesitated to discuss the term, perceiving it as identifying a group of people whose negative attributes had absolutely no correspondence to themselves:

> Hispanic? Yes, I know they call us that. I think the word Hispanic is used for everyone who speaks Spanish. But actually I don't know what it means. You see, there are different conceptions of Hispanics.

They think we are all alike. Sometimes they say, oh, yes, that's a
Hispanic. We're not going to rent to him because he's Hispanic. They
think that Hispanics are noisy; that they are badly educated; that they
have no morals. Sometimes that's because they have no education. . . .
Then others will say, oh yes, those are Hispanics. They're so dirty.
They'll point to a building and say the people in there are pigs. Why?
Because there are two or three families in a building who have the
bad habit of throwing cans into the street, or making noise. So
because of those two or three families, they call us all Hispanics.
(Rosa, El Salvador)

According to Rosa, Hispanic is a term that "they" [Americans] use as a
synonym for pigs, for people who are dirty, have bad habits, and are
noisy. In trying to evade these negative connotations, it is not surprising that many find reasons to simply distance themselves from the
term:

It's wrong to call us Hispanic. Because that word applies to the
Spaniards. We're not Spaniards. We're from Latin America. (Alicia,
Colombia)

In so doing, they signaled their deep disapproval of those they con-
ceive of as Hispanics in this society:

Americans think that we come here to take away something that
belongs to them. A lot of people give them that image. Many go into
drugs, some don't work and so on. No wonder they think badly of
Hispanics. (Verónica, Dominican Republic)

I know Americans think that we don't like to work, that we're
disorganized and messy. It's because wherever there is something
broken or dirty there's always a Hispanic. (Milagros, Peru)

Indeed, sometimes the discussion on the negative meaning attributed
to the term Hispanics brings out prejudices that one national group
might have about another:

I don't want to mention specific nationalities but it is true that there
are people who put music on really loud; they drink beer and throw
the cans out on the street. (Rosa, El Salvador)

Thus, not surprisingly, several informants like Alicia, quoted earlier,
rejected the definition of Hispanic for themselves and for others from
Latin America:

I will call myself by my nationality, no matter where I live. (Irene,
Ecuador)

We should be called South Americans, or Central Americans. It depends on where you're from. (Julián, Peru)

Rosa explicitly linked her understanding of the meaning of the term Hispanic to her knowledge of the Spanish language:

When someone asks me what I am, I say I'm Salvadorean. I'm Central American from El Salvador, and that's it. (Rosa, El Salvador)

What if someone answers you by asking, "Then you are a Hispanic?"

No, I don't think that. I just think, "Oh well, maybe they call me that because I speak Spanish." Because the first thing I say to an American if I'm lost on the street, or if I have to go to an office is "Do you speak Spanish?" So, it probably comes from that. (Rosa, El Salvador)

Refusing to identify herself as a Hispanic, she thus negatively assesses its social value. Rosa's statement concerning Americans' use of the term Hispanic as being due to the fact that she always asks Americans "Do you speak Spanish?" sounds almost naive when contrasted to her harsher evaluation that the label results from the "lack of morals" of "two or three families." In this respect Rosa, like others in this study, shows her fear of having the connotations of the label imposed on her sense of self and life and, in so doing, openly distances herself from the label in personal rather than in the broad sociological terms adopted by Francisco and Soledad.

Culture, Language, and Discrimination

> "It would be madness to forget our culture
> and language!"

Regardless of their social class, all of the men and women in this study emphasized the importance of learning the English language. No matter how difficult it was to learn, they simultaneously struggled to maintain their own language and customs. Across the board, their comments reinforced the statement by Arturo (El Salvador), quoted earlier, as they explained that one should never forget one's customs and language: "How could we leave our customs and culture aside? We're not machines to be reprogrammed! We are human beings born into a culture and educated with love for our home" (Soledad, Colombia). "The roots of language and customs never die," Julieta (Mexico) affirmed. "We never forget our culture of origin." Indeed, knowing several languages was viewed by many in very positive terms:

If you speak two languages you're worth twice as much. What is so wrong about knowing more than one language? You can never have too much knowledge about anything. Besides, the people of at least twenty-one countries in the world speak Spanish. (Dolores, Guatemala)

Not surprisingly, bilingualism was also the ideal expressed by the informants in relation to their own children's upbringing:

I've always liked languages. I think that the more languages people know, the more opportunities they'll have to develop themselves. My language is Spanish. I want my children to speak it so that they'll know their culture and so that they'll never be ashamed of being Latin American. Because I know a lot of families here who are ashamed of being Colombian. (Alicia, Colombia)

Many noted either explicitly or implicitly, as in Alicia's comment, their awareness of the effects of the existing prejudice against Hispanics in their daily lives. It is interesting to observe in this respect that several theorists have noted the link Alicia established between language and culture as a significant approach to staving off the effects of prejudice on children. Sotomayor, for example, has shown the importance of recognizing the value of the relationship among "language, culture and ethnicity in developing self-concept," discussing the low self-image that Spanish speakers have as a result of the negative views of the Spanish language prevailing in U.S. society. Others have stressed that culture is an essential component to consider in the acquisition or maintenance of a language.[12]

Most of the workers interviewed in this study perceived bilingualism as valuable in people's lives. For them, learning English was as essential as maintaining Spanish. Most emphasized the importance of learning English, and for many the reason was self-evident. As Jaime (Honduras) put it, "I have to learn English because in this country, people speak English." Ofelia (Colombia) said, "I'm studying English because I live in a country in which speaking English is a necessity." Others explicitly associated learning English with getting a better job and hence improving their social positions. One woman couldn't seem to stop listing all the reasons why she was learning English:

Because I like it and because I want to get a good profession, a good job and I want to know more about the culture of this country, and I have to relate to people who speak English. It's the language you have to use in this country. Besides, of all the languages, it is the one that is spoken the most all over the world. (Verónica, Dominican Republic)

Several commented on the value of speaking English for establishing better communications with English-language speakers:

> I'm studying English in order to understand and to make myself understood. I want to be able to take care of myself when I need to. (Dolores, Guatemala)

> I want to talk to Americans. (Milagros, Peru)

> I want to get ahead and also be able to respond and understand well when people talk to me and ask me questions. (Teresa, Puerto Rico)

As the above comments make clear, learning English is perceived as a ticket of entry into U.S. society. And this access in turn is perceived primarily in terms of material advancement. However, as Joshua Fishman has argued, it is important to note in this regard that "mastery of English is almost as inoperative with respect to Hispanic social mobility as it is with respect to black social mobility."[13] At the same time, learning English is also perceived as a means for improving relations between Spanish and English speakers. These findings, of course, contradict the claims about Hispanics made by organizations such as U.S. English who are lobbying to add an English Language Amendment to the Constitution of the United States.[14]

Some people in this study believed that because Americans "read about Latin America and the Caribbean," as Julieta (Mexico) noted, they do understand their cultures, a point with which Arturo (El Salvador), for example, agreed, although he suggested that this was because "the United States has had many years of relations with Central America and Latin America." Others sought to give balanced views on Americans' perceptions of Latinos:[15]

> It's true that most of them don't know our culture. But I think Americans who have relations with us and know us do understand us; but most of us don't relate to them because we don't know their language and we don't have any American friends. (Verónica, Dominican Republic)

But the more common statements made in the interviews related to the importance of communicating with Americans because "most of them" (Americans) seemed to have such limited understanding of the cultures of Latin America. In general terms, they expressed their perception of this as resulting from a "lack of interest in our cultures" (Dolores, Guatemala).

Interestingly, education or lack of it was cited by many as the reason why they felt that Americans did or did not understand Latin American culture: "They don't understand us because they haven't studied the culture of Latin America and the Caribbean" (Jorge, Puerto Rico). The idea that Americans "don't understand us" led most of the informants to express their belief that people with ties to Latin America experience a great deal of prejudice in their daily lives:

> They have such a poor image of us. They don't understand anything about us because if they did they'd treat us better. (Teresa, Puerto Rico)

> They think that we are very backward because we don't have their customs. They think that we are good for work, rather ignorant or at times even stupid, but with a strong character. (Paulo, Nicaragua)

A few attempted to explain why Americans might be prejudiced against them:

> They don't understand us. Our cultures are different from theirs. They think we are less intellectual than they are, because they think they're better than we are, and more intelligent because they are from North America. (Irene, Ecuador)

Still others emphasized their belief that lack of knowledge of Latin American culture led Americans to be prejudiced in their understanding of difference:

> I know that they don't understand us because they discriminate against us just because we are Hispanics. (Ofelia, Colombia).

And while Mónica stated that Americans do understand the culture of Latin America "because they are intelligent people and they like to read and are in those countries," she also noted that the image Americans draw from their understanding is simplistic:

> Americans think that all Latinos are ignorant. Because they say that we have small minds ... they think everyone is the same. (Mónica, Dominican Republic)

To a certain extent, the working-class people in this study also tended to attribute some of the cause of this prejudice to their own lack of knowledge of English. The perception of the prejudice against Latin Americans as resulting from lack of language skills led many, like

Verónica and Alicia, quoted earlier, to suggest that learning the language would certainly help to bridge the gap between Americans and Latin Americans in the United States. In fact, several believed that their going to school to learn English would solve the problem of prejudice against them once and for all. Indeed, one of the reasons they were in the English classes was to overcome the prejudice they experienced in their daily lives. Comments such as the following one were echoed in many interviews:

> If I have problems in this country, it's not because I'm from Ecuador but because of the language. Because in this country, when you don't speak the language, they think you won't complain; they think you won't be able to find the right office, or the right person. But if I have a problem, even with my bad English, I get around. That's why it's important to learn English: so that they can't take advantage of you. (Irene, Ecuador)

In this respect, they echo the feelings expressed by the Polish writer, Eva Hoffman, concerning her own struggles with the English language:

> I know that language will be a crucial instrument, that I can overcome the stigma of my marginality, the weight of presumption against me, only if the reassuringly right sounds come out of my mouth. . . .
>   It's not that we all want to speak the King's English, but whether we speak Appalachian or Harlem English, or Cockney or Jamaican Creole we want to be at home in our tongue.[16]

Almost all of the people I interviewed noted that the best thing about life in the United States was, as Teresa (Puerto Rico) put it, "that you're always working," or in the words of Verónica (Dominican Republic), it is easier "to achieve what you want here." For Julieta (Mexico), who preferred life in her country because it was "more peaceful," living in the United States was better in terms of its "better employment opportunities" and thus "economically." Yet she too noted that the worst thing about this country was "the racism." Indeed, their positive views about the economic possibilities opened to them in the United States was weighed against the prejudice they experienced as Spanish-speaking Latin Americans in this country. Many, particularly among the working-class immigrants, could point to some incident in their daily life experiences that exemplifed prejudice against Latinos. Invariably, their views of the prejudice against Hispanics were tempered by their appreciation for what they have achieved in the United

States. María's testimony encapsulates the effects of the stigmatizing labeled Hispanic in this respect:

> I would like my children to go into the U.S. army. You know why?
> Because what I've achieved here I've gotten thanks in part to this
> country. I did it with my efforts, but they gave me the opportunity to
> come, to survive. So to show my gratitude I would like that. . . . The
> problem is that in the army, or in the navy, Hispanics are always
> given the worst jobs. If my daughter is educated and qualified, why
> should the Americans give her the worst positions just because she
> speaks Spanish? (María, Dominican Republic)

Like many immigrants, she values the opportunities that exist in the United States. Yet she is critical of the discrimination against Hispanics. The result, then, is the constant expression of ambivalent feelings and thoughts about their lives in the United States. Although some understood the existing prejudice against them as stemming from simplistic generalizations about "those two or three families," as Rosa put it, the ambivalence expressed by most also reflected their belief that, nevertheless, the prejudice of Americans toward Hispanics was unwarranted and the result of the *social and class* distance they perceived between Hispanics and "Americans." María, for example, noted that prejudice begins early in children's lives at schools. She commented that parents like herself have to fight hard against American teachers' reinforcement of the negative connotations associated with the label Hispanic, which invariably affect the self-image of second-generation Latinos growing up in this country:

> The American teachers are always trying to sidetrack my daughter.
> They give her bad advice. They tell her she'll never make it. I
> remember staying up so many nights talking with her. I always said
> to her: Look, life is like this. Some people don't want others to go up
> in life, because the more uneducated people there are, the more
> people there are to be exploited. Imagine if we were all professionals:
> Who would wash their clothes? Who would clean their apartments?
> (María, Dominican Republic)

Given their awareness of the stereotypes associated with the Spanish language, it is not surprising that many of the working-class men and women shunned the term Hispanic as a means of self-identification. Indeed, as the next section shows, the negative social value and meaning that they attributed to the homogenizing nature of the term is pitted against the positive value attributed to their national and cultural diversity, as represented by their emphasis on their respective nationalities as a means of self-identification.

Reimagining the American Continent

"We have to differentiate ourselves."

As discussed in chapter 2, Latin Americans' identity in continental terms is still being debated and is yet to be fully forged. It is thus not surprising that the existence of a shared identity among Latin American people and the exploring of its meaning and value were new to some of the people in this study, regardless of their time of arrival in the United States. This became apparent to me when Rosa dropped into my office a few days after our first interview, and said:

> I have to talk to you. I have to tell you something. . . . I went to the factory the very next day after our last conversation and I asked my colleagues at work what they understood by Hispanic. I asked an Ecuadorian, a Dominican, and a Puerto Rican. They all gave me the same answer. They said it was because we all speak Spanish. . . . They didn't seem to care what the Americans call us. But I think it's interesting. I think we should know why they call us Hispanic. So I began to think about it. (Rosa, El Salvador)

Nevertheless, the idea of self-identifying in terms of Hispanic seemed difficult for her to accept. Asked whether she thought of herself in those terms, she answered:

> No, I don't. I'm Central American. Because you know there's the North Americans and the Central Americans and the South Americans. We're all Americans, right? But then we have to differentiate ourselves. Some are in the North, some in the Center, and others in the South, right? So when someone asks me what I am, I say I'm Salvadorean. I'm Central American from El Salvador, and that's it. A Colombian can say I'm South American, from Colombia. (Rosa, El Salvador)

Like most of the people interviewed, Rosa defines herself in terms of her nationality, Salvadorean. Her reluctance to use the term Hispanic was at least partly due to the negative connotations that others associated with the term and her consequent perception of the stigma attached to it. At the same time, she contextualized her national identity in terms of the continent's geography, narrowing the latter down to particular nationalities. This was an approach echoed by most of the others in this study as they sought to define their identities in the U.S. context.

Indeed, in many ways, the "Hispanic" was the external other. At the same time, through its negation, the label Hispanic became the basis on which the sense of one's self and identity was being constructed in the new context. For the people in this study, the root of the problem with the term Hispanic was the stigmatizing stereotypes resulting from reducing all Spanish-speaking people to one homogenizing idea. In addition, most were aware that along with showing Americans' lack of knowledge about the other countries in the hemisphere, labels such as this also efface what are for them obvious national, ethnic, and social distinctions:

> Neither Americans or Europeans know much about geography. In this respect they are very ignorant. That's why they group us all together. They don't know the difference, because they don't know their geography. Because for example, just because you speak Spanish, they immediately ask, "You Puerto Rican?" And I tell them, "No, I'm South American or Colombian but I speak Spanish and the Puerto Rican people do too." Because they think that everyone who speaks Spanish is Puerto Rican . . . or, for example, the Dominicans will say, "We are Caribbeans," because they identify with the Caribbean, and the Americans can't relate to that because culturally they only know about themselves. (Soledad, Colombia)

The extent to which Latin Americans resented what they perceived as Americans' lack of knowledge about their respective cultures can be seen in the ways they defined their identity in the U.S. context—"We are all of us Americans," as Julián (Peru) put it. It is also clear in the relationship they established between people's self-identification and their insistence on specifying the continent's geography:

> I never call people from this country "Americans." I use that word for everyone from Alaska to Patagonia. In my city—I can only speak of my city, because you know, each one has its own customs—we call them yanquis or gringos, but not Americans.
>
> I only know one America. Its geographical position may be North America, Central America, or South America. But we're all American. Colombia isn't located in Europe, it isn't located in Asia, and it isn't in Africa either. So, if they take the name of the entire continent for their country, what is left for ours? What is the name of the continent that Colombia is on? (Alicia, Colombia)

Like Alicia, many of the men and women in this study stressed the fact that they are as American as U.S. citizens. The use of the term Latin

American in this sense becomes simply the counterweight of the term North American. In fact, comments such as Alicia's point to some of the tensions, discussed in chapter 2, that were shaped by the Monroe Doctrine early in the hemisphere's history. These are visible to this day in the relations between the populations of the Latin American nations, on the one hand, and the United States, on the other. Not surprisingly, they too were addressed in several of the interviews. Dolores, for example, told me:

> The problems of Latin America can't be solved by the U.S. army going to fight there, but instead by not providing arms to either side in the conflicts, and by creating sources of employment. Besides I think that no country, however powerful it might be, should intervene in the internal affairs of any of the countries of Latin America. (Dolores, Guatemala)

It was clear that for Juan, a U.S.-born Puerto Rican, the tensions had specific political and historical antecedents:

> I'm American only by accident, because Puerto Rico's a territory of the United States. I don't think that's by choice, because they've got American bases there. (Juan, Puerto Rico, U.S.-born)

Asked about his American citizenship and passport, Juan continued to deny that he was "American," explaining, "I'm Americanized, but I'm not American." Asked what he meant by "Americanized," Juan specified, "I believe like they say, work hard, you get ahead, you get whatever you want, you get your house, your cars, your mortgages."

Although he acknowledges that he is Americanized, however, Juan refuses the identity of "American," recognizing it as having been imposed on Puerto Ricans as much as the word Hispanics had been. As he explained, "Puerto Ricans never call each other Hispanics," just as "they never called each other spics." Not surprisingly, Juan defined his identity in national (Puerto Rican) rather than ethnic (Hispanic or Latino) terms:

> First I'd say I'm Puerto Rican. I would consider myself that because that's what I was taught to believe in . . . You know, to be proud of your nationality. You're proud of what you are and what the people in your country fought for. (Juan, Puerto Rico, U.S.-born)

For the most part, among the non–Puerto Ricans in this study, the tension between the "two Americas" is also manifested in the need to recognize the boundaries of the identity of the Other in the process of shaping one's own identity in the United States context:

> I once had a discussion with a Puerto Rican who said to me, "I'm American," and I answered, "I'm as American as you are, because there is only one America." (María, Dominican Republic)

Thus, particularly in the process of defining the group's internal boundaries and their own identity within it, this study's Latin American population affirmed the significance of specifying their respective national origins among themselves. Verónica told me:

> If I introduce you to someone I would say "This is my friend, she's from Peru." Or else, I'd say, "She's South American, or Peruvian." (Verónica, Dominican Republic)

Regardless of social class, while the men and women clearly understood the implications of the label Hispanic and their own reasons for its existence, they did not necessarily see the purpose in their personal lives of homogenizing the various nationalities under the label Hispanic. Asked how she would call people in this country who don't have her nationality but whose families come from Latin America or who speak Spanish, Soledad's response reinforced Verónica's above, as the following excerpt from my interview with her exemplifies:

> Soledad: I always call people according to their country: a Salvadorean, an Uruguayan, an Argentinean.
>
> *But not a Hispanic?*
>
> Soledad: No, I identify them according to their country.
>
> *Why wouldn't you say they're Hispanic?*
>
> Soledad: Well, it just doesn't sound right to me. For example, if I'm with my people, I might say South Americans, like others would say Central Americans or Caribbeans.
>
> *So there's a difference?*
>
> Soledad: Yes, we're not just a lump, we know who everyone is—because even though we may use the same language, our cultures are different and we have to think about what we're going to say to each other. . . . What I most admire is our cultural differences. Because you know, I look at people through the eyes of an artist—I look at people and their things. We have to see each other. Many of the things we might say in Spanish is offensive to one person, funny to another.

> Another thing is the food. . . . For example, we have to learn to eat
> what [Central Americans] eat. (Soledad, Colombia)

The Weight of Race, Class, National Origins, and Language in the Label Hispanic

In defining the meaning that the term Hispanic in the United States has for themselves, the men and women in this study showed that they were conscious of the differences among the various Latin American nationalities. Yet they were also aware of the effects that the assumptions and prejudices stemming from the indiscriminate grouping of Hispanics in the United States had on their lives. This was particularly noted in these terms by Jorge, an island-born Puerto Rican. He emphasized that the recognition of his identity as a Puerto Rican had to include acknowledgment that Puerto Rico's populations were Spanish speaking, even though the island might be part of the United States. Therefore, he perceived the expectation that he speak English as an act of discrimination, and explained what he meant by saying:

> At the beginning, when I arrived, my boss wanted me to speak
> English, even though I didn't know the language. I think he thought
> that I was a Latino. (Jorge, Puerto Rico, island-born)

It is not surprising, then, that within the attempts made by this study's group of men and women to define the term Hispanic in the U.S. context, many identified a variety of elements in its definition. Moreover, they discussed and even speculated about the weight of its various geographical, linguistic, national, and racial aspects. Inevitably, as they tried to make sense of the weight of these various aspects in defining the value of the term Hispanic in their everyday lives, they included their life experiences as immigrants. Some, for example, made specific reference to the term's linguistic element and discussed it in terms of people who speak Spanish:

> Maybe they call me that because I speak Spanish. (Rosa, El Salvador)

> They call us Hispanics because we speak Spanish. (Julián, Peru)

Others related the term specifically to the issue of nationality, emphasizing the importance of an individual's birthplace as an element in defining who belongs to the category of Hispanics:

> I don't really know what Hispanic means: I think it's all the people
> who come from Latin America. But I'm not sure. I know that people

who are born here in the United States aren't Hispanic. So, for
example, one of my children, the one born in Peru, is Hispanic; the
other isn't because she was born in this country. (Milagros, Peru)

Asked how she would categorize the child born in the United States,
Milagros didn't hesitate to answer, "Well, if she was born here, of
course she's an American." Thus, she views the term Hispanic as having a precise regional connotation, although she perceives its meaning
to be strictly tied to people's birthplace, rather than to their ethnicity.
Another version of this approach combined the regional and the linguistic elements of the term: "It's an undefined group name given to all
the countries where Spanish is spoken" (Mónica, Dominican Republic).

And, recognizing the origin of the term as imposed by Americans,
Jorge also made an implicit reference to the idea of a linguistic hierarchy among Spanish-language countries that is sometimes raised within
the Latin American context: "It's the nickname that the Americans
have given to us because some countries speak Spanish almost per-
fectly" (Jorge, Puerto Rico, island-born).

A certain cynicism was also not absent from the sometimes lengthy
explanations of the origins and meaning of the term:

White people have a name for everybody else. From whites you came
up with the word Hispanics, and spic. I mean, Puerto Ricans never
call each other Hispanic. They never called each other spics. They
never did. When they said Hispanics, that's just a group of people
that they've just put together that speaks Spanish. . . .

They just count all Latin people in one bunch. They do it to the
blacks, too. I mean, come on, they're more than just blacks. You got
your American blacks, you got your African, your Jamaican; then you
got your Puerto Rican blacks; some guys are darker than me. Then
you got your Dominican blacks, you got white people that are dark
skinned. And it's just that they clump 'em all together just so they
can generalize everybody. . . .

So you got your Hispanics over here which includes whatever race
you want to put in it south of the border. Then you got your blacks,
anything from the Congo down. Then you got your whites which is
Americans. (Juan, Puerto Rico, U.S.-born)

In view of the prevalence of race-related representations in New
York City, where he grew up, it is not surprising that a New York–born
Puerto Rican discussed the meaning of Hispanic in strictly racial-ethnic terms. Although Juan recognized the diversity within the various
groups, he also had a firm perception of a two-tiered racial hierarchy

made up of "whites" and "everybody else" in the United States. He defined Hispanics as including "whatever race you want to put in it south of the border," while singling out "whites" as "Americans": his interpretation, then, clearly recognizes that in this country race and nationality are conflated. Indeed, although he clearly rejected Hispanic as a term of self-identification and focused instead on his nationality rather than race, Juan (who is very fair skinned) nevertheless implicitly recognized that in this society, and insofar as his nationality and his race *are* conflated, his identity as a Puerto Rican is not "white."[17]

Interpreting the weight of the various components of the term Hispanic—race, class, national origins, and language—becomes an essential part of people's self-definition and strategies of survival. Perhaps the clearest example of the extent to which this is true can be seen in the following description of the problems that the 1990 census questionnaire raised for Hispanics:

> If I were black and I spoke Spanish, I don't know how I would have answered that census questionnaire. They put black down as a race and separated it from people who speak Spanish. And they didn't have anything down for mestizos or for white Latin Americans. So when I was answering the census I said to myself, "Whoever did this made a lot of mistakes. Whoever did the census form wasn't educated enough about race." Because *how could someone who is really black but speaks Spanish write down that he's black?* I kept wondering about that. (Soledad, Colombia)

Here Soledad defines race as incorporating both culture and language, as well as phenotype. In fact, Soledad's criticism of the race and Hispanics section of the census questionnaire clearly showed the greater social value that Latin Americans *publicly* place on cultural and linguistic attributes (speaking Spanish) than they do on skin color. Soledad's criticism of the separation of race and language in the census thus also points to the process through which Latin Americans are forced to recognize the prevalence of racial classifications in the United States. As they come to terms with the consequent subsuming of their own Latin American–based national cultural and linguistic forms of understanding and affirming their identities, they confront prejudices internalized from their socialization in their own societies.[18]

What emerges from the testimonies of the men and women interviewed for this study is the extent to which they drew on their social and cultural backgrounds and their life experiences as they tried to come to terms with the label Hispanic in their lives. The cynicism of

Juan, a Puerto Rican born in New York, about the classification of Hispanics, for example, is the result of his lived experience in the racially charged environment of New York City, where he grew up. Soledad's questions stem from her own Latin American socially and culturally shaped perception that "whoever did the census form wasn't educated enough about race." For in Colombia, where she comes from, as in other Latin American countries, the discourse on race distinctions is much more gradated and each gradation is strictly related to the individual's status and social class position.

Again, the study is not representative of the immigrant populations from Latin America nor of the Puerto Ricans in New York City. At the same time, these interviews contribute to understanding some of the ways that Latinos do construct their social and racial identities in the United States. Further research on this question is essential, for the interviews make clear that the ways the members of this group choose to identify themselves in this country are less a matter of cultural imperative and more a reflection of their direct experiences and their needs at a given conjuncture in their lives. To a large extent, their choice of identity expresses their expectations of and strategies for incorporation into the U.S. social structure. While, as Latin Americans, they may insist that they are as American as the "gringos," their confrontation with race and class representations in U.S. society forces them to incorporate these dimensions both in the way they imagine the "American community" and in their own lived experience as Hispanics in the United States.

Chapter 7

Imagined Communities Revisited

Recently, I went to a literature conference at an East Coast university, focusing on new writers and writing in Mexico. One of the panels was made up of Mexican writers who talked about the development of their lives as writers in Mexico. Following their presentations, a Chicana college senior asked one of the panelists how she defined "Mexican writers."

When that student asked her question, there was a ripple in the room. The audience was largely made up of Spanish-speaking Latino and Latina professors, students, and community members of several different national backgrounds, including Chicano, Puerto Rican, Dominican, Peruvian, Spanish, and Colombian. All of us shared in common the fact that we lived, worked, or studied in the United States, so that as Latinos, we understood the young participant's question in terms of the discussion of ethnicity and nationality in this country. In this sense, the question might be rephrased as follows: If she were to take up writing as a career, would she, as a Chicana and as a member of a new generation of Latinos born or raised in the United States, be considered to be a Mexican writer, too? So everyone leaned forward in anticipation of hearing the verdict on this young Chicana's "Mexicanness" by a "real" Mexican author from Mexico. After all, literature, as Eliana Ortega and Nancy Saporta have said, is not so much a search as it is an articulation and affirmation of people's identities. Indeed, writers have historically played a significant role in the creation and affirmation of national cultures and identities.[1]

But the Mexican author to whom the question was directed had only arrived in the United States a few days before to be on this panel. She seemed rather perplexed by the question, which, after all, was the product of the debate on ethnicity and nationality as it is played out in the U.S. context. Her answer was both brief and concise: "A Mexican author," she said, "is somebody born in Mexico, or somebody who has been raised there since a very young age."

The audience leaned back. The disappointment in the room—either because of the brevity of her response, or maybe even the finality and self-evidence of her tone—was palpable. The resolution of the confusion of U.S.-born Latinos' national identity would have to wait for another time.

Moments such as this capture one of the dilemmas that the new generations of Latinas and Latinos born and raised in the United States confront with respect to their personal identities and their understanding of the meaning of cultural and ethnic identities and national affiliations. This is not surprising given the continued absence in their daily lives of an articulated recognition of the relationship between diversity and political inclusion made manifest in full rights of citizenship and equality.[2] The new generation of Latinos cannot root their identity in a nation that lumps them indiscriminately together under the stigmatizing label "Hispanic" and treats them as second-class "foreign Others." Insofar as they are perceived as members of a Hispanic community— which, lacking historical and contextual grounding, is nebulously defined—the implicit suggestion that Latinos are not *really* Americans ultimately undermines the very notion of the right to equality and justice under the law.

There is no doubt that Latinos and Latinas in the United States have cultural, linguistic, and historical ties to various nations in Latin America and that those ties have to be reaffirmed through grounded knowledge of their respective national histories and the consequent recognition of the continent's diversity. At the same time it seems to me that it is equally important to research and study the histories, cultures, and experiences that have shaped the varied and multiple meanings and social values of being Latinos and Latinas in the United States. Only in that way can we understand the ways that the historical legacies and cultures of Latin Americans and Latinos are articulated and reaffirmed in everyday life. Only in that way can Latinos solidify the ties of commonality that bind them to Latin America, on the one hand, and also recognize the particular context that distinguishes their realities and experiences from Latin America, on the other.[3]

I have heard that young Chicana's question in various forms echoed in the discourse of many of the new generations of Latinos, particularly in the context of the Northeast, where, outside of urban centers like Boston or even New York, there are relatively small communities of Latinos, and thus a grounded notion of Latino identity lacks contextualization and cultural reinforcement. Yet that question, in whatever form it takes, makes it clear that the representations forged during the nineteenth century of the "American national community" to a large extent continue to shape the way people living in this country today imagine inclusion and exclusion in the society and the way they live their sense of belonging to this nation. It is not surprising, for example, that Juan, a young U.S.-born Puerto Rican, equated "American" with "white," to the exclusion of other racial groups.

As I discussed in chapter 2, these representations were shaped *in relation to Latin Americans* on the basis of nineteenth-century ideological justifications of the "national" superiority of the United States against "foreign Others" in the hemisphere. The perception of a North-South continental hierarchy based on an ideology of national superiority also appears to continue to prevail today. As Irene said in her interview, "They think they're better than we are, and more intelligent because they are from North America."

Yet the aftermath of the Mexican-American War was not the first time that the Latin American reality had been homogenized in the perceptions and through the actions of an external power. As early as the sixteenth century, the fragmented regional realities and demographic differences of the continent had already ensured that the New World, as conceived by early Renaissance Europeans, proved all too often to be no more than "a fragile construct of the mind."[4] In fact, the extent to which the vision of a homogenized Latin American reality continues to reflect no more than a "fragile construct of the mind" on the part of Americans today has been well described by the Uruguayan writer Mario Benedetti:

> Europe and the United States often evaluate Latin America as a large pot of folklore, an attractive and picturesque human geography, but also as a somewhat homogeneous whole with barely visible hues, which correspond, in a way, to the various provincial traits of a single nation. There is, it is true, a past that is more or less shared and, in vast areas, an official language common to all. *But beyond these similarities, each sector has its own distinct past and present, a different social context, and a language with varying resonances and modulations.*[5]

But what distinguishes the homogenizing of Latin Americans by the United States from the previous homogenization they had been subjected to by Spain (and Europe as a whole) was that the nineteenth-century process of constructing the image of an "American imagined community" did not make allowances for the racial, social, or national differences of the Latin American peoples in relation to whom it was being forged.

Almost 150 years after the Mexican-American War, the process of ideologically structuring the nationalities, languages, class-based experiences, and races of people with ties to Latin America continues in the United States—now publicly and officially endorsed and reinforced in terms of an ethnic label, Hispanic. Indeed, the way this study's particular group of men and women perceived the intersection of the various elements of the label points to the difficult "fit" between the label and the deeply diverse populations it seeks to encompass. Similarly, the debates on these racial and ethnic categories in mainstream institutions include confronting this difficulty whenever the attempt to clarify the definition of the Hispanic category is made:

> Was it [the Hispanic population] to be defined as those persons who had ancestors from Mexico; if so how many ancestors? Was it those persons who spoke Spanish? Or was it those who called themselves Mexican-Americans or some other Hispanic name? What if someone had parents from Mexico but did not consider himself or herself to be Hispanic?[6]

Like politicians and policymakers, researchers, statisticians, interest groups, the media, business and advertising concerns, and the public at large, the men and women in this study also attributed a different weight to the various elements that compose the term Hispanic. But unlike the sectors listed above, they were also struggling to avoid an intransigent, prejudiced, and monolithic classification that would directly and negatively affect their daily lives.

The strategies they adopted as they coped with this stigmatizing label and situated themselves in U.S. society differed primarily according to their social class backgrounds and status in their country of origin. The working-class people evaluated their lives in this country in positive terms, relative to what they perceived to be their life chances in their home countries. Nevertheless, they were not naive about the extent to which they could advance in economic and social terms in U.S. society. The ambivalence they expressed toward both white Europeans and U.S. society points to their awareness of the limits imposed on their upward mobility by what they perceived as prejudice and discrimination against those labeled as Hispanics. They identified these limits as caused as much by their Spanish language and lack of English skills as by the general lack of knowledge in the United States about the rest of the hemisphere. Their interviews strongly suggest that they perceived the negative connotations of the term as placing a ceiling on how much they could achieve in the United States. As their interview data suggests, ambivalence became a way for them to position themselves in relation to both their old and the new societies.

The middle-class people in this study did not express the same ambivalence, but manifested more openly their desire to integrate into U.S. society. To do so, they were willing to subscribe to the idea that people with ties to Latin America must unite and fight together to achieve the privileges of the white middle class in the United States. "We must join together" was a phrase that continually punctuated Francisco's comments on the social status of Hispanics in this country, while Soledad made every effort to emphasize the unity of the small group of Latinos in her workplace. Nevertheless, the cultural difficulties resulting from class and national differences, raised by Fernando, continue to hinder the forging of Latino unity in the United States. Some of his concerns are reflected in the words of B. E. Aguirre and Rogelio Saenz:

> The common cultural ground is too remote, the structural actions of the state are too specific and inconsistent, the ethnocentrism of the various groups is too strong, to give realistic hope for the emergence of a new Latino ethnicity out of the unguided process of collective experience. Left to its own devices, Latinismo will not become a new ethnicity.[7]

In other words, Latin American immigrants in the United States, like people everywhere, are a very complex group whose class and race values, differentiated gender experiences, national differences, and political convictions and beliefs may interfere again and again with the construction of group solidarity among themselves. There are, of course, many among the middle-class sectors whose life experiences, combined with their political analysis and vision of the kind of society they would like to build for future generations of Latinos, will lead them to turn their attention and efforts to work with and for "la comunidad." But middle-class people of Latin American descent also bring with them their socialization within Latin American hierarchical societies. Given their particular insertion into their own stratified societies, their social status in their own countries, like their very class and educational backgrounds, may lead some, like Fernando, to expect immediate incorporation into the upper echelons of U.S. society, far from the daily lives and experiences of working-class communities.

In thinking about the construction of Latino social movements, of Latinismo, it is thus important to incorporate the idea that they may also share class backgrounds and status, racial and ethnic prejudices and values that, as Martha Giménez has suggested, can unite middle-class people beyond their nationalities. These can often work against establishing ties with working-class people, whether in their own countries or abroad.[8] As a result, like the ethnic label Hispanic itself, this kind of unifying discourse, for a variety of ideological, national, social, and personal reasons, is pitted against the cultural, social, ethnic, and racial diversity that reinforces political differences within Latin American populations. Given this diversity, to identify oneself with the issues that Latinos confront in U.S. society today is *also* a conscious choice to acknowledge one's history and sociocultural background, as well as the need to struggle for social justice. In other words, more than solely a culturally dictated fact of life, identifying oneself as Latino or Latina and participating in a Latino social movement is also a *political* decision, one that aims to strengthen *la comunidad* in those terms.

Within this framework, it is important to examine the meaning and social value of the term Hispanic in varied contexts and among different social sectors, as well as the ways in which actions aimed at reinforcing an *assumed* collective Hispanic ethnic identity affects people's lives. For, even when specific sectors of the Latino population might choose to impute and celebrate a common heritage in their struggle for a greater numerical voice in the distribution of resources in this country, this should by no means obscure the ways that class, race, national origins, gender, and language are articulated such that the experiences and identities of people with ties to Latin America are also structurally and culturally differentiated.

As my data suggest, the concept Hispanic does not necessarily correspond to the diverse ways the Latin Americans I interviewed perceive themselves or their status and histories in this society. Scholars working with qualitative research have often suggested that in-depth studies of small groups such as this one can pinpoint the web of subtle interstices in the multiple ways that a particular group of men and women understand their lived experiences.[9] Because these dimensions are often not fully portrayed in quantitative research, studies of this kind can serve to suggest areas of further research or to complement the findings of larger survey studies, such as the recent *Latino Voices* by

Rodolfo de la Garza and others, which usefully portrays the broader trends within the group or in the larger society. In pointing to the ways that the group of men and women I interviewed differentially interpret and negotiate the meaning and value of the label Hispanic, my study suggests the need for further research about the gap between the label and the diverse characteristics and experiences of the people to whom it is applied. Specifically, it suggests a more detailed exploration of what Aguirre and Saenz have referred to as "the factors that hinder the emergence of Latino culture" and of the meaning of the notion of a "Latino social movement," suggested by Juan Flores and George Yudice.[10]

Latino versus Hispanic: Is Terminology the Issue?

As I noted in chapter 1, "Hispanics" are often perceived to be responsible for many of the ills of modern life in the United States: drugs, unemployment, taking jobs away from "Americans," declining educational standards, teenage pregnancies, and so on. Moreover, sectors in the United States, represented by the various English Only movements, have taken a firm stance that the English language is seriously threatened primarily by the presence of large Spanish-speaking groups in the United States. But some mainstream institutions, such as Hollywood and other business and advertising concerns, and even sectors in the group itself believe Latinos need to be identified as a homogeneous community, whether to constitute a market segment or to provide legitimacy for a potentially powerful voting block. In this respect, Coco Fusco has pointed out that "as consumers [Latinos] outspend the average North American by more than 30%. . . . Hollywood's renewed interest in exploiting the Latino market in the 1980s occurs at a time when traditional political parties are recognizing Latinos as an actual and potential voting population with specific political needs and problems (such as immigration)."[11]

At the same time, some scholars are increasingly suggesting that along with social and cultural differences, the local problems and national concerns differentially affect the various national groups, for their experiences are also shaped by their respective citizenship status, the reasons for their presence in the United States, and the historical period and varied forms of incorporation into the national economy.[12] For example, beyond the varied social and economic concerns of the various national populations, the political issues currently raised by the issue of immigration—to cite just one example—take on a different institutional connotation for Mexican immigrants than they might for

Cuban exiles and refugees, for whom open immigration to the United States has long been restricted. Given the particular history of the United States' relations with Cuba, the specificity of the issues involved in political immigration became even more clearly manifested through the differentiated reception of refugees from other Latin American countries, such as those fleeing El Salvador during the 1980s. Puerto Ricans, on the other hand, are U.S. citizens and can come and go to the island at will. Thus they do not personally experience the effects of the Immigration and Naturalization Service (INS) and are not necessarily on the same side of the issue in political and economic terms as these or other groups, such as, for example, the Dominicans or other immigrants from Central or South American countries.

Thus, within the Latino communities themselves, U.S. immigration debates centering on well-publicized efforts in the hemisphere to restrict immigration are also influenced by geographical factors. Moreover, the proximity of the Caribbean would certainly give the notion of the circularity of migration a different connotation to those with ties to the Caribbean islands than it might acquire for populations coming from the more distant Central American nations and certainly for those who leave their homelands in South America. Distance similarly differentiates the meaning that the issues raised by the immigration debates will have among Latin Americans from what it has acquired in the border region of the Southwest, particularly in the context of the dubious North American Free Trade Agreement (NAFTA) accords. Along with neglected historical, geographical, and regional factors, these differences have also been shaped by race, gender, and generational considerations that reinforce Latinos' diverse experiences and cultural formations and affect their understanding of particular issues. They also influence the political positions people adopt and their experience of others identified as Hispanics in the United States.

Seen in this light, the various meanings and social values attributed to the ethnic label Hispanic and to "Hispanic ethnicity" point to how far the label can be from expressing the social and cultural diversity of people of Latin America in the United States today. Consequently, the discussion over the appropriate terminology for this group (that is, Hispanic versus Latino) becomes a false debate—insofar as, like the label Hispanic, the term Latino or Latina, or even Latin American, does not solve the problems raised by existing national and linguistic, class and racial differences in the U.S. context.

It is difficult to ignore the fact that the term Latino is in many ways as much of a neologism as the word Hispanic. For, just as Hispanic refers to a specific population and culture on the Iberian Peninsula, so, too, the word Latin or Latino (originally corresponding to the Latin language)—outside of perhaps the most conservative religious orders—finds little correspondence in contemporary Latin American realities: both terms in fact exclude much of the historical experiences and linguistic traditions of the African, Asian, and indigenous populations of the American continent.

Still, the fact remains that several of the men and women in this study expressed a preference for the term Latino, Latin American, or even Central and South American over the label Hispanic. This is not surprising if one recalls that these terms also reflect their awareness that *everyone* in the Americas—regardless of race, class, language, or national origin—is as American as the "gringos," as Alicia (Colombia) put it, adding, "I only know one America. Its geographical position may be North America, Central America, or South America. But we're all American." On the other hand, however, unlike the stigmatizing attributes of the label Hispanic, the connotations of the term Latino in no way include the implicit negatively perceived class and race connotations that the label Hispanic connotes today in the United States.

In this respect, Edward Murguia makes the point that "the term Hispanic fundamentally is integrationist with some amount of pluralism within it, while Latino is fundamentally pluralist with some amount of integration within it." He suggests that whatever term is designated must incorporate both pluralism and integration, insofar as "some degree of both is desired by most of this minority."[13]

The debate on terminology is important, for there is no doubt that the names we choose with which to identify ourselves in the public sphere are as fundamental to the construction of our political and social identity as are our own personal names. At times it seems to me that it also raises the question of whether it is possible to live in a society as large and complex as the United States *without* labeling and stereotyping diverse populations. It is true that this debate may never be resolved—whether one is referring to Hispanics or to Latinos, or even to other groups currently known as Arabs, African Americans or blacks, Asian Americans, Jews, native Americans, or white Europeans. Nevertheless, it is important to understand the many historically constructed meanings and social values that these "ethnic labels" can and have acquired over time. As I suggested in chapters 2 and 3, the names adopted by different groups or imposed on them by others emerge as a result of particular historical and political contexts. Hence the importance of understanding their meanings and values in different sectors

of society and contextualizing their use in terms of the political and demographic realities through which they come into being. Rather than
continue to adhere to simplistic connotations of homogenizing "ethnic" labels, it is essential to turn to history and everyday life as sources
from which to address the diversity within and among different populations' experiences. In so doing, the ways in which the intersections
of gender, race, language, class, and national origins have historically
served to exclude various populations from full participation and citizenship rights in the "national community" of the United States can be
more fully documented, analyzed, and understood.

Indeed the need to examine the implications of these labels has become more pressing today, particularly in terms of the process of personal, social, and political identity formation of the children of the citizens, residents, and immigrants of Latin American descent growing
up in the United States today. For, as I mentioned in the introduction,
unlike the people in this study, these new generations of Latinos were
born in the post-1970 period together with the label Hispanic, its connotations, and the invented but now traditional celebrations of a homogenized "Hispanic Heritage" in the United States. They are the first
generation to grow up officially identified *as Hispanics* in the United
States, rather than by their national origins or legacy.

Reflections and Refractions of the Latino Experience: The New Generations

The continuous insistence on homogenizing Latinos' social, historical,
and cultural experiences in the United States raises the issue of the extent to which the "myth of homogeneity" could someday prevail—
particularly among the second and later generations, given the continued exclusion of the presence and role of people of Latin American
descent from the mainstream representations of this nation's history.
Contrary to the intensive efforts to "Americanize" varied populations
in the past, the descendants of long-established Chicano and Puerto Rican populations, like those of more recent Latin American immigrants,
are increasingly socialized and recognized primarily as members of a
Hispanic ethnic group, regardless of their parents' nationalities, race,
and class, and with no reference to the respective historical periods or
ways in which their ancestors came to be living in the United States.

Indeed, unlike their descendants, first-generation Latin American
immigrants to the United States have the benefit of their experiences
and memories to affirm their respective national identities—whose

meaning, as Julián's story in the Introduction illustrates, they largely came to discover once they had left their countries. With the exception of Juan, a New York–born Puerto Rican, the men and women in my study were representatives of the first generation arriving in the United States: they were not, after all, born and raised in this country. Those born and raised abroad can thus resort to a national identity and cultural experience derived from their homeland in order to distance themselves from the negative connotations of both the label Hispanic and its corollary, an imputed collective Hispanic experience, distinct from their own.

For the second and subsequent generations, however, the problem and means of both defining and affirming a national identity remains, as seen in the case of the young Chicana I described at the beginning of this chapter. Given the historical conflation of race and nationality discussed in chapter 2 and Latinos' continued exclusion from the way the "American community" is imagined, these later generations are not necessarily perceived as "Americans." Yet when they go to their parents' countries in Latin America, although they often find some commonalities in the cultural and religious traditions as well as in the family stories they might share with relatives abroad, they also encounter significant cultural and linguistic gaps, particularly in the public sphere, between their lived experience in the United States and that of their parents' respective homeland populations.[14] Born and raised in the United States, the later generations are often unable to recognize their U.S.-Latino experiences in the Latin American context, and are simultaneously not fully acknowledged as part of the populations of those societies. Commenting on her recent Latin American lecture tour on U.S. Latino films, Coco Fusco states:

> Perhaps even more disturbing was the way so many members of the audience rejected any identification with the dark-skinned Mexican American students [in the film *Stand and Deliver*] and seemed uncomfortable with using the term "Latino" as all-inclusive. Most of the audiences I spoke to were white and middle class. If nothing else, my lecture tour compelled me to understand the relativity of notions of Latino cultural identity, and the uneven development of racial debates in different parts of Latin America and the U.S.[15]

The issue of the national and cultural identities of these second and subsequent generations in the United States thus remains to be explored. In so doing it is important to take into account the complex and sometimes contradictory social and cultural positions in which they

are caught, in relation both to their own antecedents and to mainstream society. While on the one hand their parents continually tell
them stories and traditions of their homeland, emphasizing that their
roots are in particular countries in Latin America, mainstream institutions, on the other hand, simultaneously reinforce, often but not exclusively through the schools and the media, the negatively conceived
message that they are "Hispanics in the U.S.A."—without providing
them with historical explanations of their roots and communities here.
Future research on the national and cultural identity of the U.S.-born
descendants of Latin American immigrants thus requires consideration of the impact of two "myths," for lack of a better term, which
along with the socioeconomic factors in their communities are today
also structuring the identities and experiences of second and subsequent generations of Latinos.

The first is the myth spun by memory—the memories of the first
generation of immigrants about their lives in their homelands. Women
have long taken on a fundamental role not only in the fight for daily
survival but also in maintaining the historical memory of the silenced
in the Americas. For, as in the United States, the official history of Latin
American countries has also been written largely as a history of exclusion of various groups based on race, class, and status. Moreover, given
the lack of literacy, the oral tradition in those countries is an important
and, for many, the only history library they'll ever get.

Latin American women—mothers like María, for example, or *las
abuelitas* (grandmothers), aunts, and sisters—now living in the United
States are fighting to make sure that their children survive the poverty,
racism, and violence of ghetto life in this society. At the same time, they
are also resorting to their national and cultural traditions, the myths,
dreams, and hopes similar to those reinforced during the Chicano and
Puerto Rican movements of the sixties discussed in chapter 3. Keeping
the cultural traditions of their homelands alive, they are retelling to
their children their experiences, stories, and histories in the United
States. In the process, many are also altering traditional perceptions of
Latina women as passive victims of their experience.[16] As they forge
the future of both their male and female children in this country, these
women also provide them with the cultural and historical resources
and the sense of self that the schools and the national community as a
whole have denied them. Although these memories are in turn translated and filtered by the following generations through their own experiences here, they nevertheless continue to be an important source of

self-affirmation and identity for Latinas and Latinos growing up in this country.

The second myth stems from the fact that regardless of the meaning and value attributed to the label, the concept of Hispanic—or its "Latino" alternative—is today firmly entrenched in the everyday language used by many people in this country. Spun by the mainstream institutions' insistence on imposing a homogenizing label and identity, it is a myth that someday may indeed generate a "generic Hispanic," to borrow Cafferty and McCready's phrase.

The complexity of these two myths—the myth of memory and the myth of homogeneity—has been stated in different terms by Michael Fischer, who has noted that "ethnicity is something reinvented and reinterpreted in each generation by each individual and that it is often something quite puzzling to the individual, something over which he or she lacks control.[17] Yet it is important to qualify this statement. "Ethnicity" may indeed be "quite puzzling," particularly for this generation, because, as Joan Vincent suggests (see chapter 4), the adoption of ethnic identity is an option limited to those who, particularly in racial terms, are in a position to opt for alternative forms of self-identification in the U.S. context. Given the conflation of race and nationality in this country, the majority of the Latino populations are assigned a minority status and put under the stigmatizing label Hispanic, imposed from above, regardless of their own self-identification, their phenotype, or their English language skills. Moreover, racial and racialized groups as a whole live their status in the public sphere of this society in terms of an invisibility reinforced through lack of knowledge of their respective histories. Added to this, in the case of the Latinos, are new "invented traditions" based on a homogenized past in this country. Thus, it is not surprising that for many second-generation minorities, the relationship between their adherence to the post-1960s ideology about ethnicity and their rights as native-born U.S. citizens could indeed be quite puzzling, for today that ideology assumes that the ideals of "justice and equality for all" are embedded in the "equality of difference" of all ethnic groups.

In an otherwise insightful and important book, Werner Sollors noted that "the categorical separation of race and ethnicity too easily lends itself to false generalizations about America." Theoretically, this statement may indeed pertain to the histories and lives of those for whom that separation is an option. But for others, their histories in this country and their daily reality of racial and racialized differences make it more difficult to "keep looking at race as one aspect of ethnicity," particularly given that these differences have now been reinforced in the society's daily and political life in the form of entrenched and stigmatizing ethnic labels.[18]

The effects of the historical conflation of race and nationality through ethnic labels today can be seen clearly within the Latino community itself. It is true that in some ways, U.S.-born Chicanos and Puerto Ricans do stand out as "different" from the more recent immigrant groups from Latin America and their children. Puerto Ricans like Juan, for example, have to contend with their continued colonial ties between Puerto Rico and the United States, which differentiate their legacy from that of other people of Latin American descent. Similarly, the experiences of the descendants of earlier Mexican populations have also been shaped by a past and present in this country that is different from that of other Latin Americans, given the history of complex border relations between the United States and Mexico. The ongoing exclusion of these two historical minorities from the historical memory of the American imagined community means that Puerto Ricans and many second and later generations of Mexican Americans/Chicanos continue to be treated as second-class citizens when they are not perceived as newly arrived immigrants. At the same time, however, insofar as Latin American immigrants today become "instant Hispanics" as soon as they cross the border into the United States, their experiences and identities, like those of their children, are also homogenized and are being shaped by the stigmatizing label Hispanic, constructed in relation to the presence—albeit unacknowledged—of Mexican Americans/Chicanos and Puerto Ricans as historical minorities in this nation. In short, then, Latinos have been racialized such that they experience the effects of invisibility in social and political institutions that should instead ensure full rights of citizenship and justice for all people in the United States.

Given the context of ethnic labels endorsed by state policies and practices, or, as Sollors put it, "the complicated ethnic scene today," questions concerning the specificity of the meaning of the terms *race* and *ethnicity* are commonly heard and debated in the society. It seems to me that a critical question we must address in the current context is, Do minorities—whether they have an ambiguous racial status or are explicitly identified on the basis of race—have access to full citizenship rights, equality, and social justice in the same terms as all other citizens and residents who are not identified as racialized minorities in the United States?

Finally, as the Dominican sociologists Ramona Hernandez and Silvio Torres-Saillant have said: "People in the dominant sector of society enjoy the privilege of individuality. But people at the margins tend to be construed as representative specimens. The tendency to view them as representative units of a collective alterity cancels out their claim to individuality."[19] What does it mean to claim our individuality? Doesn't it mean speaking out about our experiences and in the process recognizing, as the women of the Chicano and Puerto Rican movements did during the 1960s, that difference and diversity is the strength of the group? In recent years, I have noted that when young Latinos leave their communities to go to college, for example, and are confronted with other groups, they look for one another and "find each other" in various educational settings. Yet what sometimes seems to happen, particularly in residential campuses away from urban centers with a large Latino presence, is the need to establish who is the "real Latino," the "real Latina." In so doing, each person's individuality and uniqueness is subsumed to a higher group image defined on the basis of their own version of homogeneity. As many students try to fit into this new Latino stereotype in various ways, they seek to explain to themselves and others why, for example, their parents did not teach them Spanish, or why they did not learn it by themselves, without a full understanding of the strength of the socialization forces in the society. At the same time, they minimize the fact that they do not know the history of their own group or that of other Latinos' groups—forgetting or not knowing that they are all the result of a school system that silenced that knowledge of their specific and heterogeneous histories for them and for others.

In other words, in the interest of ensuring unity, they sometimes forget that because of the ways that race, class, gender, language, sexuality, and ethnicity are articulated, their experience shapes, defines, and affirms themselves to themselves and others in unique ways. Instead of recognizing diversity, they opt to emphasize a nebulous definition of the Latino group's identity—creating, for example, the "ideal Latina" or "Latino," the stereotyped version of a homogenized Latino or Latina self. As some of my students have described her to me, for example, the Latina mythical self is not too tall, not too short. She wears red lipstick and red nail polish. She has straight hair, is not too dark, but neither is she too light. She's very poor, not too educated, *pero habla inglés*. And *español*. She's subservient to men and certainly not gay. She's a good salsa dancer, shapely, flirtatious, but always Latina virgin—*siempre, si Dios quiere* (God willing), of course. And then, the struggle to compete about who is the ideal Latina sets in. Those who don't fit the mold, those who are not reflected in this created Latina mirror—because they are too dark or too light, or they are lesbians, or they don't like to dance, or they don't speak Spanish—become marginalized. Thus, the new generations end up doing to themselves what the society has done to all Latinos: they homogenize, they stereotype, they categorize—and ultimately they divide themselves. They fracture the community. They break the self, not the mirror. And then—contrary to the last line of the "Ending Poem" by Rosario Morales and Aurora Levins Morales—they are not "whole."[20]

The number of diverse experiences that shape the personal identities and experiences among the new generations of Latinos is matched only by the social forces that shape their lives and communities. But the issues that young men and women confront are not just related to their own personal diversity. In order to affirm their identities, their experiences in this country, they must affirm that they are citizens with "the right to have rights" in their daily lives. They must fight against the experience of invisibility to ensure social justice for themselves, for all Latinos, and ultimately for all U.S. citizens and residents. Part of that struggle as students is to learn the history of their nation, but it is also to insist that that history recognize and acknowledge the respective experiences of Mexican Americans/Chicanos, Puerto Ricans, and the other groups of Latin American descent, as a crucial part of this nation's formation. Equally important is the acknowledgment of each national group's experience as part of a long history of survival, of cultural resistance, of cultural affirmation, rather than as a deviation of a stereotype or a confirmation of the stigmas attached to the label Hispanic.

In other words, the invisibility of Latinos must also be addressed by the educational institutions in the country. It is true that at least at the present time, the new generation of Latinos identify themselves in terms of their parents' national identities and ties to Latin American countries. Yet, in order to fully understand their identity formation and concerns, it is important to recognize that they have grown up in this country as Latinos or "Hispanics." Thus, their schooling, socialization experiences, and sense of belonging to the United States (in short, their national identity and citizenship allegiances) have tied their immediate personal concerns and intellectual interests to the social, economic, political, and cultural conditions of the communities in which they have been brought up in this country. As U.S. citizens and residents, the new generations have a right to learn the history of their communities and to demand that it be taught, not just for their own sake, but for everyone who lives in the United States. While some, like Ernest Boyer, cited in chapter 2, may view educational institutions primarily as "a battle ground" that reflect the social tensions of the society, I see them primarily as a significant site, although by no means the only one, in which students can be encouraged to be curious about contradictions, to learn to examine the complexity of their society and the nation's social life. In short, through open access to all forms of knowledge about the various groups in society, students will be better able to formulate their questions about the meaning of the ideals of equality and justice for all.

Yet the postsixties rise in ethnic and racial group consciousness in U.S. society has not been matched by any significant accompanying curriculum changes in high school or college textbooks. Moreover, as evidenced by recruitment efforts, actual student enrollments, and hiring practices relative to the changing demographics in the United States, many universities are still not fully cognizant of the implications of the changing composition of the U.S.-born populations. Yet the fact that Latinos will become the largest minority group in the country by the turn of the century—and thus for the first time in U.S. history, the largest minority group will not be African Americans—does have serious consequences for the future of this country and for all educators, regardless of their fields of specialization.

Clearly, increased numbers do not necessarily signify increased political power. Nevertheless a number of issues are raised by perpetuating the black-white framework traditionally used to understand the tensions in society. For example, although the media portrayal of the Los Angeles riots focused on the history of black-white tensions, a significant number of the protestors arrested were Latinos. Similarly, the tensions in New York City's Washington Heights neighborhood in July 1992, or those in Washington, D.C., and Miami in the 1980s, are evidence of the growing frustration concerning the persistent invisibility and socioeconomic conditions in Latino communities. Regardless of one's ethnicity or field of specialization, knowledge and further research of these conditions as well as of Latinos' cultural specificity is as essential in dealing with societal problems such as AIDS or teenage pregnancy, for example, as it is in understanding the importance of Latinos today to political developments in the Southwest and California or to those that led to the elections of Mayor Washington in Chicago and Mayor Dinkins in New York. In other words, Latinos are increasingly present and involved in shaping regional political outcomes throughout the country.

This trend is not likely to be reversed. In spite of the different national origins encompassed by the federally created term Hispanic, the fact is that according to the 1980 census, 59 percent of the 23.5 million Latinos were mainland-born. An additional 8 percent were U.S. citizens born in Puerto Rico. The actual figures are much higher given that these percentages are from the 1980 census and do not include naturalized citizens. Still, even then, the fact remains that the majority of Latinos today are U.S. citizens. Together with the ultimate aim of the controversial North American Free Trade Agreement—the development of a common market throughout the hemisphere—this means that the visibility and presence of Latinos in U.S. society and politics will certainly increase.

Thus, the implications of these trends for liberal arts education *both include and go beyond* the issue of whether or not students themselves recognize their particular racial or ethnic community's experience in the curriculum of their educational institutions. They also direct our attention to the pressing need to ensure that the experiences of Latinos, like those of all other minority groups, are incorporated as part of *all* students' understandings of the society into which they will enter at the end of their education. In making this commitment, educators and indeed the national community as a whole will be in a better position to understand and evaluate the consequences of the demographic phenomena I referred to earlier. What is at issue then is the means of enriching the curriculum and the broader society in ways that will enable everyone to deal more appropriately with the overall socioethnic and political changes currently underway. It seems to me that these changes affect all citizens of this country and in many ways reflect and refract the experience of the people of the Americas as a whole.

Notes

Introduction. Hispanics in the United States: "We All Sing a Different Song"

1. This narrative is based on oral interviews conducted in February and March 1990 with Julián, one of fourteen immigrants who left Peru in February 1985. His name, like that of all the people interviewed (see chapter 5), has been changed to protect his privacy.

2. Eric Hobsbawm, *The Age of Empire, 1875-1914*, 53.

3. While my preference is for the terms Chicano and Chicana, in this study I use both the terms Mexican American and Chicano to refer to this population, mindful that different sectors prefer to self-identify in different ways. Hence, my usage of both terms signals recognition that both terms are used within the group in the current period. As Beatríz Pesquera and Adela de la Torre state in "A Note on Ethnic Labels," introducing their anthology on Chicana studies, "Among the numerous ethnic labels used to describe persons of Mexican origin in the United States, none is unanimously regarded—by scholars or the population at large—as the 'most appropriate' or the 'most correct' one." See Adela de la Torre and Beatríz Pesquera, eds., *Building with Our Hands: New Directions in Chicana Studies*, xiii.

In chapter 3, I address some of the roots of the preference for each term in my discussion of the emergence of the movements within this national-origin group, who adopted and defined the meaning of the term Chicano in the specific political context of the civil rights struggles of the 1960s. See also C. H. Arce and A. Hurtado, "Mexicans, Chicanos, Mexican Americans, or Pochos . . . Que Somos? The Impact of Language and Nativity on Ethnic Labeling," 103-30.

4. David Reimers, "An Unintended Reform: The 1965 Immigration Act and Third World Immigration to the United States," 9-25; Rubén G. Rumbaut, "The Americans: Latin American and Caribbean Peoples in the United States," in *Americas: New Interpretive Essays*, ed. Alfred Stepan, 275-307; Miguel Tinker Salas, "El Immigrante Latino: Latin American Immigration and Pan-Ethnicity," 58-71; and Alejandro Portes, "From South of the Border: Hispanic Minorities in the United States," in *Immigration Reconsidered: History, Sociology, and Politics*, ed. Virginia Yans-McLaughlin, 160-86. "People of Latin American descent" refers to populations with past and or present ties to Puerto Rico, Mexico, the former Spanish colonies in Central and South America, and the Spanish-speaking Caribbean nations of Cuba and the Dominican Republic.

5. Although heard sporadically before, the term Latino was created "from below" during the 1980s and is generally used by progressive, grassroots sectors of the population. It emerged primarily in urban areas such as Los Angeles, New York City, and Chicago, where there are now significant numbers of people from various Latin American nations. As in the case of the term Hispanic, however, there are those who object to "Latino." For an example of the complex and different uses and connotations of these two terms, see Edward Murguia, "On Latino/Hispanic Ethnic Identity," 8-18.

6. Carl J. Mora, "Americans of Hispanic Origin," letter to the editor, *New York Times*, February 25, 1985.

7. Joshua Fishman, " 'English Only': Its Ghosts, Myths and Dangers," 125-40; and Calvin Veltman, *Language Shift in the United States*. In a recent survey on language skills, Rodolfo O. de la Garza, Louis deSipio, F. Chris García, John García, and Angelo Falcón found that "no more than 10 percent of [the] U.S. citizen respondents from any of the national-origin groups [surveyed] were monolingual in either Spanish or English. . . . The majority of U.S. citizen respondents were either bilingual or English-dominant." See Rodolfo O. de la Garza et al., *Latino Voices: Mexican, Puerto Rican, and Cuban Perspectives on American Politics*, 64.

8. Gloria Anzaldúa, "En Rapport, In Opposition: Cobrando cuentas a las nuestras," in *Making Face, Making Soul: Haciendo Caras: Creative and Critical Perspectives by Women of Color*, 142, 145.

9. Similarly, as I argue in chapter 3, the indifference to diversity within the various Puerto Rican and Chicano/Mexican-American movements of the sixties—regardless of whether the emphasis on the group's homogeneity was a politically necessary strategy at that particular historical moment—ultimately led to the varied groups' fragmentaton.

10. Félix Padilla, *Latino Ethnic Consciousness: The Case of Mexican Americans and Puerto Ricans in Chicago*; and Juan Flores and George Yudice, "Living Borders/Buscando América: Languages of Latino Self-Formation," 57-84.

Chapter 1. "Hispanics? That's What *They* Call Us"

1. U.S. Bureau of the Census, Population Division, *Development of the Race and Ethnic Items for the 1990 Census*, 51.

2. J. Jorge Klor de Alva, "Telling Hispanics Apart: Latino Sociocultural Diversity," in *The Hispanic Experience in the United States: Contemporary Issues and Perspectives*, ed. Edna Acosta-Belén and Barbara R. Sjostrom, 107-36.

3. Martha Giménez, " 'Latino/Hispanic'—Who Needs a Name? The Case against a Standardized Terminology," 41.

4. C. Nelson and Marta Tienda, "The Structuring of Hispanic Identity," 49-74.

5. Ira S. Lowry, "The Science and Politics of Ethnic Enumeration," in *Ethnicity and Public Policy*, ed. W. Van Horne, 42-61; J. Harvey M. Choldin, "Statistics and Politics: The 'Hispanic' Issue in the 1980 Census," 403-18; and Marta Tienda and V. Ortiz, " 'Hispanicity' and the 1980 Census," 3-20.

According to Sullivan, the identifiers historically used for the Hispanic population by the Bureau of the Census have included the following: country of birth: Mexico, Cuba, Central or South America, other (1880-1980), Puerto Rican (1950-80); country of birth of parents (1880-1970); Mexican "race" (1930); Spanish surname (five southwestern states, 1950-80); Spanish mother tongue (1940-70); language other than English (1980); self-identification of Spanish origin: Mexican, Puerto Rican, Cuban, Central or South American, other (1970) (the terms Mexican, Mexican-American, and Chicano were all coded as "Mexican"); and Puerto Rican, Cuban, other Spanish/Hispanic (1980). See Teresa A. Sullivan, "A Demographic Portrait," in *Hispanics in the U.S.A.*, ed. Pastora San Juan Cafferty and William C. McCready, 12.

6. G. Anzaldúa, ed., *Making Faces*, 1990; Cherríe Moraga, *Loving in the War Years: Lo que nunca pasó por sus labios*; Gloria Anzaldúa and Cherríe Moraga, eds., *This Bridge Called My Back: Writings by Radical Women of Color*; and Maxine Baca Zinn, "Gender and Ethnic Identity among Chicanos," 18-24.

7. Joan Moore and Harry Pachon, *Hispanics in the United States*, 3.

8. Pastora San Juan Cafferty and William C. McCready, eds., *Hispanics in the United States: A New Social Agenda*, 253.

9. David E. Hayes-Bautista and Jorge Chapa, "Latino Terminology: Conceptual Basis for Standardized Terminology," 66.

10. Fernando M. Treviño, "Standardized Terminology for Standardized Populations," 69.

11. Ibid., 71.

12. Giménez, " 'Latino/Hispanic,' " 559.

13. Ibid., 559-60.

14. Félix Padilla, *Latino Ethnic Consciousness*, 13.

15. Padilla, *Latino Ethnic Consciousness*; and B. E. Aguirre and Rogelio Saenz, "A Futuristic Assessment of Latino Ethnic Identity," 19-32. On the issue of panethnicity, see *Latino Studies Journal* 2, and Martha E. Giménez, Fred A. López III, and Carlos Muñoz, eds., "The Politics of Ethnic Construction: Hispanic, Chicano, Latino . . . ?" Special Issue of *Latin American Perspectives* 19, no. 4 (Fall 1992).

16. Werner Sollors, *Beyond Ethnicity: Consent and Descent in American Culture*, 36; and Michael Omi and Howard Winant, *Racial Formation in the United States: From the 1960s to the 1980s*, x and 57. For an excellent recent critique of the race and ethnicity debates, see E. San Juan Jr., *Racial Formations/Critical Transformations: Articulations of Power in Ethnic and Racial Studies in the United States*.

17. Milton Gordon, *Assimilation in American Life*; Nathan Glazer and Daniel Moynihan, *Beyond the Melting Pot: The Negroes, Puerto Ricans, Jews, Italians and Irish in New York City*; Thomas Kessner, *The Golden Door: Italians and Jewish Immigrant Mobility in New York City, 1880-1915*; Leonard Dinnerstein and David M. Reimers, *Ethnic Americans: A History of Immigration*; David Muga, "Academic Sub-Cultural Theory and the Problematic of Ethnicity: A Tentative Critique," 1-51; Shih-Shan Henry Tsai, *The Chinese Experience in America*; William Peterson, Michael Novak, and Phillip Gleason, *Concepts of Ethnicity*; and Stephan Thernstrom, Ann Orlov, and Oscar Handlin, eds., *Harvard Encyclopedia of American Ethnic Groups*.

18. Daniel Moynihan, *Counting Our Blessings: Reflections on the Future of America*.

19. See, for example, Edna Acosta-Belén and Barbara R. Sjostrom, eds., *The Hispanic Experience in the United States*; Gastón Fernández, Beverly Nagel, and León Narváez, eds., *Hispanic Migration and the United States: A Study in Politics*; and Martha Giménez, "U.S. Ethnic Politics: Implications for Latin Americans." Available bibliography varies according to each group. For overviews of Chicanos, for example, see Ricardo Romo, *East Los Angeles: History of a Barrio*; Carey McWilliams, *North from Mexico: The Spanish Speaking People of the United States*; Albert Camarillo, *Chicanos in a Changing Society*; Rodolfo Acuña, *Occupied America: A History of Chicanos*; and the works cited in chapters 2 and 3. On Puerto Ricans, see Alfredo López, *Doña Licha's Island: Modern Colonialism in Puerto Rico*; Clara E. Rodríguez, *Puerto Ricans: Born in the U.S.A.*; History Task Force, *Labor Migration under Capitalism: The Puerto Rican Experience*; Adalberto López, ed., *The Puerto Ricans: Their History, Culture and Society*; Manuel Maldonado-Denis, *The Emigration Dialectic: Puerto Rico and the U.S.A.*; and the works cited in chapters 2 and 3. For overviews of the Cuban migration, see Alejandro Portes and Roberto Bach, *Latin Journey: Cuban and Mexican Immigrants in the United States*; Silvia Pedraza-Bailey, *Political and Economic Migrants in America: Cubans and Mexicans*; Eleanor Meyer Rogg, *The Assimilation of Cuban Exiles: The Role of Community and Class*; and Silvia Pedraza-Bailey, "Cuba's Exiles: Portrait of a Refugee Migration." On Dominican immigration, see Patricia Pessar and S. Grasmuck, *Between Two Islands: Dominican International Migration*; and S. Torres-Saillant, "Dominicans as a New York Community: A Social Appraisal," 7-25. On Central and South Americans, see A. Orlov and Reed Ueda, "Central and South Americans," in *Harvard Encyclopedia*, ed. Thernstrom, Orlov, and Handlin, 210-17; M. L. Leitch and L. Leslie, "A Demographic Profile of Recent Central American Immigrants: Clinical and Service Im-

plications," 315-29; S. Wallace, "Central American and Mexican Immigrant Characteristics and Economic Incorporation in California," 657-70; Allan F. Burns, *Maya in Exile: Guatemalans in Florida*; Teófilo Altamirano, *Los que se fueron: Peruanos en Estados Unidos*; A. Marshall, "Emigration of Argentines to the United States," in *When Borders Don't Divide: Labor Migration and Refugee Movements in the Americas*, ed. Patricia Pessar, 129-41; and Elsa Chaney, "Colombians in New York City: Theoretical and Policy Issues," in *Sourcebook on the New Immigration: Implications for the U.S. and the International Community*, ed. Roy Simon Bryce-Laporte, 285-94.

20. Mario Barrera, *Race and Class in the Southwest: A Theory of Racial Inequality*, 17.

21. Howard Zinn, *A People's History of the United States*, 292.

22. Adalberto López, *Puerto Ricans*, 314.

23. Annette Fuentes and Barbara Ehrenreich, *Women in the Global Factory*, 12; Saskia Sassen, *The Mobility of Labor and Capital: A Study in International Investment and Labor Flow*; and Julie Nash and María Patricia Fernández-Kelly, eds., *Women, Men, and the International Division of Labor*.

24. Eduardo Galeano, *Open Veins of Latin America: Five Centuries of the Pillage of a Continent*; Walter LaFeber, *Inevitable Revolutions: The United States in Central America*; George Black, *Good Neighbor: How the United States Wrote the History of Central America and the Caribbean*; and Victor Valenzuela, *Anti-United States Sentiment in Latin American Literature*.

25. Pedraza-Bailey, "Cuba's Exiles," and "Cuban Political Immigrants and Mexican Economic Immigrants: The Role of Government Policy in Their Assimilation," in *Hispanic Migration and the United States*, ed. Fernandez, Nagel, and Narvaez, 68-101; and Portes and Bach, *Latin Journey*.

26. Juan Flores, " 'Que Assimilated, Brother, yo soy assimilao': The Structuring of Puerto Rican Identity in the U.S.," 4.

27. J. Attinassi, Juan Flores, and Pedro Pedraza, "La Carreta Made a U-Turn: Puerto Rican Language and Culture in the United States," 193-218; Flores and Yudice, "Living Borders"; and Hayes-Bautista and Chapa, "Latino Terminology."

28. Oxford Analytica, *America in Perspective*, Similarly, people from other lands currently in the United States have never had to confront the imposition of a language on their territory, as was the case for the Puerto Ricans and the nineteenth-century Mexicans. See Guadalupe San Miguel Jr., "Conflict and Controversy in the Evolution of Bilingual Education in the United States—An Interpretation," in *The Mexican-American Experience*, ed. Rodolfo O. de la Garza et al., 267-79; and López, ed., *Puerto Ricans*.

29. Gloria Anzaldúa, *Borderlands/La Frontera*, 77-91; Guillermo Gómez-Peña, "Documented/Undocumented," in *The Graywolf Annual Five: Multi-Cultural Literacy*, ed. Rick Simonson and Scott Walker, 127-34; and Flores and Yudice, "Living Borders."

30. Flores, " 'Que Assimilated, Brother, yo soy assimilao,' " 4.

31. See chapter 4.

32. R. E. Butler, *On Creating a Hispanic America: A Nation within a Nation?*

33. U.S. Congressional Record, *Bilingual Education*, 98th Cong., 2nd sess., April 3, 1984, (Washington, D.C.: GPO), 130 (42).

34. Fishman, " 'English Only.' "

35. P. Baptista-Fernandez and B. S. Greenberg, "Hispanic-Americans: The New Minority on Television," in *Life on Television: Content Analyses of U.S. Television Drama*, ed. B. S. Greenberg, 4.

36. "Advertisers Learn to Speak Spanish—the Hard Way," *Television/Radio Age*, special issue (July 1988); Strategy Research Corporation, "Spanish Language Advertising," *M.M.A.*, January 1989, 2-3; and I. Herrera, "U.S. Advertisers Talking Hispanics' Language," *Washington Post*, Aug. 28, 1985, 16.

37. Yankelovich, Skelly & White, *Spanish America: A Study of the Hispanic Market*, 10.

38. Eric Hobsbawm, "Mass-Producing Traditions: Europe, 1879-1914," in *The Invention of Tradition*, ed. Eric Hobsbawm and Terence Ranger, 263-308.

39. Carlos E. Cortés, " 'Greaser's Revenge' to 'Boulevard Nights,' " in *Chicano Studies in the 1980s*, ed. National Association for Chicano Studies, 130. On issues of representation in film, see also Coco Fusco, "The Latino 'Boom' in Hollywood," 48-56; and Chon Noriega, ed., *Chicanos and Film: Representation and Resistance*.

40. Governor's Advisory Committee for Hispanic Affairs, *New York State Hispanics: A Challenging Minority*, v.

41. Ibid.; see also J. Johnson, "Hispanic Dropout Rate Is Put at 35%," *New York Times*, Sept. 15, 1989, 12; C. Potler, *State of the Prisons: Conditions inside the Walls*; C. Russell, "Blacks and Hispanics Suffer High AIDS Rate," *Washington Post*, Oct. 24, 1986, 17; and "Hispanic Poverty Rate Nears That of Blacks," *New York Times*, Sept. 1986, 14.

42. N. Pierce and J. Hagstrom, "The Hispanic Community: A Growing Force to Be Reckoned With," in *Latinos and the Political System*, ed. F. Chris García, 11-27.

43. Giménez, " 'Latino/Hispanic'—Who Needs a Name?" 559.

44. B. E. Aguirre and Rogelio Saenz, "A Futuristic Assessment of Latino Ethnic Identity," 19-32

Chapter 2. "So Far from God, So Close to the United States": The Roots of Hispanic Homogenization

1. Discussing the confusion raised by the definition of *Hispanic*, Carl Mora remarks: "What do our statisticians and government officials do? They refer to all these people as being 'of Spanish origin' (except the Brazilians) when it is obvious that a great many Spanish-speaking Latin Americans have no ancestral connection at all to Spain (but some Portuguese-speaking Brazilians do).... The term 'non-Hispanic white' is ... used to denote one of European origin; but where then, did the 'Hispanic whites' originate if not also in Europe?" Carl J. Mora, "Americans of Hispanic Origin."

2. Simón Bolívar, *Para nosotros la patria es América*; José Martí, *Páginas escogidas*, ed. Roberto Fernández Retamar; J. Giordano and D. Torres, eds., *La identidad cultural de Hispanoamerica: Discusión actual*; Angel Rama, *Transculturación narrativa en América Latina*; Gabriel García Márquez, *El general en su laberinto*; Julio Cortázar, *Rayuela*; and Leopoldo Zea, ed., *América Latina en sus ideas*.

3. See chapter 4.

4. See Robert Berkhofer's discussion of the exclusion of Native Americans in *The White Man's Indian: Images of the American Indian from Columbus to the Present* for an analogous argument, and for overviews of the histories of racial minorities in the United States, see, for example, Ronald Takaki, *A Different Mirror: A History of Multicultural America*; Takaki, *Iron Cages: Race and Culture in Nineteenth Century America*; and B. Ringer, *"We the People" and Others: Duality and America's Treatment of Its Racial Minorities*.

5. For accounts of the Spanish colonial heritage in Latin America, see, for example, S. J. Stein and B. H. Stein, *The Colonial Heritage of Latin America: Essays on Economic Dependence in Perspective*; Mark Burkholder and Lyman Johnson, *Colonial Latin America*; and Richard Morse, "The Heritage of Latin America," in *The Founding of New Societies*, ed. L. Hartz, 123-77.

6. Morner, *Race Mixture in the History of Latin America*; and Carlos Fuentes, *Latin America at War with the Past*.

7. Fuentes, *Latin America at War with the Past*, 27.

8. Ibid., 28.

9. New Mexico is perhaps the clearest example of the coexistence of differentiated land and social structural arrangements present elsewhere in colonial Spanish America.

By the early nineteenth century, the bulk of what was to become the Mexican population was concentrated in the northernmost region of the Spanish Empire, known today as northern New Mexico. As in other parts of Mexico and the Andean region of South America, "communal villages" were organized in northern New Mexico on the basis of collective land grants given to communities as a whole. But, as Richard Morse notes, while small private farmers were few and far between in most of Spanish America, in northern Mexico they did coexist with the hacienda and *ejidos* (or communal land ownership). In this case, most of the acquired land was equally divided for private farming, but a part of the land grant remained commonly owned, and grazing and water were shared communally (Mario Barrera, *Race and Class in the Southwest*).

Unlike the case in northern New Mexico, the sheepherding industry of the rest of the area (today known as the "ovine nursery of the nation") was organized on the basis of "a traditional social structure and a well-defined division of labor." Two or three *pastores* or sheepherders were under the command of a mounted rider (*vaquero*), who in turn was supervised by a range boss (*caporal*). The superintendent or *major-domo* was over the *caporal*. At the top of the pyramid was the owner or patron, a member of the small but wealthy "Hispano" elite that, in New Mexico, became known as the *ricos* (see Carey McWilliams, "Heritage of the Southwest," in *Chicano: The Evolution of a People*, ed. Renato Rosaldo, Robert Calvert, and Gustav Seligman, 5). These regional patterns of land ownership and of social and racial organization and status, exemplified by the variations found in New Mexico, extended from the southern reaches of the Spanish empire to sparsely populated California. See Stanley J. Stein and Barbara H. Stein, *The Colonial Heritage of Latin America*.

10. Morner, *Race Mixture*, 6.

11. Verena Stolke, "Conquered Women," 23-28; and Ramón Gutiérrez, *When Jesus Came, the Corn Mothers Went Away: Marriage, Sexuality, and Power in New Mexico, 1500-1846*.

12. Morse, "The Heritage of Latin America."

13. This, too, enhanced the social status of both the "white" Latin American–born Spaniards (criollos) and the mestizos born in wedlock to either "pure" Spaniards or criollo families, while the consequent disdain for the large numbers of illegitimate mestizos and mulattoes in colonial society simultaneously became increasingly entrenched in the laws and customs of Spain's New World colonies. See Morner, *Race Mixture*.

14. Alejandro Lipschütz, *El indoamericanismo y el problema racial en las Américas* (Santiago, 1944), 75.

15. Gutiérrez, *When Jesus Came, the Corn Mothers Went Away*, 198-99.

16. Morner, *Race Mixture*, 36-40.

17. See Gutiérrez, *When Jesus Came, the Corn Mothers Went Away*, chaps. 5 and 6. Griswold del Castillo notes that "Spanish laws . . . frequently described the relationship between husband and wife in monarchical terms: 'the husband is, as it were, the Lord and Head of his wife.' " Richard Griswold del Castillo, *La Familia: Chicano Families in the Urban Southwest, 1848 to the Present*, 28.

18. See Morse, "Heritage of Latin America"; and Roberto R. Da Matta, "Do You Know Who You're Talking To?" in *Carnivals, Rogues and Heroes: An Anthropology of the Brazilian Dilemma*, 429-42.

19. F. González del Cossío, quoted in Morner, *Race Mixture*, 109; see also Richard Graham, ed., *The Idea of Race in Latin America, 1870-1940*.

20. "Entre el zar de Rusia y un mujik creo que habría menos distancia que entre un comunero de Andahuaylas (mi pueblo natal) y cualquiera de los presidentes del Perú." Quoted in William Rowe, ed., *José María Arguedas: Los ríos profundos*, xvii; my translation.

21. Juan A. Oddone, "Regionalismo y Nacionalismo," in *América Latina en sus ideas*, ed. Leopoldo Zea, 236.

22. Peter Wade, "Race and Class: The Case of South American Blacks," 233. Indeed the very existence of the notion of "continuum," with its attending hierarchical status at each point along the way, points to the entrenched racial prejudices inherited from colonial Spanish society. This continuum "allows mulattoes to dissociate themselves from blacks and be accepted as socially distinct and . . . permits some of them to 'marry up' racially." Ibid.

23. Richard Griswold del Castillo. *The Treaty of Guadalupe Hidalgo: A Legacy of Conflict.* For general overviews of the consequences of the Mexican-American War for the Spanish-speaking populations of the Southwest and California, see, for example, Carey McWilliams, *North from Mexico*; Barrera, *Race and Class in the Southwest*; and Acuña, *Occupied America*. On the complexity and diversity of the effects of the Mexican-American War upon different Mexican populations in specific regions, see, for example, Sarah Deutsch, *No Separate Refuge: Culture, Class, and Gender on an Anglo Hispanic Frontier in the American Southwest, 1880-1940*; David Montejano, *Anglos and Mexicans in the Making of Texas, 1836-1986*; Mario T. Garcia, *Desert Immigrants: The Mexicans of El Paso*; Leonard Pitt, *The Decline of the Californios: A Social History of the Spanish-Speaking Californians, 1846-1890*; and Arnoldo de León, *They Called Them Greasers: Anglo Attitudes toward Mexicans in Texas, 1821-1900.*

24. Takaki, *Iron Cages*, 161.

25. Barrera, *Race and Class in the Southwest*, 26. See also Pitt, *Decline of the Californios.*

26. Griswold del Castillo, *Treaty of Guadalupe Hidalgo*; Manuel G. Gonzáles, *The Hispanic Elite of the Southwest*; Acuña, *Occupied America*; and Barrera, *Race and Class in the Southwest.*

27. The *pobres'* forms of resistance to the disruptive encroaching penetration of Anglo-Americans into their communities and communally owned lands took a different form, graphically described by Rosenbaum: "On the morning of April 27, 1889, the owners of a ranch near San Geronimo, twelve miles west of Las Vegas, awoke to find their four miles of new barbed wire fence cut. Cut is a mild word. It was destroyed, the fence posts chopped to kindling and the wire strewn in glittering fragments. The partners—two English adventurers trying their luck at Wild West ranching—were the first victims of a civil war that raged across San Miguel County for the next eighteen months. Wearing white masks or caps—*gorras blancas*—bands of native New Mexicans—*mexicanos*—struck at night, leveling fences, destroying crops, burning buildings, and not infrequently, shooting people. By the summer of 1890, according to one English language newspaper, *Las Gorras Blancas* had brought business in Las Vegas to a standstill." Robert J. Rosenbaum, "Las Gorras Blancas of San Miguel County, 1884-1890," in *Chicano: The Evolution of a People*, ed. Renato Rosaldo, Robert Calvert, and Gustav Seligman, 129. See also Rosenbaum's *Mexicano Resistance in the Southwest: The Sacred Right of Self-Preservation* for a fuller treatment of the Mexicano resistance strategies.

28. Deutsch, *No Separate Refuge*; and Rosenbaum, *Mexicano Resistance*. Many of the efforts to resist the Anglos have been recorded in the Mexican *Corridos*, or ballads, about the period. The classic text on this question is Américo Paredes, *With His Pistol in His Hand: A Border Ballad and Its Hero*. See also José E. Limón, *Mexican Ballads, Chicano Poems: History and Influence in Mexican-American Social Poetry.*

29. Montejano, *Anglos and Mexicans*, 84; and Barrera, *Race and Class.*

30. Montejano, *Anglos and Mexicans*, 84. Not surprisingly, this statement rings true beyond the border region to include the Southwest as a whole. See de León, *They Called Them Greasers*; Acuña, *Occupied America*; and Barrera, *Race and Class.*

31. Acuña, *Occupied America*, 55.

32. McWilliams, *North from Mexico*, chap. 2, as quoted by Acuña, *Occupied America*, 55.

33. Nancie Gonzalez, *The Spanish Americans of New Mexico*, 205, quoted in Acuña, *Occupied America*, 56. Similarly, although the numbers of Puerto Ricans in the United States did not reach 1,600 in the census of 1910, Bernardo Vega notes that the rampant racism and discrimination against "everything foreign" and particularly against Puerto Ricans in New York led many of the elite to prefer to pass as Spaniards or to not speak Spanish and to deny their origins in the early-twentieth-century Latino community in New York. Bernardo Vega, *Memoirs of Bernardo Vega: A Contribution to the History of the Puerto Rican Community in New York*, ed. César Andreu Iglesias, 97.

34. Quoted in Montejano, *Anglos and Mexicans*, 115; my emphasis.

35. Pitt, *Decline of the Californios*, 14.

36. Wade, *Race and Class*, 233.

37. Benedict Anderson, *Imagined Communities: Reflections on the Origin and Spread of Nationalism*, 14-15.

38. Stephan Thernstrom, "Ethnic Groups in American History," in *Ethnic Relations in America*, ed. American Assembly, 3-27.

39. Gordon, *Assimilation in American Life*, 115.

40. Thernstrom, "Ethnic Groups in American History," 3.

41. Joshua Fishman, *Language Loyalty in the United States*, 32.

42. In some ways, the Dred Scott case of 1857 exemplifies this difference. The Supreme Court did not address the issue raised by Scott of whether he, a freed slave, could be sold into slavery again. Instead it focused on the larger question of whether blacks had the legal right to recourse to the U.S. system of justice at all. In the court's decision, the 84-year-old chief justice, Roger Brook Taney, recognized that "the words 'people of the United States' and 'citizens' are synonymous terms and mean the same thing." Yet arguing that the writers of the Constitution did not intend to recognize blacks as "people" of the United States or to recognize them as citizens of this country, the majority ruling concluded that Dred Scott did not have the right to appeal to the U.S. system of justice in the first place. Hence he was denied legal recognition of his freedom from slavery. In denying the humanity of African Americans, the Dred Scott case thus served to confirm that they were in fact not "citizens" and therefore not entitled to other Americans' right to constitutional protection. As I discuss in the following pages, the case of the Mexican Americans who were granted citizenship through the Treaty of Guadalupe Hidalgo following the Mexican-American War is very different. On the Dred Scott case, see Ringer, *"We the People,"* 103-7, 1110-14; National Advisory Commission on Civil Disorders, *The Kerner Report, 1968*, 211; and, for a fuller discussion of the arguments presented in this case, Vincent C. Hopkins, S. J., *Dred Scott's Case*.

43. Robert F. Foerster, *The Racial Problems Involved in Immigration from Latin America and the West Indies to the United States*, A Report Submitted to the Secretary of Labor, 55.

44. Quoted in E. Fiske, "One Language or Two?" *New York Times*, fall survey on education, Nov. 10, 1985, 1. For an overview of bilingual education in the United States, see Gary Keller and K. S. Van Hooft, "Chronology of Bilingualism and Bilingual Education"; Guadalupe San Miguel Jr., *"Let All of Them Take Heed": Mexican-Americans and the Campaign for Educational Equity in Texas, 1910-1981*; R. Padilla, *Bilingual Education and Public Policy in the United States*, vol. 1; and Guadalupe San Miguel Jr., "Conflict and Controversy in the Evolution of Bilingual Education in the United States—An Interpretation," in *The Mexican-American Experience*, ed. R. O. de la Garza et al., 267-79. For debates on the language question in the United States, see, for example, Ana Celia Zentella, "Language Politics in the U.S.A.: The English Only Movement," in *Literature, Language and Politics*, ed. B. J. Craige, 39-51; Fishman, " 'English Only' "; J. Crawford, ed., *Language Loyalties: A*

Source Book on the Official English Controversy; and C. Cazden and C. E. Snow, *English Plus: Issues in Bilingual Education.*

45. Eric Hobsbawm, "Mass-Producing Traditions."

46. Thus, although referring to the 1870-1914 period, Hobsbawm's explanation of the roots of national identity of Americans continued to be confirmed in the hearings of the "House Committee on *Un-American* Activities" of the 1950s; see Marty Jezer, *The Dark Ages: Life in the United States, 1945-1960,* 77-106.

47. Hannah Arendt, "Lawlessness Is Inherent in the Uprooted," *New York Times Magazine,* Apr. 28, 1968, 24; my emphasis. Benedict Anderson's distinction between the nature of nationalism and racism is helpful: "The fact of the matter is that nationalism thinks in terms of historical destinies, while racism dreams of eternal contaminations, transmitted from the origins of time through an endless sequence of loathsome copulations: outside history." Anderson, *Imagined Communities,* 136.

48. Even late-eighteenth-century appeals by white Americans such as Thomas Jefferson that African Americans should be deported from the newly created nation of the United States were often grounded on a perceived racial incompatibility rather than on their birthplace. See Ronald Takaki, "Reflections on Racial Patterns in America: An Historical Perspective," in *Ethnicity and Public Policy,* ed. W. Van Horne, 1-24.

49. National Advisory Commission on Civil Disorders, *Kerner Report,* 215; my emphasis.

50. Quoted in Ringer, *"We the People,"* 220-24. See also Richard Kluger, *Simple Justice: The History of Brown v. Board of Education and Black America's Struggle for Education.* I thank Anani Dzidzienyo for bringing to my attention some of the nuanced implications of the location of the case in Louisiana.

51. As early as 1826, Senator John Randolph, for example, emphasized in a U.S. Senate speech "that his countrymen ought not to associate as equals with the people of Latin America, some of whom had descended from Africans." Quoted in the Mexican newspaper *El Sol,* cited in Brack, 1973, 64. De León makes a similar case in *They Called Them Greasers.*

52. Tomás Almaguer, "Ideological Distortions in Recent Chicano Historiography: The Internal Model and Chicano Historical Interpretations," 7-28.

53. Acuña, *Occupied America,* 38.

54. Ibid.

55. Victor M. Valenzuela, "The Monroe Doctrine," in *Anti–United States Sentiment in Latin American Literature,* 11; see also Reginald Horseman, *Race and Manifest Destiny: The Origins of American Racial Anglo-Saxonism.*

56. According to Jefferson's advice to James Monroe in a letter on the Monroe Doctrine: "[Independence] made us a nation, [the Monroe Doctrine] sets our compass and points the course which we are to steer through the ocean of time opening on us." Quoted in Sculley Bradley et al., eds., *The American Tradition in Literature* 1:330. By February 15, 1905, Roosevelt had clearly shown the unilateral nature of the Monroe Doctrine and his corollary: "The United States determines when and if the principles of the Doctrine are violated and when and if violation is threatened. We alone determine what measures if any shall be taken to vindicate the principles of the Doctrine, and we of necessity determine when the principles have been vindicated. . . . It is our Doctrine to be by us invoked and sustained, held in abeyance or abandoned, as our high international policy or vital national interests shall seem to us, and to us alone to demand." Quoted in Valenzuela, "The Monroe Doctrine," 11-12.

57. "Away, away with all these cobweb tissues of rights of discovery, exploitation, settlement, contiguity, etc. [The American claim] is by the right of our manifest destiny to overspread and to possess the whole of the continent which providence has given us for

the development of the great experiment of liberty and federative self-government entrusted to us." Quoted in Gutiérrez, *When Jesus Came, the Corn Mothers Went Away*, 340. In this sense, the Mexican-American War followed a tradition of expansionism first set in motion by early generations of Americans who had encroached on Native Americans' lands; see, for example, Horseman, *Race and Manifest Destiny*, 103-15.

58. Ronald Takaki, for example, summarizes the nationalist and racist justifications for the Mexican-American War put forth by the editor of the *Southern Quarterly Review* in his discussion of the significance of the "Conquest of California": "The Mexican-American War had clarified the national purpose, [the editor] declared. . . . United States troops had chastised arrogant and 'fraudulent' Mexicans. . . . 'There are some nations that have a doom upon them. . . . The nation that makes no onward progress . . . that wastes its treasures wantonly—that cherishes not its resources—such a nation will burn out . . . will become the easy prey of the more adventurous enemy.' " Takaki, *Iron Cages*, 161.

59. Barrera, *Race and Class*, 13.

60. See Horseman, *Race and Manifest Destiny*, 229-71. Thus, when the question of further expansion into Mexico was again raised for debate in the early 1850s, Senator John Clayton could remind his colleagues that this would involve dealing with the dangers of including Mexico's people as citizens: "Yes! Aztecs, Creoles, Half-breeds, Quadroons, Samboes, and I know not what else—'ring-streaked and speckled'—all will come in, and, instead of our governing them, they by their votes, will govern *us*." Quoted in ibid., 246.

61. Takaki, *Iron Cages*, 162.

62. Pitt, *The Decline of the Californios*, 59; and Acuña, *Occupied America*, 119ff.

63. Quoted in Zinn, *A People's History*, 292. "We want a foreign market for our surplus products," stated McKinley years before his presidency. In 1897 Senator Albert Beveridge declared: "American factories are making more than the American people can use; American soil is producing more than they can consume. Fate has written our policy for us; the trade of the world must and shall be ours." Ibid.

64. Alfredo López, *Doña Licha's Island: Modern Colonialism in Puerto Rico*. As Zinn notes, Cuba's full sovereignty was to be marred, however, by the U.S. Army, which refused to leave Cuba until it reluctantly agreed to incorporate the Platt Amendment into its constitution (1902), effectively bringing Cuba into the American sphere of influence. Zinn, *A People's History*, 305.

65. José Luis González, *Puerto Rico: The Four Storeyed Country*, 1-31; and Adalberto López, ed., *The Puerto Ricans*, 25-28.

66. Frank Bonilla, "Beyond Survival: Por qué seguiremos siendo Puertorriqueños," in Adalberto López, *The Puerto Ricans*, 453-54.

67. U.S. Congressional Record 1900, 56, 1: 2011, as quoted in Ringer, *"We the People,"* 974. For a discussion of the status of Puerto Rico since 1898, see Ringer, *"We the People,"* 945-1097; Alfredo López, *Doña Licha's Island*; Edwin Meléndez and Edgardo Meléndez, *Colonial Dilemma: Critical Perspectives on Contemporary Puerto Rico*; History Task Force, *Labor Migration under Capitalism*; and Gordon K. Lewis, *Notes on the Puerto Rican Revolution: An Essay on American Dominance and Caribbean Resistance*.

68. U.S. Congressional Record 1900, 56, 1: 2172; quoted in Ringer, *"We the People,"* 973.

69. Quoted in Montejano, *Anglos and Mexicans*, 84; my emphasis.

70. History Task Force, Centro de Estudios Puertorriqueños, *Labor Migration under Capitalism: The Puerto Rican Experience*, 127, 124ff.

71. James Cockcroft, *Outlaws in the Promised Land: Mexican Immigrant Workers and America's Future*, chap. 3. Félix Padilla discusses the effects of the bracero program in Chicago in *Latino Ethnic Consciousness*.

72. This comparison was first made by Bernardo Vega in the 1920s. Vega, *Memoirs of Bernardo Vega*, 120.

73. Tzvetan Todorov, *The Conquest of America: The Question of the Other*, 42-43.

74. Senator Thaddeus Stevens, quoted in Octavio I. Romano-V., "The Anthropology and Sociology of the Mexican-Americans," in *Voices: Readings from El Grito*, ed. Romano-V., 37.

75. McWilliams, quoted in ibid.; my emphasis.

76. See Foerster, *Racial Problems Involved in Immigration*.

77. Quoted in George I. Sánchez, "Pachucos in the Making," in *Chicano: The Evolution of a People*, ed. Renato Rosaldo, Robert Calvert, and Gustav Seligman, 208.

78. Stan Steiner, "Chicano Power: Militance among the Mexican-Americans," in *Pain and Promise: The Chicano Today*, ed. Edward Simmen, 130; my emphasis.

79. Michael B. Kane, *Minorities in Textbooks*, 138-42.

80. Bonilla, *Por qué seguiremos siendo*, 454.

81. See de León, *They Called Them Greasers*.

82. For historical descriptions and analyses of the portrayals of people of Latin American descent (regardless of nationality) as exotic lovers or violent *bandidos* in Hollywood Westerns and romantic films, see, for example, Gary Kellner, ed., *Chicano Cinema: Research, Reviews and Resources*; Allen Woll, "Bandits and Lovers: Hispanic Images in American Film," in *The Kaleidoscopic Lens: How Hollywood Views Ethnic Groups*, ed. Randall M. Miller, 54-71; Cortés, " 'Greaser's Revenge' "; and Noriega, *Chicanos and Film*.

83. For a similar statement on Anglo views of Mexicans at the turn of the century in Texas, see de León, *They Called Them Greasers*, 104.

Chapter 3. "Establishing an Identity" in the Sixties: The Mexican American/Chicano and Puerto Rican Movements

1. Elizabeth Martínez. "Histories of 'the Sixties': A Certain Absence of Color," 175-84. In discussing the sixties, I am following Martínez's periodizing of the era as extending beyond 1970. For issues of periodization, see Fredric Jameson, "Periodizing the Sixties," in *The Sixties, without Apology*, ed. Sohnya Sayres et al., 178-209; and Kobena Mercer, " '1968': Periodizing Politics and Identity," in *Cultural Studies*, ed. Lawrence Grossberg et al., 424-49. Edward Escobar's recent article exemplifies the importance of incorporating the interconnections among the various minority movements in future studies of the sixties and provides a possible framework for approaching the period: Edward Escobar, "The Dialectics of Repression: The Los Angeles Police Department and the Chicano Movement, 1968-1971," 1483-1504. Other authors have also noted the absence of minority student movements in the period's history. See, for example, Carlos Muñoz, *Youth, Identity, Power: The Chicano Movement*, 1-18.

The phrase in this chapter's title is from Cecilia Blondet, "Establishing an Identity: Women Settlers in a Poor Lima Neighbourhood," in *Women and Social Change in Latin America*, ed. Elizabeth Jelin, 12-78.

2. Hannah Arendt, *The Origins of Totalitarianism* (New York: Harcourt, Brace, Jovanovich, 1979), as quoted in María Celia Paoli, "Citizenship, Inequalities, Democracy and Rights: The Making of a Public Space in Brazil," 145.

3. Paoli, "Citizenship, Inequalities, Democracy and Rights," 145.

4. For a definition and discussion of cultural nationalism with specific reference to Mexican Americans and Puerto Ricans, see J. Jorge Klor de Alva, "Aztlán, Borinquen and

Hispanic Nationalism in the United States," in *Aztlán: Essays on the Chicano Homeland*, ed. Rudolfo A. Anaya and Francisco Lomelí; see also Genaro Padilla, "Myth and Comparative Cultural Nationalism: The Ideological Uses of Aztlán," in *Aztlán*, ed. Anaya and Lomelí, 111-34.

5. The conflict between equality and community among Mexican Americans/Chicanos is discussed by Mario Barrera, *Beyond Aztlán: Ethnic Autonomy in Comparative Perspective*. For a history of the broader political and sociocultural context of the 1945-60 period, see Jezer, *The Dark Ages*.

6. Escobar, "Dialectics of Repression," 1490. For overviews of Mexican Americans in the 1950s, see, for example, Mario García, *The Mexican Americans: Leadership, Ideology and Identity, 1930-1960*; Muñoz, *Youth, Identity, Power*, 19-46; Juan Gómez Quiñones, *Chicano Politics: Reality and Promise, 1940-1990*; and Acuña, *Occupied America*, 251-306.

7. Muñoz, *Youth, Identity, Power*; Vicki Ruiz, " 'Star Struck': Acculturation, Adolescence, and the Mexican American Woman, 1920-1950," in *Building with Our Hands: New Directions in Chicana Studies*, ed. Adela de la Torre and Beatríz Pesquera; and Eduardo Hermán Gallegos, and Julián Samora, *Mexican Americans in the Southwest*.

8. Vicki L. Ruiz, "Oral History and La Mujer: The Rosa Guerrero Story"; and Vicki L. Ruiz and Susan Tiano, *Women on the U.S.-Mexico Border: Responses to Change*, 227. On Pachucos, see Octavio Paz, *Labyrinth of Solitude: Life and Thought in Mexico*, chap. 1; and for a response, Marcos Sanchez-Tranquilino, "Mano a Mano: An Essay on the Representation of the Zoot Suit and Its Misrepresentation by Octavio Paz," 34-42.

9. See Félix Padilla, *Latino Ethnic Consciousness*, 31-37; and Cockcroft, *Outlaws in the Promised Land*, chap. 5.

10. See Muñoz, *Youth, Identity, Power*, 51.

11. Escobar, "The Dialectics of Repression."

12. Rosa Estades, *Patrones de participación política de los Puerto Riqueños en la ciudad de Nueva York*, 47.

13. Vega, *Memoirs of Bernardo Vega*, 97.

14. Virginia Sánchez Korrol, "Latinismo among Early Puerto Rican Migrants in New York City: A Sociohistoric Interpretation," in *The Hispanic Experience in the United States*, ed. Edna Acosta-Belén and Barbara R. Sjostrom, 151-63; and Estades, *Patrones de participación política*.

15. For the New York community, see, for example, Roberto P. Rodríguez-Morazzani, "Puerto Rican Political Generations in New York: Pioneros, Young Turks and Radicals," 102-7. Félix Padilla, *Latino Ethnic Consciousness*, 38-54, discusses the case of Puerto Ricans in Chicago; see also Estades, *Patrones de Participación Política*.

16. See Félix Padilla, *Latino Ethnic Consciousness*; Alfredo López, *Doña Licha's Island*; P. J. Soto, *Spiks*; and Adalberto López, "The Puerto Rican Diaspora: A Survey," in *The Puerto Ricans: Their History, Culture and Society*, ed. Adalberto López, 313-44.

17. Piri Thomas, *Down These Mean Streets*, 143-44. On the issue of race on the island and in the United States within the Puerto Rican community, see José Luis González, *Puerto Rico: The Four-Storeyed Country*; Rodríguez, *Puerto Ricans*, chap. 3; Clara Rodríguez, "Puerto Ricans: Between Black and White," in *The Puerto Rican Struggle: Essays on Survival in the U.S.*, ed. Clara Rodríguez, Virginia Sánchez Korrol, and J. Oscar Alers, 20-46; Samuel Betances, "Race and the Search for Identity," in *Race, Class and Gender*, ed. Margaret Anderson and Patricia Hill Collins, 277-86; and Eduardo Seda Bonilla, "El problema de la identidad de los Niuyorricans."

18. Ruiz, " 'Starstruck.' "

19. See, for example, Ruiz, ibid.; Patricia Zavella, *Women's Work and Chicano Families: Cannery Workers of the Santa Clara Valley*; Ernesto Galarza, Hermán Gallegos, and Julián Samora, *Mexican Americans in the Southwest*; and Guadalupe San Miguel, Jr., "*Let All of*

Them Take Heed": Mexican Americans and the Campaign for Educational Equality in Texas, 1910-1981. On Chicanos and the political system, see Rodolfo de la Garza, "And Then There Were Some . . . : Chicanos as National Political Actors, 1967-1980," 1-23; and Joan Moore, *Mexican Americans.*

20. Da Matta, "Do You Know Who You're Talking To?"

21. Thernstrom, "Ethnic Groups in American History."

22. Asian Americans and the sectors of the Mexican-American communities who arrived at the turn of the century are the exception here in terms of having at one time been immigrants to this country. Yet they entered a society whose racial formation quickly placed them outside the boundaries of the "national community" imagined in white Anglo-Saxon terms (see chapter 2). On the question of racial formation, see Michael Omi and Howard Winant, *Racial Formation in the United States*, especially 57-69.

23. Felipe Luciano, "America should never have taught us how to read, she should never have given us eyes to see," in Young Lords Party and Michael Abramson, *Palante: The Young Lords Party*, 29.

24. "Carmen," "It was just escape . . . the easiest cop-out there is at this point is drugs," in Young Lords Party and Abramson, *Palante*, 36.

25. The words are by Reies López Tijerina, the son of a migrant worker who later led the movement to restore legal ownership of Spanish and Mexican land grants to Mexican-American small farmers in New Mexico. He goes on to describe what I am here calling the "profound experience of exploitation," saying, "And I was just a little boy. I didn't know any better, all my friends were the same, and I was content. I only had about six months of school in all, because we were always on the move, and the only books I read were Jack and Nancy and so forth. I didn't think anything of going with my brothers to the garbage cans of the rich people, and we would find half a loaf of bread and meat and make our own lunch and go to school." Richard Gardner, *Grito! Reies Tijerina and the New Mexico Land Grant War of 1967*, 36.

26. Martínez, "Histories of the 'Sixties,' " 183. The Young Lords in particular made liberation of all third world people part of their party and program. See Young Lords Party and Abramson, *Palante.*

27. Although not the focus of this study, it is important to take up the challenge posed by Elizabeth Martínez and begin to explore more fully both the interconnections and divisive factors affecting movement unity in the sixties. Some authors have begun to think about these connections; see, for example, Escobar, "Dialectics of Repression"; Manning Marable, *Race Reform and Rebellion: The Second Reconstruction in Black America, 1945-1990*; and Rodríguez-Morazzani, "Puerto Rican Political Generations."

28. Pablo "Yoruba" Guzmán, "Before people called me a spic, they called me a nigger," in Young Lords Party and Abramson, *Palante*, 75.

29. See Rodríguez-Morazzani, "Puerto Rican Political Generations"; Muñoz, *Youth, Identity, Power*; and Ricardo Perez, "La marcha de la reconquista."

30. Piri Thomas, "Puerto Ricans in the Promised Land," *Civil Rights Digest* 6, no. 2 (1972), special issue devoted to an account of the hearing on Puerto Rican problems held by the U.S. Commission on Civil Rights in New York, 5-39.

31. Writing in the late 1970s, Pablo Yoruba Guzmán noted that the different strategies and approaches of the various organizations can be best understood in terms of the ideological differences between the Young Lords and other radical groups of the time, namely the Puerto Rican Socialist party or PSP. See Guzmán, "Puerto Rican Barrio Politics in the United States," in *The Puerto Rican Struggle: Essays on Survival in the United States*, ed. Rodríguez, Sánchez Korrol, and Alers. Although there were other student and community groups at the time, in this section I focus on the Young Lords party as an example of the kinds of political manifestations that emerged at the time. This decision,

to a large extent, is influenced by the still-neglected study of Puerto Rican activism during the period.

32. Iris Morales, "I became the one that translated . . . the go-between," in Young Lords Party and Abramson, *Palante*, 24.

33. Originally an affiliate of Chicago's Young Lords Organization, the New York Young Lords were later to found the party. For a history of the Young Lords, see Young Lords Party and Abramson, *Palante*; David Perez, *Long Road from Lares: An Oral History*; Puerto Rican Revolutionary Workers Organization (Young Lords Party), *Resolutions and Speeches: First Congress*, November, 1972; Juan González, et al., *The Ideology of the Young Lords Party*; Rodríguez-Morazzani, "Puerto Rican Political Generations"; Luciano, "The Young Lords Party"; José Iglesias, "Right On with the Young Lords," *New York Times Magazine*, June 7, 1970; and Guzmán, "Puerto Rican Barrio Politics in the United States."

34. Frank Bonilla, "Beyond Survival"; and Adalberto López, "The Puerto Rican Diaspora."

35. Luciano, in Young Lords Party and Abramson, *Palante*, 29.

36. Iris Morales, "I became the one that translated," in Young Lords Party and Abramson, *Palante*, 24 and 27.

37. Pedro Pietri, *Puerto Rican Obituary*, 1-11.

38. Felipe Luciano, "Dedication," *Caribe* 7, no. 4 (1983), 4.

39. Rodríguez-Morazzani, "Puerto Rican Political Generations," 98.

40. See Vega, *Memoirs of Bernardo Vega*.

41. Pérez, *Long Road from Lares*, 7-8.

42. As I will discuss below, my understanding of both the Puerto Rican and the Mexican American/Chicano movements is in this sense influenced by Richard King's *Civil Rights and the Idea of Freedom*, although his discussion focuses on the very different experience of the African-American community.

43. Guzmán, "Before people called me a spic," in Young Lords and Abramson, *Palante*, 74.

44. Ibid., 76.

45. Ibid., 75.

46. Gloria Gonzáles, "It's not medical care our people get, but a test tube kind of thing," in Young Lords Party and Abramson, *Palante*, passim; and Yglesias, "Right On with the Young Lords," 68-71.

47. Denise Oliver, "When you look to any group to find out who's the most oppressed, it's always gonna be the women," in Young Lords Party and Abramson, *Palante*, 52; and Estades, *Patrones de participación política*, 51.

48. Guzmán, "We're saying that . . . it would be healthy for a man, if he wanted to cry, to go ahead and cry. It would also be healthy for a woman to pick up the gun," in Young Lords Party and Abramson, *Palante*, 46-47.

49. Morales, "I became the one," in Young Lords Party and Abramson, *Palante*, 28.

50. Oliver, "When you look to any group," in Young Lords Party and Abramson, *Palante*, 50-51.

51. Richie Pérez, "From Assimilation to Annihilation: Puerto Rican Images in U.S. films," 8-27; Alberto Sandoval Sánchez, "Una lectura puertorriqueña de la América de West Side Story," 30-45; and Oscar Lewis, *La Vida: A Puerto Rican Family in the Culture of Poverty*.

52. Rodríguez-Morazzani, "Puerto Rican Political Generations," 110-11. For a discussion on the questions raised by the issue of citizenship among Puerto Ricans, see Frank Bonilla, "Migrants, Citizenship and Social Pacts," 81-90. See Vega, *Memoirs*, on early Puerto Rican and Cuban political organization in New York City, and Virginia Sánchez Korrol, *From Colonia to Community: History of Puerto Ricans in New York City, 1917-1948*.

53. On Lolita Lebrón, see Federico Ribes Tovar, *Lolita Lebrón la prisionera*. Tovar's portrait provides an interesting contrast to the negative press accounts of both the March 1 event and of Lebrón; see, for example, C. Knowles, "Five Congressmen Shot in House by Three Puerto Rican Nationalists," *New York Times*, Mar. 2, 1954; C. P. Trussel, "Witness Describes Shooting, Capture," *New York Times*, Mar. 2, 1954, 1; C. P. Trussel, "Shooting in House Causes Increase in Capitol Guards," Mar. 3, 1954, 1; William Blair, "Regrets Voiced by Muñoz-Marin," *New York Times*, Mar. 3, 1954, 1, 14; and C. P. Trussell, "Capital Assassins Resistant on Plea," Mar. 6, 1954. *Time* magazine describes Lebrón "jabbering in Spanish" as she "waved a Puerto Rican flag": "The Capitol: Puerto Rico Is Not Free," Mar. 8, 1954, 19. P. Kihss includes some nationalist responses in "Sublime Heroism Cited in Shooting," *New York Times*, Mar. 3, 1954, 14; while *Newsweek* portrays the nationalists as "fanatics" on an "insane" mission: "Congress: Bloody Session," Mar. 8, 1954, 22-23. Lebrón's refusal to request parole from a government she did not recognize and the positive response to Lebrón by people on the island is described by Anne Nelson, "Lolita Lebrón Would Rather Die in Prison," *Nation*, Aug. 11, 1979, 103-4. I thank Elizabeth García for her research assistance.

On Pedro Albizu Campos, see Carlos Rodríguez Fraticelli, "Pedro Albizu Campos: Strategies of Struggle and Strategic Struggles," 24-33; and Amílcar Tirado Avilés, "La forja de un líder: Pedro Albizu Campos, 1924-1930," 12-23. See also Alfredo López, *Doña Licha's Island*.

54. Klor de Alva adds that the Young Lords party became the Puerto Rican Revolutionary Workers Organization. "Aztlán, Borinquen and Hispanic Nationalism," 156.

55. Guzmán, in Young Lords Party and Abramson, *Palante*; see also "A Report to the Mayor of a Citizen, Julio Roldán," *New York Times*, Oct. 16, 1970, 51; "Hundreds in East Harlem Rampage," *New York Times*, June 15, 1970, 31; "Victim Blames 'Kids' Not Young Lords for East Harlem Looting," *New York Times*, June 16, 1970, 42; "East Harlem Looting," *New York Times*, June 26, 1970, 44; Michael Knight, "Young Lords and Police Clash at Newark Puerto Rican March," *New York Times*, July 19, 1970, 33; and Walter Waggoner, "Young Lords in Newark Accuse Police of 'Brutality' in Parade," *New York Times*, July 20, 1970, 16.

56. Klor de Alva, "Aztlán, Borinquen and Hispanic Nationalism," 158.

57. Guzmán in Young Lords and Abramson, *Palante*, 76; and Estades, *Patrones de participación política*, 50-53.

58. Rodríguez-Morazzani, "Puerto Rican Political Generations," 19; Adalberto López, "The Puerto Rican Diaspora"; and Alfredo López, *Doña Licha's Island*.

59. Blanca Vasquez, quoted in Alberto Sandoval Sánchez, "La identidad especular del allá y del acá: Nuestra propia imagen puertorriqueña en cuestión," 28-43.

60. For a comprehensive study of the Chicano movement, see Muñoz, *Youth, Identity, Power*. Ramón Gutiérrez examines the role of gender relations in shaping the movement participants' goals and ideology in "Community, Patriarchy and Individualism: The Politics of Chicano History and the Dream of Equality." For overviews of the Mexican-American and Chicano movements in the 1960s and 70s, see, for example, Gómez Quiñones, *Chicano Politics: Reality and Promise, 1940-1990*; Acuña, *Occupied America*, 307-412; and Tony Castro, *Chicano Power: The Emergence of Mexican America*, 79-167. I am using the term Chicano to refer to the student movements to emphasize the specificity of the youth movement.

61. On the farmworkers' movement, see Margaret Rose, "Traditional and Non-traditional Patterns of Female Activism in the United Farm Workers of America, 1962-1980," 26-30; "Jessie López de la Cruz, The Battle for Farmworkers Rights," in *Moving the Mountain: Women Working for Social Change*, ed. Ellen Cantarow, with Susan Gushee O'Malley and Sharon Hartman Strom, 95-151; Craig Jenkins, *The Politics of Insurgency: The Farm*

Worker Movement in the 1960s; Dick Meister and Anne Loftis, *A Long Time Coming: The Struggle to Unionize America's Farm Workers*; M. Dubofsky and W. Van Tine, eds., *Labor Leaders in America*; Jacques Levy, *César Chávez: Autobiography of La Causa*; Peter Mattheisen, *Sal si puedes*; J. London and H. Anderson, "Man of Fire: Ernesto Galarza," in *Chicano: The Evolution of a People*, ed. Renato Rosaldo, Robert Calvert, and Gustav Seligman, 278-92; César Chávez, "The California Farm Workers' Struggle," 16-19; and "Farm Workers—the Union Makes Them Strong," *International: Official Publication of the Seafarers International Union of North America, AFL-CIO* (New York, February 1968). For López Tijerina's movement, see Frances Swadesh, "The Alianza Movement: Catalyst for Social Change in New Mexico," in *Chicano: The Evolution of a People*, ed. Renato Rosaldo, Robert Calvert, and Gustav Seligman, 267-77; and Gardner, *Grito!*

62. See Muñoz, *Youth, Identity, Power*, 10; John Hammerback, Richard Jensen, and José Angel Gutiérrez, *A War on Words*.

63. César Chávez, "An Organizer's Tale," *Ramparts Magazine*: "Huelga! Tales of the Delano Revolution," July 1966. Little is known about the women in the UFW and Chavez's organizing efforts. See Rose, "Traditional and Non-traditional Patterns"; Dolores Huerta, "Dolores Huerta Talks: About Republicans, Cesar, Children and Her Home Town," 20-24; "An Interview with Dolores Huerta," *El Chicano*, Jan. 25, 1973, 3, 15; Barbara L. Baer and Glenna Matthews, " 'You Find a Way': The Women of the Boycott," *Nation*, Feb. 23, 1974, 232-38; Barbara L. Baer, "Stopping Traffic: One Woman's Cause," *Progressive*, Sept. 1975, 38-40; María Moreno. "Before Delano . . . 'I'm Talking for Justice,' " 12-13; Jean Murphy, "Unsung Heroine of La Causa," 20; Enriqueta Longeaux y Vasquez, "The Woman of La Raza," *El Grito del Norte*, July 2, 1969, 8-10; and López de la Cruz, "The Battle for Farmworkers' Rights," 95-151.

64. Quoted in "Grapes of Wrath," *Newsweek*, Dec. 27, 1965.

65. Quoted in "Nonviolence Still Works: César Chávez: A Controversial Labor Leader Talks about a New Kind of Unionism," *Look*, Apr. 1, 1969, 52-57.

66. On Luis Valdez and the Teatro Campesino, see Yolanda Julia Broyles, "Women in El Teatro Campesino: ¿Apoco Estaba Molacha La Virgen de Guadalupe?" in *Chicana Voices: Intersections of Class, Race and Gender*, ed. National Association for Chicano Studies, 162-87; Yolanda Broyles-González, "The Living Legacy of Chicana Performers: Preserving History through Oral Testimony," *Frontiers* 11, no. 1 (1990): 46-52; Luis Valdez, *Luis Valdez—Early Works: Actos, Bernabé and Pensamiento Serpentino*; and N. Kannellos, "Luis Miguel Valdez," in *Dictionary of Literary Biography: Chicano Writers*, vol. 122, ed. Francisco A. Lomelí and C. R. Shirley (Detroit, Mich.: Gale Research, 1979).

67. Luis Valdez, "The Tale of the Raza," *Ramparts Magazine*: "Huelga! Tales of the Delano Revolution," July 1966, 40.

68. Ibid., 39.

69. For discussions of the symbolism of the Chicano movement, see Luis Leal, "In Search of Aztlán," in *Aztlán: Essays on the Chicano Homeland*, ed. Rudolfo Anaya and Francisco Lomelí, 6-14; and Gutiérrez, "Community, Patriarchy and Individualism."

70. As Frances Swadesh describes, since the U.S. government does not recognize collective ownership claims, much of the common-use lands had been assigned to the public domain. Moreover since the nineteenth century, corruption in the legal system had ensured that court battles between heirs and the state of New Mexico had repeatedly resulted in lost cases for the plaintiffs and fortunes for the lawyers. As a result, López Tijerina's Alianza insisted on taking the land grant decisions to the Supreme Court. Swadesh, "The Alianza Movement," in Rosaldo, Calvert, and Seligman, eds.

71. Gardner, *Grito!* 120-21.

72. Swadesh, "The Alianza Movement," in Rosaldo, Calvert, and Seligman, eds.

73. Gardner, *Grito!* 9. For accounts of the courthouse raid, see Gardner, ibid., 1-8, and Swadesh, "The Alianza Movement," in Rosaldo, Calvert, and Seligman, eds.

74. Gardner, *Grito!* 205-7.

75. Ibid., 209; and Acuña, *Occupied America*, 340. As Galarza, Gallegos, and Samora noted in 1970, "latent hostility" among some Mexican Americans toward "the Negro" was not always due to economic competition in the labor market. Nor was it indigenous to "the culture of poverty among Mexicans." Rather, it was "abetted, if it does not indeed stem from, their uncritical acceptance of American middle class racial contagion." Ernesto Galarza, Hermán Gallegos, and Julián Samora, *Mexican Americans in the Southwest*, 63.

76. Muñoz, *Youth, Identity, Power*, 15, 59-60.

77. Ibid., 15. For a review essay on recent interpretations of the Chicano movement, see Fred López, "Reflections on the Chicano Movement," *Latin American Perspectives*, issue 75, vol. 19, no. 4 (Fall 1992): 79-102.

78. Quoted in Muñoz, *Youth, Identity, Power*, 78.

79. For a comparison of Black Nationalism and the Chicano Power movement, see Marable, *Race, Reform, and Rebellion*, 141-45.

80. Jameson, "Periodizing the Sixties." Along with the books reviewed by Elizabeth Martínez (see n. 1), an excellent discussion of the period's civil rights and student new left movements is Edward P. Morgan, *The 60s Experience: Hard Lessons about Modern America*. See also Mercer, " '1968' "; and Klor de Alva, "Aztlán, Borinquen and Hispanic Nationalism." See King, *Civil Rights*, 153-59, for a critique of the black liberation movement's "colonial analogy" with third world liberation movements.

81. Muñoz, *Youth, Identity, Power*, 146-48. On the institutionalization of Chicano Studies, see ibid., 127-90. For recent critiques of the resulting Chicano historiography based on the internal colonialism model, see Almaguer, "Ideological Distortions in Recent Chicano Historiography," and Alex M. Saragoza, "Recent Chicano Historiography: An Interpretive Essay," *Aztlán: A Journal of Chicano Studies*, 1-78. The classic conceptualization of "internal colonialism" can be found in Robert Blauner's *Racial Oppression in America*.

82. King, *Civil Rights*; and Muñoz, "El Plan de Santa Barbara," in *Youth, Identity, Power*, 191-202. Muñoz notes that the adoption of cultural nationalism was not without its critics within the student movement (91-94).

83. Gutiérrez, "Community, Patriarchy and Individualism." Gutiérrez provides an excellent analysis of gender relations in this period. See also Alma M. García, "The Development of Chicana Feminist Discourse, 1970-1980," 217-138; and Beatríz Pesquera and Denise Segura, "Beyond Indifference and Antipathy: The Chicana Movement and Chicana Feminist Discourse." For various perspectives and approaches to the concept of Aztlán, see the anthology edited by Rudolfo Anaya and Francisco Lomelí, *Aztlán: Essays on the Chicano Homeland*.

84. Pérez, "La marcha de la reconquista," 10. On the death of Rubén Salazar, see Earl Shorris, *Latinos!*; and Acuña, *Occupied America*, 345-50. For reactions during this period, see, for example, Francisca Flores, "There Will Be No Prosecution for the Death of Rubén Salazar," *Regeneración* 1, no. 7: 1-3. *Regeneración* 1, no. 6, also has various articles analyzing the incident. Jaime J. Delgado, "National Chicano Moratorium, August 29, 1970" (Providence, R.I., 1993), provides an extensive logbook compilation of the varied coverage by mainstream and alternative media of the incident and its aftermath.

85. Muñoz, *Youth, Identity, Power*, 79.

86. Anthony Smith, *Theories of Nationalism*, as cited in Michael Pina, "The Archaic, Historical and Mythicized Dimensions of Aztlán," in *Aztlán: Essays on the Chicano Homeland*, ed. Anaya and Lomelí, 38.

87. Klor de Alva, "Aztlán, Borinquen and Hispanic Nationalism," 151.

88. Muñoz, *Youth, Identity, Power*, 101. For accounts of La Raza Unida party, see *ibid.*, 99-126; Mario Barrera and Carlos Muñoz Jr., "La Raza Unida Party and the Chicano Student Movement in California," 101-19; J. Shockley, "Crystal City: Los Cinco Mexicanos," in *Chicano: The Evolution of a People*, ed. Rosaldo, Calvert, and Seligman, 303-14; and J. Shockley, "Crystal City: La Raza Unida Party and the Second Revolt," in Rosaldo, Calvert, and Seligman, eds., 314-27.

89. Muñoz, *Youth, Identity, Power*, 101. On the party's platform on women's participation, see ibid., 105-6.

90. "José Angel Gutiérrez," *Regeneración*, 1, no. 3 (1970): 4.

91. See Muñoz, *Youth, Identity, Power*; Barrera and Muñoz, "La Raza Unida Party"; and Richard García, as quoted in Marable, *Race, Reform, and Rebellion*, 143-45.

92. Quoted in Marable, *Race, Reform, and Rebellion*, 143.

93. Gutiérrez, "Community, Patriarchy and Individualism."

94. Marable, *Race, Reform and Rebellion*, 144; and Estades, *Patrones de participación política*.

95. This analysis is partially influenced by King's *Civil Rights and the Idea of Freedom*. See also Paoli, "Citizenship, Inequalities, Democracy and Rights"; and Blondet, "Establishing an Identity." For an excellent discussion on the concept of "experience" in historiography, see Joan Scott, "Experience," in *Feminists Theorize the Political*, ed. Judith Butler and Joan Scott, 22-40.

96. Huerta, "Dolores Huerta Talks," 21.

97. Paul Jacobs in *Ramparts Magazine*, July 1966, 39. The Citizens for Farm Labor was created by Ann Draper of Amalgamated Clothing and Textile Workers Union (ACTWU).

98. See Escobar, "The Dialectics of Repression"; Marable, *Race, Reform, and Rebellion*; Muñoz, *Youth, Identity, Power*; and Morgan, *The 60s Experience*.

99. Escobar, "The Dialectics of Repression."

100. King, *Civil Rights*, 50-51ff.

101. Martha P. Cotera, *The Chicana Feminist*, 11.

102. Chavez, "An Organizer's Tale."

103. Quoted in Barbara L. Baer and Glenna Matthews, " 'You Find a Way.' " *Nation*, Feb. 23, 1974, 237.

104. Swadesh, "The Alianza Movement," in Rosaldo, Calvert, and Seligman, eds.

105. Cotera, *The Chicana Feminist*, 20.

106. Blanca Vásquez, "Mi gente: Antónia Pantoja and Esperanza Martell," 48-55.

107. López de la Cruz. "The Battle for Farmworkers' Rights," in *Moving the Mountain*, ed. Cantarow, 134. For a discussion on the role of participation of family units in strengthening the movement and simultaneously redefining gender relations, see Maxine Baca Zinn, "Political Familism: Toward Sex Role Equality in Chicano Families," 13-26.

108. Quoted in Ellen Cantarow and Susan Gushee O'Malley, eds., "Ella Baker: Organizing for Civil Rights," in *Moving the Mountain: Women Working for Social Change*, 53.

109. Gutiérrez, "Community, Patriarchy and Individualism," 54.

110. Esperanza Martell, quoted in Vásquez, "Mi gente," 53.

111. Isabelle Navar, "La Mexicana: An Image of Strength," 4. Homophobia, however, remained unacknowledged by many Chicanas and within the broader movements. See Anzaldúa and Moraga, *This Bridge*.

112. King, *Civil Rights*, 71-72.

113. Navar. "La Mexicana," 4.

114. Francisca Flores, "Conference of Mexican Women, Un Remolino," 2.

115. Rudolfo Gonzáles, "Chicano Nationalism: The Key to Unity for La Raza," in *Chicano: The Evolution of a People*, ed. Renato Rosaldo, Robert Calvert, and Gustav Seligman, 424-25.

116. Leticia Hernández, "Chicanas Identify," 9. For a discussion of this point, see Alma García, "Development of Chicana Feminist Discourse."

117. Hernández, "Chicanas Identify," 2; and Beatríz Pesquera and Denise Segura, "Beyond Indifference and Antipathy: The Chicana Movement and Chicana Feminist Discourse," 73. See also Gutiérrez, "Community, Patriarchy and Individualism."

118. José Vasconcelos, *La Raza Cósmica. Misión de la Raza Iberoamericana* (Mexico: Espasa-Calpe Mexicana, [1948] 1990).

119. Vasquez, "Mi gente," 53.

120. Angela Jorge, "The Black Puerto Rican Woman in Contemporary American Society," in *The Puerto Rican Woman: Perspectives on Culture, History and Society*, ed. Edna Acosta-Belén and Barbara R. Sjostrom, 180-81.

121. See Edna Acosta-Belén, "From Settlers to Newcomers: The Hispanic Legacy in the United States," in *The Hispanic Experience in the United States*, ed. Edna Acosta-Belén and Barbara R. Sjostrom, 99.

Chapter 4. Hispanic Ethnicity, the Ethnic Revival, and Its Critique

1. Quoted in Edward Simmen, ed., *Pain and Promise: The Chicano Today*, 122.

2. Sarah Deutsch, *No Separate Refuge*; Louise Año Nuevo Kerr, "Chicanas in the Great Depression," in *Between Borders: Essays on Mexicana/Chicana History*, ed. Adelaida R. del Castillo, 257-68; Roberto R. Calderón and Emilio Zamora, "Manuela Solís Sager and Emma B. Tenayuca: A Tribute," in *Between Borders: Essays on Mexicana/Chicana History*, ed. del Castillo, 269-80; Mario Barrera, *Beyond Aztlán*; Vicki L. Ruiz, *Cannery Women, Cannery Lives*; and Rodolfo Acuña, *Occupied America*.

3. "Hispanic Heritage Week Set," *New York Times*, Sept. 13, 1969, 1, 17.

4. Joint Resolution, Sept. 17, 1968 (36 U.S.C., 169ff), quoted in Isidro Lucas, "Political Demands of Spanish-speaking Communities in the United States," in *Politics and Language: Spanish and English in the United States*, ed. D. J. R. Bruckner, 133-54.

5. H. J. Abramson, "Assimilation and Pluralism," in *Harvard Encyclopedia of American Ethnic Groups*, ed. Stephan Thernstrom, Ann Orlov, and Oscar Handlin, 150-60.

6. On Cubans in the United States, see, for example, Alejandro Portes and R. Bach, *Latin Journey*; Silvia Pedraza-Bailey, *Political and Economic Migrants in America: Cubans and Mexicans*; Eleanor Meyer Rogg, *The Assimilation of Cuban Exiles*; Pedraza-Bailey, "Cuba's Exiles"; Robert Bach, "The New Cuban Immigrants: Their Background and Prospects," 39-46; Silvia Pedraza-Bailey, "Cuban Political Immigrants and Mexican Economic Immigrants: The Role of Government Policy in Their Assimilation," in *Hispanic Migration and the United States*, ed. Gastón Fernández, Beverly Nagel, and León Narvaez, 68-101.

7. Margarita Melville, "Hispanics: Race, Class, or Ethnicity?" 67-83.

8. See "National Hispanic Heritage Week, 1969," Proclamation 3930, Sept. 12, 1969, in *Weekly Compilations of Presidential Documents* 5, no. 37 (Sept. 15, 1969): 1252. Also see Laura E. Gómez, "The Birth of the 'Hispanic' Generation: Attitudes of Mexican-American Political Elites toward the Hispanic Label."

9. Jack Forbes, "The Hispanic Spin: Party Politics and Governmental Manipulation of Ethnic Identity," 67. On the political implications for Hispanics of the ethnic and racial categories used by the census, see J. Harvey M. Choldin, "Statistics and Politics: The 'Hispanic' Issue in the 1980 Census," and Ira S. Lowry, "The Science and Politics of Ethnic Enumeration," in *Ethnicity and Public Policy*, ed. W. Van Horne.

10. Eric Hobsbawm, "Mass-Producing Traditions," in *The Invention of Tradition*, ed. Eric Hobsbawm and Terence Ranger.

11. Edna Acosta-Belén, "From Settlers to Newcomers," in *The Hispanic Experience in the United States*, ed. Acosta-Belén and Barbara R. Sjostrom, 81.

12. Milton Gordon, *Assimilation in American Life*.

13. Stephan Thernstrom, "Ethnic Groups in American History," 16.

14. Nelson and Tienda, "Structuring of Hispanic Identity," 49.

15. Glazer and Moynihan, *Beyond the Melting Pot*; and Gordon, *Assimilation in American Life*.

16. Thernstrom, "Ethnic Groups in American History," 3.

17. Nelson and Tienda, "The Structuring of Hispanic Identity," 49.

18. Thernstrom, "Ethnic Groups in American History," 10, 5, 27.

19. Omi and Winant, *Racial Formation in the United States*; Stephen Greer, "The Ethnic Question," in *The Sixties, without Apology*, ed. Sohnya Sayres et al., 119-36; Muga, "Academic Sub-Cultural Theory and the Problematic of Ethnicity"; Joan Moore, "Minorities in the American Class System," in *Majority and Minority: The Dynamics of Race and Ethnicity in American Life*, ed. N. R. Yetman, 278-85.

20. See, for example, Glazer and Moynihan, *Beyond the Melting Pot*; Michael Novak, *The Rise of the Unmeltable Ethnics*; Andrew Greely, *Why Can't They Be Like Us? America's White Ethnic Groups*; Kessner, *The Golden Door*; Deborah Dash Moore, *Home in America: Second Generation New York Jews*; Shih-Shan Henry Tsai, *The Chinese Experience in America*; Joshua Fishman, *The Rise and Fall of the Ethnic Revival*; and Nathan Glazer, *Ethnic Dilemmas, 1964-1982*.

21. Moynihan, *Counting Our Blessings*, 205. See also Glazer and Moynihan, *Beyond the Melting Pot*.

22. Gordon, *Assimilation in American Life*, 234-35.

23. Leonard Dinnerstein and David M. Reimers, *Ethnic Americans: A History of Immigration*.

24. Joshua Fishman, *Language Loyalty in the United States*. See also Fishman, *The Rise and Fall of the Ethnic Revival*.

25. Kessner, *The Golden Door*; and Moore, *Home in America*.

26. Pedraza-Bailey, "Cuban Political Immigrants and Mexican Economic Immigrants," in Fernandez, Nagel, and Narvaez, eds., 71-72.

27. Tsai, *The Chinese Experience*, xiii. Joseph Fitzpatrick, *Puerto Ricans: The Meaning of Migration to the Mainland*.

28. Michael S. Laguerre, *American Odyssey: Haitians in New York City*, 155, 158; and Clara E. Rodríguez, *Puerto Ricans: Born in the U.S.A.*, esp. chap. 3.

29. Constance R. Sutton, "The Caribbeanization of New York City and the Emergence of a Transnational Socio-Cultural System," in *Caribbean Life in New York City: Sociocultural Dimensions*, ed. Constance R. Sutton and Elsa Chaney. On transnationalism, see Michael Kearney, "Borders and Boundaries of Self at the End of Empire," *Journal of Historical Sociology* 4, no. 1 (March 1991): 51-74; *Caribbean Life in New York City*, ed. Sutton and Chaney; and Nina Glick Schiller, Linda Basch, and Cristina Blanc-Szanton, eds., *Towards a Transnational Perspective on Migration: Race, Class, Ethnicity and Nationalism Reconsidered*.

30. Roger Rouse, "Mexican Migration and the Social Space of Postmodernism," 8.

31. Abramson, "Assimilation and Pluralism," 150.

32. Greer, "The Ethnic Question," in Sayres et al., eds. 124-25.

33. Muga, "Academic Sub-Cultural Theory," 18.

34. Moore, "Minorities in the American Class System," 278.

35. Omi and Winant, *Racial Formation*, 62.

36. Ibid., 20.

37. Takaki, "Reflections on Racial Patterns in America," in *Ethnicity and Public Policy*, ed. W. Van Horne.

38. Omi and Winant, *Racial Formation*, 20.

39. E. San Juan Jr., *Racial Formations/Critical Transformations*, 33. San Juan Jr. provides an excellent overview and critique of ethnicity theory from this perspective. See also Takaki, "Reflections on Racial Patterns in America," and Omi and Winant, *Racial Formation*, 9-25.

40. William Julius Wilson, "The Black Community in the 1980s: Questions of Race, Class, and Public Policy," in *Majority and Minority: The Dynamics of Race and Ethnicity in American Life*, ed. N. R. Yetman, 492.

41. H. Cruse, *Plural but Equal: A Critical Study of Blacks and Minorities and America's Plural Society*, 28.

42. See San Juan Jr., *Racial Formations/Critical Transformations*; Omi and Winant, *Racial Formation*; and Ronald Takaki, ed., *From Different Shores: Perspectives on Race and Ethnicity in America*.

43. Greer, "The Ethnic Question," in Sayres et al., eds.

44. Quoted in Isaura Santiago Santiago, *A Community's Struggle for Equal Educational Opportunity: Aspira v. Board of Ed.*, 10.

45. U.S. Commission on Civil Rights, "A Better Chance to Learn: Bilingual-Bicultural Education," 9, 143.

46. Fishman, *The Rise and Fall of the Ethnic Revival*.

47. Fishman, *Language Loyalty*, 30, and " 'English Only,' " 130.

48. S. Diamond, "Discussion of Barry and Breton Presentations," in *Politics and Language: Spanish and English in the United States*, ed. D. J. R. Bruckner.

49. Maria Eugenia Matute-Bianchi, "The Federal Mandate for Bilingual Education," in *Bilingual Education and Public Policy in the United States I*, ed. R. Padilla, 18.

50. Henry Perkinson, *The Imperfect Panacea: American Faith in Education, 1865-1976*.

51. Matute-Bianchi, "The Federal Mandate for Bilingual Education," in Padilla, ed.

52. Steven R. Applewhite, "The Legal Dialectic of Bilingual Education," in *Bilingual Education and Public Policy in the United States*, ed. R. Padilla, 3-16.

53. For a critique of this case, see Peter B. Kutner, "Keyes v. School District Number One: A Constitutional Right to Equal Educational Opportunity?" 1-40.

54. Applewhite, "The Legal Dialect," in Padilla, ed. See also Herbert Teitelbaum and Richard J. Hiller, "Bilingual Education: The Legal Mandate," 138-71.

55. Applewhite, "The Legal Dialect."

56. Ibid., 10.

57. Ibid., 12.

58. Lily Wong Fillmore, "Against Our Best Interest: The Attempt to Sabotage Bilingual Education," in *Language Loyalties: A Source Book on the Official English Controversy*, ed. J. Crawford, 367-76; Teitelbaum and Hiller, "Bilingual Education"; Richard T. Castro, " 'English Only' Bills Undercut Rights of Ethnic Minorities," *In These Times*, Feb. 18, 1987, 16; and Edward M. Chen and Wade Henderson, "New 'English-Only' Movement Reflects Old Fear of Immigrants," *Civil Liberties*, Summer-Fall 1986, 8.

59. Amado Padilla, "Bilingual Schools: Gateways to Integration or Roads to Separation," 52-67.

60. On the debates on evaluation, see Ann C. Willig, "A Meta-Analysis of Selected Studies on Effectiveness of Bilingual Education"; Keith Baker, "Ideological Bias in Bilingual Education Research"; and the response by Stanley Seidner, *Political Expedience or Educational Research: An Analysis of Baker and Dekanter's Review of the Literature of Bilingual Education*.

61. Fishman, " 'English Only,' " 128.

62. Shirley Brice Heath and Frederick Mandabach, "Language Status Decisions and the Law in the United States," in *Progress in Language Planning*, ed. Juán Corrubias and Joshua Fishman, 87-105.

63. Senator Ralph Yarborough, "Introducing the Bilingual Education Act," excerpts from speech delivered in Congress on Jan. 17, 1967, in *Language Loyalties*, ed. J. Crawford, 322-25; and "Law and Policy in the Lau Era: The Emerging Politics of Language," *Education Week*, Feb. 8, 1984, 12-16.

64. Veltman, *Language Shift in the United States*.

65. Fishman, " 'English Only' "; and Zentella, "Language Politics in the U.S.A."

66. Fishman, " 'English Only,' " 132.

67. Joan Vincent, "The Structuring of Ethnicity," 377.

68. Martha E. Giménez, "Minorities and the World-System: Theoretical and Political Implications of the Internationalization of Minorities," in *Racism, Sexism and the World-System*, ed. J. Smith et al., 49; my emphasis.

Chapter 5. Hispanics and the Dynamics of Race and Class: The Fieldwork Data

1. On the notion of ethnic identity as a continuous process of articulation, see Vincent, "The Structuring of Ethnicity."

2. See Félix Padilla, *Latino Ethnic Consciousness*, on the emergence of Latinismo among Puerto Ricans and Mexican-Americans. Padilla focuses on "situations involving inequality experienced in common" in Chicago (68). Defining Latinismo as *"political ethnicity*, a manipulative device for the pursuit of collective political, economic, and social interests in society" (163), Padilla's study centers on Latino ethnic consciousness resulting from interest-group articulation. Of particular relevance here is his discussion of the implications of regional differences in the United States, as well as his point that Latino interests may sometimes conflict with the interests of national groups. As he notes, the fact that different national-origin groups are settling in different areas of the United States and have diverse needs and varied historical reasons for being in this country requires more localized research into the different possibilities for and meanings of Latino identity, as well as of Latinismo as situational ethnicity. See also Flores and Yudice, "Living Borders/Buscando America."

3. Michael Rose, *Lives on the Boundary*.

4. This was confirmed by some who, like Rosa, wanted to continue the interview sessions even after I had finished collecting the data for this study: "I came by to see if you needed to know anything else. Our conversation the other day was so interesting. Can we go on?" (Rosa, El Salvador).

5. Elliot George Mishler, *Research Interviewing: Context and Narrative*.

6. Ibid., 139.

7. A. M. Rodrigues, *Operário, Operária*.

8. James Clifford and George Marcus, eds., *Writing Culture: The Poetics and Politics of Ethnography*.

9. Stuart Hall, "Encoding/Decoding," in *Culture, Media, Language*, ed. Stuart Hall, 128-38; and David Morley, "Texts, Readers, Subjects," in *Culture, Media, Language*, ed. Hall, 163-73.

10. Raymond Williams, *Marxism and Literature*. This is also exemplified in Julio Cortázar, *Rayuela*.

11. Hall, "Encoding/Decoding"; Basil Bernstein, "Elaborated and Restricted Codes: Their Social Origins and Some Consequences," 113-33; and Morley, "Texts, Readers, Subjects."

12. Edmund Leach, *Political Systems of Highland Burma*.

13. J. Van Velsen, "The Extended Case Method and Situational Analysis," in *The Social Craft of Anthropology*, ed. J. Mitchell, 147.

14. Victor Turner, "Social Dramas and Stories about Them," in *On Narrative*, ed. W. J. T. Mitchell, 168.

15. Cary Davis, Carl Haub, and JoAnne Willette, "U.S. Hispanics: Changing the Face of America," in *The Hispanic Experience in the United States*, ed. Edna Acosta-Belén and Barbara R. Sjostrom. Although noting that detailed 1990 census information was unavailable at the time he wrote, Rubén Rumbaut has provided a useful overview of the demographic characteristics of people with ties to Latin America and the Caribbean in the United States today; see Rubén G. Rumbaut, "The Americans," in *Americas: New Interpretive Essays*, ed. Alfred Stepan.

16. Klor de Alva, "Telling Hispanics Apart," in *The Hispanic Experience in the United States*, ed. Edna Acosta-Belén and Barbara R. Sjostrom, 121.

17. Davis, Haub, and Willette, "U.S. Hispanics," 12.

18. Klor de Alva, "Telling Hispanics Apart," 118-19.

19. Sassen, *The Mobility of Labor and Capital*, 279.

20. Eleanor Leacock and Helen I. Safa, eds., *Women's Work*.

21. S. E. Brown, "Love Unites Them and Hunger Separates Them: Poor Women in the Dominican Republic," in *Toward an Anthropology of Women*, ed. Rayna Rapp; and Anna Rubbo, "The Spread of Capitalism in Rural Colombia: Effects on Poor Women," in *Toward an Anthropology of Women*, ed. R. Rapp, 333-57.

22. L. B. Rubin, *Worlds of Pain*, 171.

23. Pessar, "The Dominicans."

24. Patricia Pessar, ed., *When Borders Don't Divide: Labor Migration and Refugee Movements in the Americas*, 258.

25. For an excellent study of a different process through which one group of women established their identities to themselves and others, see Cecilia Blondet, "Establishing an Identity," in *Women and Social Change in Latin America*, ed. Elizabeth Jelin.

26. Patricia Pessar and Sherri Grasmuck, *Between Two Islands: Dominican International Migration*.

27. María Patricia Fernández-Kelly and Alejandro Portes, "Continent on the Move: Immigrants and Refugees in the Americas," in *Americas: New Interpretive Essays*, ed. Alfred Stepan, 248-74; Leacock and Safa, eds., *Women's Work*; Fuentes and Ehrenreich, *Women in the Global Factory*; P. Portocarrero, ed., *Mujer en desarrollo: Balance y propuestas*; and Arthur MacEwen, "The Current Crisis in Latin America and the International Economy," 1-17.

28. Fernández-Kelly and Portes, "Continent on the Move," in Stepan, ed., 272.

29. Alejandro Portes and R. Bach, *Latin Journey*, chap. 1.

30. Fernández-Kelly and Portes, "Continent on the Move," in Stepan, ed.; Klor de Alva, "Telling Hispanics Apart," 108; and Sassen, *The Mobility of Labor and Capital*.

31. Glick Schiller, Basch, and Blanc-Szanton, eds., *Towards a Transnational Perspective on Migration*; and Rouse, "Mexican Migration and the Social Space of Postmodernism."

32. See, for example, C. Raymond, "Global Migration Will Have Widespread Impact on Society, Scholars Say," *Chronicle of Higher Education*, Sept. 12, 1990, 1; Portes and Bach, *Latin Journey*; Pessar, "Introduction: Migration Myths and New Realities," in *When Borders Don't Divide*; Pessar and Grasmuck, *Between Two Islands*; and Glick Schiller, Basch, and Blanc-Szanton, eds., *Towards a Transnational Perspective on Migration*.

33. Pedraza-Bailey, "Cuba's Exiles," 7.

34. Rumbaut, "The Americans," in Stepan, ed.

35. Michael Piore, *Birds of Passage: Migrant Labor and Industrial Societies*, 17-19.

36. Teófilo Altamirano, *Los que se fueron: Peruanos en Estados Unidos*.

37. William F. Stinner, Klaus de Albuquerque, and Roy S. Bryce-Laporte, eds., *Return Migration and Remittances: Developing a Caribbean Perspective*.

38. Roberta Ann Johnson, "The Newyorican Comes Home to Puerto Rico: Description and Consequences," in *Return Migration and Remittances*, ed. Stinner, de Albuquerque, and Bryce-Laporte, 129-56.

Chapter 6. Language, National Identity, and the Ethnic Label Hispanic

1. Eva Hoffman, *Lost in Translation: A Life in a New Language*, 116.

2. Thomas Kessner, *The Golden Door*.

3. Gilberto Velho, *Individualismo e cultura*.

4. Roberto Da Matta, "Do You Know Who You're Talking To?" in *Carnivals, Rogues and Heroes: An Anthropology of the Brazilian Dilemma*, 186-87.

5. Renato Ortiz, *Cultura e identidade nacional*, 36; Morner, *Race Mixture in the History of Latin America*; Richard Graham, ed., *The Idea of Race in Latin America, 1870-1940*; and Leslie Rout, *African Experience in Spanish America, 1512 to the Present*.

6. Garifunas are black Caribs who settled along the Central American coast. According to Nancie González, "Although generally indistinguishable from other Afro-Americans, they are unusual in that they speak a South American Indian language and share about one-quarter of their genetic makeup with native Americans" (150). For an overview of this group in New York City, see Nancie González, "Garifuna Settlement in New York: A New Frontier," in *Caribbean Life in New York City: Sociocultural Dimensions*, ed. Constance R. Sutton and Elsa Chaney.

7. Altamirano, *Los que se fueron*, 24.

8. This thus illustrates Martha Giménez's point that "middle and upper-middle class immigrants are more likely to share the values of the dominant classes including class, racial and ethnic prejudices." Martha E. Giménez, "Minorities and the World-System," in *Racism, Sexism and the World-System*, ed. Smith et al., 49.

9. Murguia, "On Latino/Hispanic Ethnic Identity," 13.

10. See, for example, B. E. Aguirre and Rogelio Saenz, "A Futuristic Assessment of Latino Ethnic Identity," 99.

11. G. Moura, *Tio Sam chega ao Brasil: A penetração cultural americana* (São Paulo: Brasiliense, 1984); and Altamirano, *Los que se fueron*.

12. Marta Sotomayor, "Language, Culture and Ethnicity in Developing Self-Concept," 207-19; Stephen D. Krashen, *The Input Hypothesis*.

13. Fishman, " 'English Only,' " 131.

14. D. F. Marshall, "The Question of an Official Language: Language Rights and the English Language Amendment."

15. Again it is important to keep in mind the notion of social distance, as a result of which, in these interviews, "Americans" were understood as "white" English speakers.

16. Hoffman, *Lost In Translation*, 123-24.

17. See chapter 2.

18. For a nuanced analysis of different racial classifications adopted by various Latinos in the United States, see Clara E. Rodríguez, Aida Castro, Oscar Garcia, and Analisa Torres, "Latino Racial Identity: In the Eye of the Beholder?" See also Clara Rodríguez, *Puerto Ricans*, chap. 3.

Chapter 7. Imagined Communities Revisited

1. Eliana Ortega and Nancy Saporta Sternbach, "At the Threshhold of the Un-

named: Latina Literary Discourse in the Eighties," in *Breaking Boundaries: Latina Writings and Critical Readings*, ed. Asunción Horno-Delgado et al.

2. See Rina Benmayor et al., eds., *Responses to Poverty among Puerto Rican Women: Identity, Community and Cultural Citizenship*.

3. This argument is exemplified well in José David Saldívar, *The Dialectics of Our America: Genealogy, Cultural Critique, and Literary History*; Aguirre and Saenz, "A Futuristic Assessment of Latino Ethnic Identity"; Hayes-Bautista and Chapa, "Latino Terminology"; and Flores and Yudice, "Living Borders/Buscando America."

4. John Elliot, *The Old World and the New, 1492-1650*, 28.

5. Mario Benedetti, "Temas y Problemas," in *América Latína en su literatura*, ed. C. Fernandez Moreno, 357; my emphasis and translation.

6. Choldin, "Statistics and Politics."

7. Aguirre and Saenz, "A Futuristic Assessment of Latino Ethnic Identity," 19.

8. Giménez, " 'Latino/Hispanic'—Who Needs a Name?" and "Minorities and the World-System."

9. See, for example, Faye Ginsburg, *Contested Lives: The Abortion Debate in an American Community*, and George Marcus and Michael Fischer, *Anthropology as Cultural Critique*.

10. Rodolfo O. de la Garza et al., *Latino Voices*; Aguirre and Saenz, "A Futuristic Assessment of Latino Ethnic Identity"; and Flores and Yudice, "Living Borders/Buscando America."

11. Fusco, "The Latino 'Boom' in Hollywood," 50.

12. For a fuller examination of these differences, see the special issue edited by Edward Murguia and P. Cancilla Martinelli, "Latino/Hispanic Ethnic Identity," and the special issue edited by Martha E. Giménez, Fred A. López III, and Carlos Muñoz Jr., "The Politics of Ethnic Construction: Hispanic, Chicano, Latino. . .?" *Latin American Perspectives*, issue 75, vol. 19, no. 4 (Fall 1992).

13. Murguia, "On Latino/Hispanic Ethnic Identity," 11.

14. These differences are beginning to be explored in novels written by Latinos. For two recent and well-publicized examples, see Julia Alvarez, *How the García Girls Lost Their Accents*, and Cristina García, *Dreaming in Cuban*.

15. Fusco, "The Latino 'Boom' in Hollywood," 49.

16. Benmayor et al., *Responses to Poverty among Puerto Rican Women*.

17. Michael M. J. Fischer, "Ethnicity and the Post-Modern Arts of Memory," in *Writing Culture: The Poetics and Politics of Ethnography*, ed. James Clifford and George Marcus, 195.

18. Sollors, *Beyond Ethnicity*, 38.

19. Ramona Hernandez and Silvio Torres-Saillant, eds., special issue, "Minorities, Education, Empowerment," esp. 1-8.

20. Rosario Morales and Aurora Levins Morales, *Getting Home Alive*.

Selected Bibliography

Abramson, H. J. "Assimilation and Pluralism." In *Harvard Encyclopedia of American Ethnic Groups*, edited by Stephan Thernstrom, Ann Orlov, and Oscar Handlin, 150-60. Cambridge: Mass.: Harvard University Press, 1980.

Acosta-Belén, Edna. "From Settlers to Newcomers: The Hispanic Legacy in the United States." In *The Hispanic Experience in the United States*, edited by Edna Acosta-Belén and Barbara R. Sjostrom. New York: Praeger, 1988.

———. ed. *The Puerto Rican Woman: Perspectives on Culture, History and Society*. New York: Praeger, 1986.

Acosta-Belén, Edna, and Barbara R. Sjostrom, eds. *The Hispanic Experience in the United States*. New York: Praeger, 1988.

Acuña, Rodolfo. *Occupied America: A History of Chicanos*. 3rd ed. New York: Harper and Row, 1988.

Aguirre, B. E., and Rogelio Saenz. "A Futuristic Assessment of Latino Ethnic Identity." *Latino Studies Journal* 2, no. 3 (1991): 19-32.

Almaguer, Tomás. "Ideological Distortions in Recent Chicano Historiography: The Internal Model and Chicano Historical Interpretations." *Aztlán: A Journal of Chicano Studies* 18, no. 1 (1988-90): 7-28.

Altamirano, Teófilo. *Los que se fueron: Peruanos en Estados Unidos*. Lima: Fondo Editorial de la Pontífica Universidad Católica del Perú, 1988.

Alvarez, Julia. *How the García Girls Lost Their Accent*. New York: Plume, 1992.

Anaya, Rudolfo, and Francisco Lomelí. *Aztlán: Essays on the Chicano Homeland*. Albuquerque: University of New Mexico Press, 1991.

Anderson, Benedict. *Imagined Communities: Reflections on the Origin and Spread of Nationalism*. New York: Verso, 1983.

Anderson, Margaret, and Patricia Hill Collins. *Race, Class and Gender*. Belmont, Calif.: Wadsworth, 1992.

Año Nuevo Kerr, Louise. "Chicanas in the Great Depression." In *Between Borders: Essays on Mexicana/Chicana History*, edited by Adelaida R. del Castillo, 257-68. Encino, Calif.: Floricanto Press, 1990.

Anzaldúa, Gloria. *Borderlands/La Frontera: The New Mestiza*. San Francisco: Spinsters/ Aunt Lute, 1987.

———. "En Rapport, In Opposition: Cobrando cuentas a las nuestras." In *Making Face, Making Soul: Haciendo Caras: Creative and Critical Perspectives by Women of Color*, edited by Gloria Anzaldúa, 142-50. San Francisco: Aunt Lute, 1990.

Anzaldúa, Gloria, and Cherríe Moraga, eds. *This Bridge Called My Back: Writings by Radical Women of Color*. New York: Kitchen Table Press, 1983.

Arce, C. H., and A. Hurtado. "Mexicans, Chicanos, Mexican Americans, or Pochos . . . Que Somos? The Impact of Language and Nativity on Ethnic Labeling." *Aztlán: A Journal of Chicano Studies* 17 (1987): 103-30.

Arendt, Hannah. "Lawlessness Is Inherent in the Uprooted." *New York Times Magazine*, April 28, 1968.

Arguedas, José María. *Los ríos profundos*. Edited by William Rowe. Oxford: Pergamon Press, 1973.

Attinassi, J., Juan Flores, and Pedro Pedraza. "La Carreta Made a U-Turn: Puerto Rican Language and Culture in the United States." *Daedalus* 110, no. 2 (1981): 193-218.

Avilés, Amílcar Tirado. "La forja de un líder: Pedro Albizu Campos, 1924-1930." *Centro Bulletin* 4, no. 1 (Winter 1991-92): 24-33.

Baca Zinn, Maxine. "Political Familism: Toward Sex Role Equality in Chicano Families." *Aztlán: A Journal of Chicano Studies* 6, no. 1 (1975): 13-26.

_____. "Gender and Ethnic Identity among Chicanos." *Frontiers: A Journal of Women's Studies* 5, no. 2 (1980): 18-24.

Bach, Robert. "The New Cuban Immigrants: Their Background and Prospects." *Monthly Labor Review* 103, no. 10 (1980): 39-46.

Baker, Keith. "Ideological Bias in Bilingual Education Research." Paper presented at the American Educational Research Association Annual Meeting, New Orleans, La., April 23-27, 1984.

Baptista-Fernández, Patricia, and Bradley S. Greenberg. "Hispanic-Americans: The New Minority on Television." In *Life on Television: Content Analyses of U.S. Television Drama*, edited by Bradley S. Greenberg, 3-12. Norwood, N.J.: Ablex, 1980.

Barrera, Mario. *Race and Class in the Southwest: A Theory of Racial Inequality*. Notre Dame, Ind.: University of Notre Dame Press, 1979.

_____. *Beyond Aztlán: Ethnic Autonomy in Comparative Perspective*. Notre Dame, Ind.: University of Notre Dame Press, 1988.

Barrera, Mario, and Carlos Muñoz Jr. "La Raza Unida Party and the Chicano Student Movement in California." *Social Science Journal* 19, no. 2 (April 1982): 101-19.

Benedetti, Mario. "Temas y problemas." In *América Latina en su literatura*, edited by César Fernández Moreno. Mexico City: Siglo XXI, 1972.

Benmayor, Rina, Rosa M. Torruellas, and Ana L. Juarbe, eds., *Responses to Poverty among Puerto Rican Women: Identity, Community and Cultural Citizenship*. New York: Centro de Estudios Puertorriqueños, Hunter College, 1992.

Berkhofer, Robert. *The White Man's Indian: Images of the American Indian from Columbus to the Present*. New York: Knopf, 1978.

Bernstein, Basil. "Elaborated and Restricted Codes: Their Social Origins and Some Consequences." *American Anthropologist* 66, no. 2 (1964): 113-33.

Black, George. *Good Neighbor: How the United States Wrote the History of Central America and the Caribbean*. New York: Pantheon Books, 1988.

Blauner, Robert. *Racial Oppression in America*. New York: Harper and Row, 1972.

Blondet, Cecilia. "Establishing an Identity: Women Settlers in a Poor Lima Neighbourhood." Translated by J. A. Zammit and M. Thomson. In *Women and Social Change in Latin America*, edited by Elizabeth Jelin, 12-78. London and New Jersey: UNRIS/Zed Books, 1990.

Bolívar, Simón. *Para nosotros la patria es América*. Caracas: Biblioteca Ayacucho, 1991.

Bonilla, Frank. "Beyond Survival: Por que seguiremos siendo Puertorriqueños." In *The Puerto Ricans: Their History, Culture and Society*, edited by Adalberto López, 453-54. Cambridge: Schenkman Books, 1980.

_____. "Migrants, Citizenship and Social Pacts." *Radical America* 23, no. 1 (Jan.-Feb. 1989): 81-90.

Boswell, Thomas D., and James R. Curtis. *The Cuban-American Experience: Culture, Images and Perspectives*. Totowa, N.J.: Rowman and Allanheld, 1984.

Bradley, Sculley, et al., eds. *The American Tradition in Literature*. Vol. 1. New York: Grosset and Dunlap, 1974.

Brice Heath, Shirley, and Frederick Mandabach. "Language Status Decisions and the Law in the United States." In *Progress in Language Planning*, edited by Juan Corrubias and Joshua Fishman, 87-105. Berlin: Mouton, 1983.

Brown, S. E. "Love Unites Them and Hunger Separates Them: Poor Women in the Dominican Republic." In *Toward an Anthropology of Women*, edited by Rayna Rapp, 322-32. New York: Monthly Review Press, 1975.

Broyles, Yolanda J. "Women in El Teatro Campesino: ¿Apoco Estaba Molacha La Virgen de Guadalupe?" In *Chicana Voices: Intersections of Class, Race and Gender*, edited by National Association for Chicano Studies, 162-87. Colorado Springs, Colo.: National Association for Chicano Studies, 1990.

Bruckner, D. J. R., ed. *Politics and Language: Spanish and English in the United States*. Chicago: University of Chicago Center for Policy Study, 1980.

Burkholder, Mark, and Lyman Johnson. *Colonial Latin America*. New York: Oxford University Press, 1990.

Burns, Allan F. *Maya in Exile: Guatemalans in Florida*. Philadelphia: Temple University Press, 1993.

Butler, R. E. *On Creating an Hispanic America: A Nation within a Nation?* Special Report. Washington, D.C.: Council for Inter-American Security, 1986.

Cafferty, Pastora San Juan, and William C. McCready, eds. *Hispanics in the United States: A New Social Agenda*. New Brunswick, N.J.: Transaction Books, 1985.

Calderón, José. " 'Hispanic' and 'Latino': The Viability of Categories for Panethnic Unity." *Latin American Perspectives*, issue 75, vol. 19, no. 4 (Fall 1992): 37-44.

Calderón, Roberto R., and Emilio Zamora. "Manuela Solis Sager and Emma B. Tenayuca: A Tribute." In *Between Borders: Essays on Mexicana/Chicana History*, edited by Adelaida R. del Castillo, 269-80. Encino, Calif.: Floricanto Press, 1990.

Camarillo, Alberto. *Chicanos in a Changing Society*. Cambridge, Mass.: Harvard University Press, 1979.

Cantarow, Ellen, Susan Gushee O'Malley, and Sharon Hartman Strom, eds. *Moving the Mountain: Women Working for Social Change*. New York: Feminist Press, 1980.

Castro, Tony. *Chicano Power: The Emergence of Mexican America*. New York: Saturday Review Press, 1974.

Cazden, C. B., and C. E. Snow. *English Plus: Issues in Bilingual Education*. Annal of the American Academy of Political and Social Science. Newbery Park, Calif.: Sage, 1990.

Chaney, Elsa. "Colombians in New York City: Theoretical and Policy Issues." In *Sourcebook on the New Immigration: Implications for the U.S. and the International Community*, edited by R. Simon Bryce-Laporte, 285-94. New Brunswick, N.J.: Transaction Books, 1980.

Chávez, César. "The California Farm Workers' Struggle." *Black Scholar* 7, no. 9 (June 1976): 16-19.

Choldin, J. Harvey M. "Statistics and Politics: The 'Hispanic' Issue in the 1980 Census." *Demography* 23 (1986): 403-18.

Clifford, James, and George Marcus, eds. *Writing Culture: The Poetics and Politics of Ethnography*. Berkeley: University of California Press, 1986.

Cockcroft, James. *Outlaws in the Promised Land: Mexican Immigrant Workers and America's Future*. New York: Grove Weidenfeld, 1986.

Cortázar, J. *Rayuela*. Buenos Aires: Ed. Sudamericana, 1967.

Cortés, Carlos E. " 'Greaser's Revenge' to "Boulevard Nights.' " In *Chicano Studies in the 1980s*, edited by the National Association for Chicano Studies, 125-40. Mich.: Bilingual Press, 1983.

Cotera, Martha P. *The Chicana Feminist*. Austin, Tex.: Information Systems Development, 1974.

Crawford, James, ed. *Language Loyalties: A Source Book on the Official English Controversy.* Chicago: University of Chicago Press, 1992.

Cruse, Harold. *Plural but Equal: A Critical Study of Blacks and Minorities and America's Plural Society.* New York: Harper and Row, 1987.

Da Matta, Roberto R. "Do You Know Who You're Talking To?" In *Carnivals, Rogues and Heroes: An Anthropology of the Brazilian Dilemma,* Notre Dame, Ind.: University of Notre Dame Press, 1991.

Davis, Cary, Carl Haub, and JoAnne Willette. "U.S. Hispanics: Changing the Face of America." In *The Hispanic Experience in the United States,* edited by Edna Acosta-Belén and Barbara R. Sjostrom, 57-136. New York: Praeger, 1988.

de la Garza, Rodolfo O. "And Then There Were Some . . . : Chicanos as National Political Actors, 1967-1980." *Aztlán: A Journal of Chicano Studies* 15, no. 1 (Spring 1984): 1-23.

de la Garza, Rodolfo O., et al., eds. *The Mexican-American Experience.* Austin: University of Texas Press, 1985.

de la Garza, Rodolfo O., Louis deSipio, F. Chris García, John García, and Angelo Falcón. *Latino Voices: Mexican, Puerto Rican, and Cuban Perspectives on American Politics.* Boulder, Colo.: Westview Press, 1992.

de la Torre, Adela, and Beatríz Pesquera, eds. *Building with Our Hands: New Directions in Chicana Studies.* Berkeley: University of California Press, 1993.

del Castillo, Adelaida R., ed. *Between Borders: Essays on Mexicana/Chicana History.* Encino, Calif.: Floricanto Press, 1990.

de León, Arnoldo. *They Called Them Greasers: Anglo Attitudes toward Mexicans in Texas, 1821-1900.* Austin: University of Texas Press, 1983.

di Leonardo, Micaela. *The Varieties of Ethnic Experience: Kinship, Class, and Gender among California Italian-Americans.* Ithaca, N.Y.: Cornell University Press, 1984.

Deutsch, Sarah. *No Separate Refuge: Culture, Class, and Gender on an Anglo Hispanic Frontier in the American Southwest, 1880-1940.* New York: Oxford University Press, 1987.

Dinnerstein, Leonard, and David M. Reimers. *Ethnic Americans: A History of Immigration.* 3rd ed. New York: Harper and Row, 1988.

Dubovsky, M., and W. Van Tine, eds. *Labor Leaders in America.* Urbana: University of Illinois, 1987.

Elliot, John. *The Old World and the New, 1492-1650.* New York: Cambridge University Press, 1976.

Escobar, Edward. "The Dialectics of Repression: The Los Angeles Police Department and the Chicano Movement, 1968-1971." *Journal of American History* 74, no. 4 (March 1993): 1483-1504.

Estades, Rosa. *Patrones de participación política de los Puerto Riqueños en la ciudad de Nueva York.* Rio Piedras: University of Puerto Rico, Editorial Universitaria, 1978.

Fernández, Gastón, Beverly Nagel, and León Narvaez, eds. *Hispanic Migration and the United States: A Study in Politics.* Bristol, Ind.: Wyndham Hall Press, 1987.

Fernández-Kelly, María Patricia, and Alejandro Portes. "Continent on the Move: Immigrants and Refugees in the Americas." In *Americas: New Interpretive Essays,* edited by Alfred Stepan, 248-74. New York: Oxford University Press, 1992.

Fillmore, Lily Wong. "Against Our Best Interest: The Attempt to Sabotage Bilingual Education." In *Language Loyalties: A Source Book on the Official English Controversy,* edited by J. Crawford, 367-76. Chicago: University of Chicago Press, 1992.

Fischer, Michael M. J. "Ethnicity and the Post-Modern Arts of Memory." In *Writing Culture: The Poetics and Politics of Ethnography,* edited by James Clifford and George Marcus. Berkeley: University of California Press, 1986.

Fishman, Joshua. *Language Loyalty in the United States.* The Hague: Mouton, 1966.

_____. *The Rise and Fall of the Ethnic Revival.* The Hague: Mouton, 1985.

_____. " 'English Only': Its Ghosts, Myths and Dangers." *International Journal of the Sociology of Language* 74 (1988): 125-40.

Fitzpatrick, Joseph. *Puerto Ricans: The Meaning of Migration to the Mainland.* Englewood Cliffs, N.J.: Prentice-Hall, 1971.

Flores, Francisca. "Conference of Mexican Women, Un Remolino." *Regeneración* 1, no. 10 (1971).

Flores, Juan. " 'Que Assimilated, Brother, Yo soy asimilao': The Structuring of Puerto Rican Identity in the U.S." *Journal of Ethnic Studies* 13, no. 3 (1985): 1-16.

Flores, Juan, and George Yudice. "Living Borders/Buscando América: Languages of Latino Self-Formation." *Social Text* 24 (1990): 57-84.

Foerster, Robert F. *The Racial Problems Involved in Immigration from Latin America and the West Indies to the United States.* Washington, D.C.: Government Printing Office, 1925.

Foner, Nancy, ed. *New Immigrants in New York.* New York: Columbia University Press, 1987.

Forbes, Jack D. "The Hispanic Spin: Party Politics and Governmental Manipulation of Ethnic Identity." *Latin American Perspectives,* issue 75, vol. 19, no. 4 (Fall 1992): 59-78.

Fraticelli, Carlos Rodriguez. "Pedro Albizu Campos: Strategies of Struggle and Strategic Struggles." *Centro Bulletin* 4, no. 1 (Winter 1991-92): 24-33.

Fuentes, Annette, and Barbara Ehrenreich. *Women in the Global Factory.* Boston: Institute for New Communications/South End Press, 1983.

Fuentes, Carlos. *Latin America at War with the Past.* Montreal: CBC Massey Lectures Series, 1985.

_____. *El espejo enterrado.* Mexico City: Fondo de Cultura Económica, 1992.

Fusco, Coco. "The Latino 'Boom' in Hollywood." *Centro* 2, no. 8 (Spring 1990): 48-56.

Galarza, Ernesto, Hermán Gallegos, and Julián Samora. *Mexican Americans in the Southwest.* Santa Barbara, Calif.: McNally and Loftin, 1970.

Galeano, Eduardo. *Open Veins of Latin America: Five Centuries of the Pillage of a Continent.* New York: Monthly Review Press, 1978.

García, Alma M. "The Development of Chicana Feminist Discourse, 1970-1980." *Gender and Society* 3 (1989): 217-38.

García, Cristina. *Dreaming in Cuban.* New York: Knopf, 1992.

García, F. Chris, ed. *Latinos and the Political System.* Notre Dame, Ind.: Notre Dame University Press, 1988.

García, Mario. *Desert Immigrants: The Mexicans of El Paso.* New Haven, Conn.: Yale University Press, 1981.

_____. *Mexican Americans: Leadership, Ideology and Identity, 1930-1960.* New Haven, Conn.: Yale University Press, 1989.

García Márquez, Gabriel. *El general en su laberinto.* Madrid: Mondadori, 1989.

Gardner, Richard. *Grito! Reies Tijerina and the New Mexico Land Grant War of 1967.* New York: Bobbs-Merrill, 1970.

Giménez, Martha E. "Minorities and the World-System: Theoretical and Political Implications of the Internationalization of Minorities." In *Racism, Sexism and the World-System,* edited by J. Smith et al., 39-56. Westport, Conn.: Greenwood Press, 1988.

_____. " 'Latino/Hispanic'—Who Needs a Name? The Case against a Standardized Terminology." *International Journal of Health Services* 19, no. 3 (1989): 557-71.

_____. "U.S. Ethnic Politics: Implications for Latin Americans." *Latin American Perspectives,* issue 75, vol. 19, no. 4 (1992): 7-17.

Giménez, Martha E., Fred A. López III, and Carlos Muñoz, eds. "The Politics of Ethnic Construction: Hispanic, Chicano, Latino . . . ?" Special issue of *Latin American Perspectives,* issue 75, vol. 19, no. 4 (Fall 1992).

Ginsburg, Faye. *Contested Lives: The Abortion Debate in an American Community*. Berkeley: University of California Press, 1989.

Giordano, J., and D. Torres, eds. *La identidad cultural de Hispanoamerica: Discusión actual*. Santiago de Chile: Monografias del Maitén, 1986.

Glazer, Nathan, ed. *Ethnic Dilemmas, 1964-1982*. Cambridge, Mass.: Harvard University Press, 1983.

Glazer, Nathan, and Daniel Moynihan. *Beyond the Melting Pot: The Negroes, Puerto Ricans, Jews, Italians and Irish in New York City*. Cambridge, Mass.: MIT Press, 1970.

Glick Schiller, Nina, Linda Basch, and Cristina Blanc-Szanton, eds. *Towards a Transnational Perspective on Migration: Race, Class, Ethnicity and Nationalism Reconsidered*. Vol. 645. New York: New York Academy of Sciences, 1992.

Gómez, Laura E. "The Birth of the 'Hispanic' Generation: Attitudes of Mexican-American Political Elites toward the Hispanic Label." *Latin American Perspectives*, issue 75, 19, no. 4 (Fall 1992): 45-58.

Gómez-Peña, Guillermo. "Documented/Undocumented." In *The Graywolf Annual Five: Multi-Cultural Literacy*, edited by Rick Simonson and Scott Walker, 127-34. Saint Paul, Minn.: Graywolf Press, 1988.

Gómez Quiñones, Juan. *Chicano Politics: Reality and Promise, 1940-1990*. Albuquerque: University of New Mexico Press, 1991.

Gonzáles, Manuel G. *The Hispanic Elite of the Southwest*. Southwestern Studies, no. 86. El Paso: Texas Western Press, 1989.

Gonzáles, Rudolfo. "Chicano Nationalism: The Key to Unity for La Raza." In *Chicano: The Evolution of a People*, edited by Renato Rosaldo, Robert Calvert, and Gustav Seligman, 424-25. Minneapolis: Winston Press, 1973.

González, José Luis. *Puerto Rico: The Four Storeyed Country*. Maplewood, N.J.: Waterfront Press, 1990.

González, Juan, et al. *The Ideology of the Young Lords Party*, New York, 1972.

González, Nancie. *The Spanish Americans of New Mexico: A Distinctive Heritage*. Los Angeles: UCLA, Mexican-American Study Project, 1967.

———. "Garifuna Settlement in New York: A New Frontier." In *Caribbean Life in New York City: Sociocultural Dimensions*, edited by C. R. Sutton and E. Chaney. Staten Island, N.Y.: Center for Migration Studies of New York, 1987.

Gordon, Milton. *Assimilation in American Life*. New York: Oxford University Press, 1964.

Governor's Advisory Committee for Hispanic Affairs. *New York State Hispanics: A Challenging Minority*. Albany: New York State Government, 1986.

Graham, Richard, ed. *The Idea of Race in Latin America, 1870-1940*. Austin: University of Texas Press, 1990.

Greeley, Andrew. *Why Can't They Be Like Us? America's White Ethnic Groups*. New York: Dutton, 1971.

Greer, Stephen. "The Ethnic Question." In *The Sixties, without Apology*, edited by Sohnya Sayres, Anders Stephanson, Stanley Aronowitz, and Fredric Jameson, 119-36. Minneapolis: University of Minnesota Press, 1984.

Griswold del Castillo, Richard. *La Familia: Chicano Families in the Urban Southwest, 1848 to the Present*. Notre Dame, Ind.: University of Notre Dame Press, 1984.

———. *The Treaty of Guadalupe Hidalgo: A Legacy of Conflict*. Norman: University of Oklahoma Press, 1990.

Grossberg, Lawrence, Nelson Cary, and Paula Treichler, eds. *Cultural Studies*. New York: Routledge, 1992.

Gutiérrez, Ramón. *When Jesus Came, the Corn Mothers Went Away: Marriage, Sexuality, and Power in New Mexico, 1500-1846*. Stanford, Calif.: Stanford University Press, 1991.

―――. "Community, Patriarchy and Individualism: The Politics of Chicano History and the Dream of Equality." *American Quarterly* 45, no. 1 (March 1993): 44-72.

Hall, Stuart. "Encoding/Decoding." In *Culture, Media, Language*, edited by Stuart Hall, 128-38. Birmingham, Ala.: Center for Contemporary Cultural Studies/Hutchinson Press, 1980.

Hammerback, John C., Richard Jensen, and José Angel Gutiérrez. *A War on Words*. Westport, Conn.: Greenwood Press, 1985.

Hayes-Bautista, David E., and Jorge Chapa. "Latino Terminology: Conceptual Basis for Standardized Terminology." *American Journal of Public Health* 77 (1987): 61-68.

Hernández, Leticia. "Chicanas Identify." *Regeneración* 1, no. 10 (1971).

Hernández, Ramona, and Silvio Torres-Saillant, eds. "Minorities, Education, Empowerment." *Punto 7 Review: A Journal of Marginal Discourse* 2, no. 2 (Fall 1992).

History Task Force, Centro de Estudios Puertorriqueños. *Labor Migration under Capitalism: The Puerto Rican Experience*. New York: Monthly Review Press, 1979.

Hobsbawm, Eric. "Mass-Producing Traditions: Europe, 1879-1914." In *The Invention of Tradition*, edited by Eric Hobsbawm and Terence Ranger, 263-308. New York: Cambridge University Press, 1983.

―――. *The Age of Empire, 1875-1914*. New York: Vintage Books, 1989.

Hoffman, Eva. *Lost in Translation: A Life in a New Language*. New York: Penguin Books, 1989.

Horno-Delgado, Asunción, Elena Ortega, Nina M. Scott, and Nancy Saporta Sternbach, eds. *Breaking Boundaries: Latina Writings and Critical Readings*. Amherst: University of Massachusetts Press, 1989.

Horseman, Reginald. *Race and Manifest Destiny: The Origins of American Racial Anglo-Saxonism*. Cambridge, Mass.: Harvard University Press, 1981.

Huerta, Dolores. "Dolores Huerta Talks: About Republicans, Cesar, Her Children and Her Home Town." *Regeneración* 2, no. 4 (1975): 20-24.

Jameson, Fredric. "Periodizing the Sixties." In *The Sixties, without Apology*, edited by Sohnya Sayres, Anders Stephanson, Stanley Aronowitz, and Fredric Jameson, 178-209. Minneapolis: University of Minnesota Press, 1984.

Jezer, Marty. *The Dark Ages: Life in the United States, 1945-1960*. Boston: South End Press, 1982.

Jorge, Angela. "The Black Puerto Rican Woman in Contemporary American Society." In *The Puerto Rican Woman: Perspectives on Culture, History and Society*, edited by Edna Acosta-Belén and Barbara R. Sjostrom, 180-81. New York: Praeger, 1986.

Kane, Michael B. *Minorities in Textbooks*. Chicago: Quadrangle Books/Anti-Defamation League of B'nai B'rith, 1970.

Keller, Gary, and K. S. Van Hooft. "A Chronology of Bilingualism and Bilingual Education in the United States." In *Bilingual Education for Hispanic Students in the U.S.A.*, edited by Joshua Fishman and Gary Keller, 3-19. New York: Teachers College, Columbia University, 1982.

Keller, Gary D., ed. *Chicano Cinema: Research, Reviews and Resources*. New York: Bilingual Press, 1985.

Kessner, Thomas. *The Golden Door: Italian and Jewish Immigrant Mobility in New York City, 1880-1915*. New York: Oxford University Press, 1977.

King, Richard. *Civil Rights and the Idea of Freedom*. New York: Oxford University Press, 1992.

Klor de Alva, J. Jorge. "Telling Hispanics Apart: Latino Sociocultural Diversity." In *The Hispanic Experience in the United States: Contemporary Issues and Perspectives*, edited by Edna Acosta-Belén and Barbara R. Sjostrom, 107-36. New York: Praeger, 1988.

_____. "Aztlán, Borinquen and Hispanic Nationalism in the United States." In *Aztlán: Essays on the Chicano Homeland*, edited by Rudolfo A. Anaya and Francisco Lomelí. Albuquerque: University of New Mexico Press, 1991.

Kluger, Richard. *Simple Justice: The History of Brown v. Board of Education and Black America's Struggle for Education*. New York: Vintage Books, 1977.

Krashen, Stephen. *The Input Hypothesis*. London: Longman, 1985.

Kutner, Peter B. "Keyes v. School District Number One: A Constitutional Right to Equal Educational Opportunity?" *Journal of Law Education* 8 (1979): 1-40.

LaFeber, Walter. *Inevitable Revolutions: The United States in Central America*. New York: Norton, 1984.

Laguerre, Michel S. *American Odyssey: Haitians in New York City*. Ithaca, N.Y.: Cornell University Press, 1984.

Leach, Edmund. *Political Systems of Highland Burma*. Boston: Beacon Press, 1959.

Leacock, E., and H. I. Safa, eds. *Women's Work: Development and the Division of Labor by Gender*. South Hadley, Mass.: Bergin and Garvin, 1986.

Leal, Luis. "In Search of Aztlán." In *Aztlán: Essays on the Chicano Homeland*, edited by Rudolfo Anaya and Francisco Lomelí, 6-14. Albuquerque: University of New Mexico Press, 1991.

Leitch, M. L., and L. Leslie. "A Demographic Profile of Recent Central American Immigrants: Clinical and Service Implications." *Hispanic Journal of Behavioral Sciences* 4 (November 1989): 315-29.

Lewis, Gordon K. *Notes on the Puerto Rican Revolution: An Essay on American Dominance and Caribbean Resistance*. New York: Monthly Review Press, 1974.

Lewis, Oscar. *La Vida: A Puerto Rican Family in the Culture of Poverty*. New York: Random House, 1966.

Limón, José E. *Mexican Ballads, Chicano Poems: History and Influence in Mexican-American Social Poetry*. Berkeley: University of California Press, 1992.

López, Adalberto. "The Puerto Rican Diaspora: A Survey." In *The Puerto Ricans: Their History, Culture and Society*, edited by Adalberto López, 313-44. Cambridge: Schenkman Books, 1980.

_____, ed. *The Puerto Ricans: Their History, Culture and Society*. Cambridge: Schenkman Books, 1980.

López, Alfredo. *Doña Licha's Island: Modern Colonialism in Puerto Rico*. Boston: South End Press, 1987.

López, Fred. "Reflections on the Chicano Movement." *Latin American Perspectives*, issue 75, vol. 19, no. 4 (Fall 1992): 79-102.

López de la Cruz, Jessie. "The Battle for Farmworkers' Rights." In *Moving the Mountain: Women Working for Social Change*, edited by Ellen Cantarow, with Susan Gushee O'Malley and Sharon Hartman Strom, 95-151. New York: Feminist Press, 1980.

Lowry, Ira S. "The Science and Politics of Ethnic Enumeration." In *Ethnicity and Public Policy*, edited by Winston Van Horne, 42-46. Madison: University of Wisconsin System, 1982.

Lucas, Isidro. "Political Demands of Spanish-speaking Communities in the United States." In *Politics and Language: Spanish and English in the United States*, ed. D. J. R. Bruckner, 133-54. Chicago: University of Chicago Center for Policy Study, 1980.

Luciano, Felipe. "The Young Lords Party." *Caribe* 7, no. 4 (1983).

MacEwen, A. "The Current Crisis in Latin America and the International Economy." *Monthly Review* 36 (1985): 1-17.

McWilliams, Carey. *North from Mexico: The Spanish Speaking People of the United States*. New York: Praeger, 1990.

Maldonado-Denis, Manuel. *The Emigration Dialectic: Puerto Rico and the USA.* New York: International Publishers, 1980.

Marable, Manning. *Race, Reform and Rebellion: The Second Reconstruction in Black America, 1945-1990.* Jackson: University Press of Mississippi, 1991.

Marcus, George, and Michael Fischer. *Anthropology as Cultural Critique.* Chicago: University of Chicago Press, 1986.

Marshall, A. "Emigration of Argentines to the United States." In *When Borders Don't Divide: Labor Migration and Refugee Movements in the Americas,* edited by Patricia Pessar, 129-41. Staten Island, N.Y.: Center for Migration Studies, 1988.

Marshall, D. F. "The Question of an Official Language: Language Rights and the English Language Amendment." *International Journal of the Sociology of Language* 60 (1986): 7-75.

Martí, José. *Páginas Escogidas,* edited by Roberto Fernández Retamar. Havana, 1985.

Martínez, Elizabeth. "Histories of 'the Sixties': A Certain Absence of Color." *Social Justice* 16, no. 4 (Winter 1989): 175-84.

Mattheisen, Peter. *Sal si puedes.* New York: Random House, 1969.

Matute-Bianchi, Maria Eugenia. "The Federal Mandate for Bilingual Education." In *Bilingual Education and Public Policy in the United States I,* edited by R. Padilla. Ypsilanti: Eastern Michigan University, 1979.

Meister, Dick, and Anne Loftis. *A Long Time Coming: The Struggle to Unionize America's Farm Workers.* New York: Macmillan, 1977.

Meléndez, Edwin, and Edgardo Meléndez, eds. *Colonial Dilemma: Critical Perspectives on Contemporary Puerto Rico.* Boston: South End Press, 1993.

Melville, Margarita. "Hispanics: Race, Class, or Ethnicity?" *Journal of Ethnic Studies* 16, no. 1 (Spring 1988): 67-83.

Mercer, Kobena. " '1968': Periodizing Politics and Identity." In *Cultural Studies,* edited by Lawrence Grossberg, Nelson Cary, and Paula Treichler, 424-49. New York: Routledge, 1992.

Mishler, Elliot G. *Research Interviewing: Context and Narrative.* Boston: Harvard University Press, 1986.

Mitchell, J., ed. *The Social Craft of Anthropology.* London: Tavistock Publishers, 1979.

Mitchell, W. J. T., ed. *On Narrative.* Chicago: University of Chicago Press, 1981.

Montejano, David. *Anglos and Mexicans in the Making of Texas, 1836-1986.* Austin: University of Texas Press, 1987.

Moore, Deborah Dash. *Home in America: Second Generation New York Jews.* New York: Columbia University Press, 1981.

Moore, Joan. *Mexican Americans.* Englewood Cliffs, N.J.: Prentice-Hall, 1976.

———. "Minorities in the American Class System." In *Majority and Minority: The Dynamics of Race and Ethnicity in American Life,* edited by Norman R. Yetman, 278-85. Boston: Allyn and Bacon, 1985.

Moore, Joan, and Harry Pachon. *Hispanics in the United States.* Englewood Cliffs, N.J.: Prentice-Hall, 1985.

Mora, Carl J. "Americans of Hispanic Origin." *New York Times,* letter to the editor, February 25, 1985.

Moraga, Cherríe. *Loving in the War Years: Lo que nunca pasó por sus labios.* Boston: South End Press, 1983.

Morales, Rosario, and Aurora Levins Morales. *Getting Home Alive.* Ithaca, N.Y.: Firebrand Books, 1989.

Moreno, María. "Before Delano ... 'I'm Talking for Justice.' " *Regeneración* 1, no. 10 (1971).

Morgan, Edward P. *The 60s Experience: Hard Lessons about Modern America*. Philadelphia: Temple University Press, 1991.

Morley, David. "Texts, Readers, Subjects." In *Culture, Media, Language*, edited by Stuart Hall, 163-73. Birmingham, Ala.: Center for Contemporary Cultural Studies/ Hutchinson Press, 1980.

Morner, Magnus. *Race Mixture in the History of Latin America*. Boston: Little, Brown, 1967.

Morse, Richard. "The Heritage of Latin America." In *The Founding of New Societies*, edited by L. Hartz, 123-77. New York: Harcourt, Brace and World, 1964.

Moura, G. *Tio Sam chega ao Brasil: A penetração cultural americana*. São Paulo: Brasiliense, 1984.

Moynihan, Daniel. *Counting Our Blessings: Reflections on the Future of America*. Boston: Little, Brown, 1980.

Muga, David. "Academic Sub-Cultural Theory and the Problematic of Ethnicity: A Tentative Critique." *Journal of Ethnic Studies* 12, no. 1 (1984): 1-51.

Muñoz, Carlos. *Youth, Identity, Power: The Chicano Movement*. London: Verso, 1989.

Murguia, Edward. "On Latino/Hispanic Ethnic Identity." *Latino Studies Journal* 2, no. 3 (September 1991): 8-18.

Murguia, Edward, and P. Cancilla Martinelli, eds. "Latino/Hispanic Ethnic Identity." *Latino Studies Journal* 2, no. 3 (1991).

Murphy, Jean. "Unsung Heroine of La Causa." *Regeneración* 1, no. 10 (1971): 20.

Nash, Julie, and María Patricia Fernández-Kelly, eds. *Women, Men and the International Division of Labor*. Albany: State University of New York Press: 1983.

National Advisory Commission on Civil Disorders. *The Kerner Report, 1968*. New York: Bantam Books, 1974.

Navar, Isabelle. "La Mexicana: An Image of Strength." *Regeneración* 1, no. 10 (1975).

Nelson, C., and Marta Tienda. "The Structuring of Hispanic Identity." *Ethnic and Racial Studies* 8, no. 1 (1985): 49-74.

Noriega, Chon, ed. *Chicanos and Film: Representation and Resistance*. Minneapolis: University of Minnesota Press, 1992.

Novak, Michael. *The Rise of the Unmeltable Ethnics*. New York: Macmillan, 1971.

Oddone, Juan A. "Regionalismo y nacionalismo." In *América Latina en sus ideas*, edited by Leopoldo Zea, 201-38. Mexico City: Siglo XXI Editores/UNESCO, 1987.

Omi, Michael, and Howard Winant. *Racial Formation in the United States: From the 1960s to the 1980s*. New York: Routledge and Kegan Paul, 1986.

Orlov, Ann, and Reed Ueda. "Central and South Americans." In *Harvard Encyclopedia of American Ethnic Groups*, edited by Stephan Thernstrom, Ann Orlov, and Oscar Handlin, 210-17. Cambridge, Mass: Harvard University Press, 1980.

Ortega, Eliana, and Nancy Saporta Sternbach. "At the Threshhold of the Unnamed: Latina Literary Discourse in the Eighties." In *Breaking Boundaries: Latina Writings and Critical Readings*, edited by Asunción Horno-Delgado, Eliana Ortega, Nina M. Scott, and Nancy Saporta Sternbach, 2-18. Amherst: University of Massachusetts Press, 1989.

Ortiz, Renato. *Cultura e identidade nacional*. São Paulo: Editora Brasiliense, 1986.

Oxford Analytica. *America in Perspective*. Boston: Houghton Mifflin, 1986.

Padilla, Amado. "Bilingual Schools: Gateways to Integration or Roads to Separation." *Bilingual Review* 4 (1977): 52-67.

Padilla, Félix. *Latino Ethnic Consciousness: The Case of Mexican Americans and Puerto Ricans in Chicago*. Notre Dame, Ind.: University of Notre Dame Press, 1985.

Padilla, R., ed. *Bilingual Education and Public Policy in the United States*. Ypsilanti: Eastern Michigan University, 1979.

Paoli, María Celia. "Citizenship, Inequalities, Democracy and Rights: The Making of a Public Space in Brazil." *Social and Legal Studies* 1 (1992): 143-59.

Paredes, Américo. *"With His Pistol in His Hand": A Border Ballad and Its Hero.* Austin: University of Texas Press, 1973.

Paz, Octavio. *Labyrinth of Solitude: Life and Thought in Mexico.* New York: Grove Press, 1961.

Pedraza-Bailey, Silvia. *Political and Economic Migrants in America: Cubans and Mexicans.* Austin: University of Texas Press, 1985.

_____. "Cuban Political Immigrants and Mexican Economic Immigrants: The Role of Government Policy in Their Assimilation." In *Hispanic Migration and the United States: A Study in Politics,* edited by G. Fernandez, B. Nagel, and L. Narvaez, 68-101. Bristol, Ind.: Wyndham Hall Press, 1987.

_____. "Cuba's Exiles: Portrait of a Refugee Migration." *International Migration Review* 19, no. 1 (1987): 4-33.

Pérez, David. *Long Road from Lares: An Oral History.* New York: Community Documentation Workshop, 1979.

Pérez, Ricardo. "La marcha de la reconquista." *Regeneración* 2, no. 1.

Pérez, Richie. "From Assimilation to Annihilation: Puerto Rican Images in U.S. Films." *Centro Bulletin* 2, no. 8 (Spring 1990): 8-27.

Perkinson, Henry. *The Imperfect Panacea: American Faith in Education, 1865-1976.* New York: Random House, 1977.

Pesquera, Beatríz, and Denise Segura. "Beyond Indifference and Antipathy: The Chicana Movement and Chicana Feminist Discourse." *Aztlán: A Journal of Chicano Studies* 19, no. 2 (Fall 1988-90): 69-92.

Pessar, Patricia R. "The Dominicans: Women in the Household and the Garment Industry." In *New Immigrants in New York,* edited by Nancy Foner, 103-30. New York: Columbia University Press, 1987.

_____, ed. *When Borders Don't Divide: Labor Migration and Refugee Movements in the Americas.* Staten Island, N.Y.: Center for Migration Studies, 1988.

Pessar, Patricia, and Sherri Grasmuck. *Between Two Islands: Dominican International Migration.* Berkeley: University of California Press, 1991.

Petersen, William. "A General Typology of Migration." *American Sociological Review* 23 (1958): 256-66.

Petersen, William, Michael Novak, and Phillip Gleason. *Concepts of Ethnicity.* Cambridge, Mass.: Harvard University Press, Belknap Press, 1982.

Pietri, Pedro. *Puerto Rican Obituary.* New York: Monthly Review Press, 1973.

Piore, Michael. *Birds of Passage: Migrant Labor and Industrial Societies.* New York: Cambridge University Press, 1979.

Pitt, Leonard. *The Decline of the Californios: A Social History of the Spanish-Speaking Californians, 1846-1890.* Berkeley: University of California Press, 1966.

Portes, Alejandro. "From South of the Border: Hispanic Minorities in the United States." In *Immigration Reconsidered: History, Sociology, and Politics,* edited by Virginia Yans-McLauglin, 160-86. New York: Oxford University Press, 1990.

Portes, Alejandro, and Robert L. Bach. *Latin Journey: Cuban and Mexican Immigrants in the United States.* Berkeley: University of California Press, 1985.

Portocarrero, P., ed. *Mujer en desarrollo: Balance y propuestas.* Lima: Flora Tristán, 1990.

Potler, C. *State of the Prisons: Conditions inside the Walls.* New York: Correctional Association of New York, 1986.

Puerto Rican Revolutionary Workers Organization and Young Lords Party. "Resolutions and Speeches: First Congress." November 1972.

Rama, Angel. *Transculturación narrativa en América Latína*. Mexico City: Siglo XXI Editores, 1982.

Rapp, Rayna, ed. *Toward an Anthropology of Women*. New York: Monthly Review Press, 1975.

Reimers, David. "An Unintended Reform: The 1965 Immigration Act and Third World Immigration to the United States." *Journal of American Ethnic History* 3, no.1 (1983): 9-25.

Ringer, Benjamin. *"We the People" and Others: Duality and America's Treatment of Its Racial Minorities*. London: Tavistock, 1983.

Rodrigues, Arakcy Martins. *Operário, Operária*. São Paulo: Editora Símbolo, 1978.

Rodríguez, Clara E. *Puerto Ricans: Born in the U.S.A.* Boston: Unwin Hyman, 1989.

Rodríguez, Clara E., Aida Castro, Oscar Garcia, and Analisa Torres. "Latino Racial Identity: In the Eye of the Beholder?" *Latino Studies Journal* 2, no. 3 (September 1991): 33-48.

Rodríguez, Clara E., Virginia Sánchez Korrol, and José Oscar Alers, eds. *The Puerto Rican Struggle: Essays on Survival in the United States*. New York: Puerto Rican Migration Research Consortium, 1980.

_____. *Mexicano Resistance in the Southwest: The Sacred Right of Self-Preservation*. Austin: University of Texas Press, 1981.

Rodríguez-Morazzani, Roberto P. "Puerto Rican Political Generations in New York: Pioneros, Young Turks and Radicals." *Centro Bulletin* 4, no. 1 (Winter 1991): 102-7.

Rogg, Eleanor Meyer. *The Assimilation of Cuban Exiles: The Role of Community and Class*. New York: Aberdeen Press, 1974.

Romano-V. Octavio. "The Anthropology and Sociology of the Mexican-Americans." In *Voices: Readings from El Grito*, edited by Octavio I. Romano-V., 26-39. Berkeley, Calif.: Quinto Sol, 1973.

Romo, Ricardo. *East Los Angeles: History of a Barrio*. Austin: University of Texas Press, 1981.

Rosaldo, Renato, Robert Calvert, and Gustav Seligman, eds. *Chicano: The Evolution of a People*. Minneapolis: Winston Press, 1973.

Rose, Margaret. "Traditional and Non-traditional Patterns of Female Activism in the United Farm Workers of America, 1962-1980." *Frontiers* 11, no. 1 (1990): 26-30.

Rose, Michael. *Lives on the Boundary*. New York: Penguin Books, 1989.

Rosenbaum, Robert. "Las Gorras Blancas of San Miguel County, 1884-1890." In *Chicano: The Evolution of a People*, edited by Renato Rosaldo, Robert Calvert, and Gustav Seligman, 128-36. Minneapolis: Winston Press, 1973.

_____. *Mexicano Resistance in the Southwest: The Sacred Right of Self-Preservation*. Austin: University of Texas Press, 1981.

Rouse, Roger. "Mexican Migration and the Social Space of Postmodernism." *Diaspora* 1, no. 1 (Spring 1991): 8-23.

Rout, Leslie B. *The African Experience in Spanish America, 1512 to the Present*. New York: Cambridge University Press, 1976.

Rubbo, Anne. "The Spread of Capitalism in Rural Colombia: Effects on Poor Women." In *Toward an Anthropology of Women*, edited by Rayna Rapp, 333-57. New York: Monthly Review Press, 1975.

Rubin, Lillian B. *Worlds of Pain*. New York: Basic Books, 1979.

Ruiz, Vicki L. *Cannery Women, Cannery Lives: Mexican Women, Unionization, and the California Food Processing Industry, 1930-1950*. Albuquerque: University of New Mexico Press, 1987.

_____. "Oral History and La Mujer: The Rosa Guerrero Story." In *Women on the U.S.-Mexico Border: Responses to Change*, edited by Vicki L. Ruiz and Susan Tiano, 219-30. Boston: Allen and Unwin, 1987.

———. " 'Star Struck': Acculturation, Adolescence, and the Mexican American Woman, 1920-1950." In *Building with Our Hands: New Directions in Chicana Studies*, edited by Adela de la Torre and Beatríz Pesquera. Berkeley: University of California Press, 1993.

Ruiz, Vicki, and Susan Tiano, eds. *Women on the U.S.-Mexico Border: Responses to Change*. Boston: Allen and Unwin, 1987.

Rumbaut, Rubén G. "The Americans: Latin American and Caribbean Peoples in the United States." In *Americas: New Interpretive Essays*, edited by Alfred Stepan, 275-307. New York: Oxford University Press, 1992.

Saldívar, José David. *The Dialectics of Our America: Genealogy, Cultural Critique, and Literary History*. Durham, N.C.: Duke University Press, 1991.

San Juan, E., Jr. *Racial Formations/Critical Transformations: Articulations of Power in Ethnic and Racial Studies in the United States*, Atlantic Highlands, N.J.: Humanities Press, 1992.

San Miguel, Guadalupe, Jr. "Conflict and Controversy in the Evolution of Bilingual Education in the United States—An Interpretation." In *The Mexican-American Experience*, edited by Rodolfo O. de la Garza et al., 267-79. Austin: University of Texas Press, 1985.

———. *"Let All of Them Take Heed": Mexican Americans and the Campaign for Educational Equality in Texas, 1910-1981*. Austin: University of Texas Press, 1987.

Sánchez Korrol, Virginia. *From Colonia to Community: History of Puerto Ricans in New York City, 1917-1948*. Westport, Conn.: Greenwood Press, 1983.

———. "Latinismo among Early Puerto Rican Migrants in New York City: A Sociohistoric Interpretation." In *The Hispanic Experience in the United States: Contemporary Issues and Perspectives*, edited by Edna Acosta-Belén and Barbara R. Sjostrom, 151-63. New York: Praeger, 1988.

Sánchez-Tranquilino, Marcos. "Mano a Mano: An Essay on the Representation of the Zoot Suit and Its Misrepresentation by Octavio Paz," *Journal*, Los Angeles Institute of Contemporary Art, Winter 1987, 34-42.

Sandoval Sánchez, Alberto. "Una lectura puertorriqueña de la América de West Side Story." *Cupey* 7 (1990): 30-45.

———. "La identidad especular del allá y del acá: Nuestra propia imagen puertorriqueña en cuestión." *Centro Bulletin* 4, no. 2 (Spring 1992): 28-43.

Santiago, Isaura S. *A Community's Struggle for Equal Educational Opportunity: Aspira v. Board of Ed*. N.J.: Office for Minority Educational Testing Services, 1978.

Saragoza, Alex M. "Recent Chicano Historiography: An Interpretive Essay." *Aztlán: A Journal of Chicano Studies* 19, no. 1 (Spring 1988-90): 1-78.

Sassen, Saskia. *The Mobility of Labor and Capital: A Study in International Investment and Labor Flow*. New York: Cambridge University Press, 1988.

Sayres, Sohnya, Anders Stephanson, Stanley Aronowitz, and Fredric Jameson, eds. *The Sixties, without Apology*. Minneapolis: University of Minnesota Press, 1984.

Scott, Joan. "Experience." In *Feminists Theorize the Political*, edited by Judith Butler and Joan Wallach Scott. New York: Routledge, 1992.

Seda Bonilla, Eduardo. "El problema de la identidad de los Niuyorricans." *Revista de Ciencias Sociales* 16, no. 4 (December 1972).

Seidner, Stanley. *Political Expedience or Educational Research: An Analysis of Baker and Dekanter's Review of the Literature of Bilingual Education*. Mimeograph. Virginia: National Clearinghouse for Bilingual Education, 1982.

Shorris, Earl. *Latinos!* New York: Norton, 1992.

Simmen, Edward, ed. *Pain and Promise: The Chicano Today*. New York: Mentor Books, 1972.

Smith, J., et al., eds. *Racism, Sexism and the World-System*. Westport, Conn.: Greenwood Press, 1988.

Sollors, Werner. *Beyond Ethnicity: Consent and Descent in American Culture*. New York: Oxford University Press, 1986.

Soto, Pedro Juan. *Spiks*. New York: Monthly Review Press, 1973.

Sotomayor, Marta. "Language, Culture and Ethnicity in Developing Self-Concept." *Social Casework* 58, no. 4 (1977): 207-19.

Stein, Stanley J., and Barbara H. Stein. *The Colonial Heritage of Latin America: Essays on Economic Dependence in Perspective*. New York: Oxford University Press, 1970.

Steiner, Stan. "Chicano Power: Militance among the Mexican-Americans." In *Pain and Promise: The Chicano Today*, edited by Edward Simmen, 122-40. New York: Mentor Books, 1972.

Stinner, William F., Klaus de Albuquerque, and Roy S. Bryce-Laporte, eds. *Return Migration and Remittances: Developing a Caribbean Perspective*. RIIES Occasional Papers no. 3. Washington, D.C.: Smithsonian Institution, 1982.

Stolke, Verena. "Conquered Women." *NACLA Report* 24, no. 5 (February 1991): 23-28.

Sullivan, Teresa A. "A Demographic Portrait." In *Hispanics in the United States: A New Social Agenda*, edited by Pastora San Juan Cafferty and William C. McCready, 7-32. New Brunswick, N.J.: Transaction Books, 1985.

Sutton, Constance R. "The Caribbeanization of New York City and the Emergence of a Transnational Socio-Cultural System." In *Caribbean Life in New York City: Sociocultural Dimensions*, edited by Constance R. Sutton and Elsa Chaney. Staten Island, N.Y.: Center for Migration Studies of New York, 1987.

Sutton, Constance R., and Elsa Chaney, eds. *Caribbean Life in New York City: Sociocultural Dimensions*. Staten Island, N.Y.: Center for Migration Studies of New York, 1987.

Takaki, Ronald. *Iron Cages: Race and Culture in Nineteenth Century America*. Seattle: University of Washington Press, 1979.

———. "Reflections on Racial Patterns in America: An Historical Perspective." In *Ethnicity and Public Policy*, edited by W. Van Horne, 1-24. Madison: University of Wisconsin System, 1982.

———. *A Different Mirror: A History of Multicultural America*. Boston: Little, Brown, 1993.

———, ed. *From Different Shores: Perspectives on Race and Ethnicity in America*. New York: Oxford University Press, 1987.

Teitelbaum, Herbert, and Richard J. Hiller. "Bilingual Education: The Legal Mandate." *Harvard Educational Review* 47, no. 2 (May 1977): 138-71.

Thernstrom, Stephan. "Ethnic Groups in American History." In *Ethnic Relations in America*, edited by the American Assembly, 3-27. Englewood Cliffs, N.J.: Prentice-Hall, 1982.

Thernstrom, Stephan, Ann Orlov, and Oscar Handlin, eds. *Harvard Encyclopedia of American Ethnic Groups*. Cambridge, Mass: Harvard University Press, 1980.

Thomas, Piri. *Down These Mean Streets*. New York: Vintage, [1967] 1991.

———. "Puerto Ricans in the Promised Land," *Civil Rights Digest* 6, no. 2 (1972).

Tienda, Marta, and V. Ortiz. " 'Hispanicity' and the 1980 Census." *Social Science Quarterly* 67 (1986): 3-20.

Tinker Salas, Miguel. "El immigrante latino: Latin American Immigration and Pan-Ethnicity." *Latino Studies Journal* 2, no. 3 (September 1991): 58-71.

Todorov, Tzvetan. *The Conquest of America: The Question of the Other*. New York: Harper and Row, 1982.

Torres-Saillant, Silvio. "Dominicans as a New York Community: A Social Appraisal." *Punto 7 Review* 2, no. 1 (Fall 1989): 7-25.

Tovar, Federico Ribes. *Lolita Lebrón la prisionera*. New York: Plus Ultra, 1974.

Treviño, Fernando M. "Standardized Terminology for Standardized Populations." *American Journal of Public Health* 77 (1987): 69-72.

Tsai, Shih-Shan Henry. *The Chinese Experience in America.* Bloomington: Indiana University Press, 1986.

Turner, Victor. "Social Dramas and Stories about Them." In *On Narrative,* edited by W. J. T. Mitchell. Chicago: University of Chicago Press, 1981.

U.S. Bureau of the Census. Population Division. *Development of the Race and Ethnic Items for the 1990 Census.* New Orleans, La.: Population Association of America, 1988.

U.S. Commission on Civil Rights. "A Better Chance to Learn: Bilingual-Bicultural Education," no. 51 (1975): 9, 143.

Valenzuela, Victor. *Anti-United States Sentiment in Latin American Literature.* Bethlehem, Pa.: Moravian Book Shop, 1982.

Van Velsen, J. "The Extended Case Method and Situational Analysis." In *The Social Craft of Anthropology,* edited by J. Mitchell. London: Tavistock, 1979.

Vásquez, Blanca. "Mi gente: Antónia Pantoja y Esperanza Martell." *Centro Bulletin* 2, no. 7 (Winter 1989-90): 48-55.

Vega, Bernardo. *Memoirs of Bernardo Vega: A Contribution to the History of the Puerto Rican Community in New York,* edited by César Andreu Iglesias. New York: Monthly Review Press, 1984.

Velho, Gilberto. *Individualismo e cultura.* Rio de Janeiro: Zahar Editores, 1981.

Veltman, Calvin. *Language Shift in the United States.* Berlin: Mouton, 1983.

Vincent, Joan. "The Structuring of Ethnicity." *Human Organization* 33, no. 4 (1974): 375-79.

Wade, Peter. "Race and Class: The Case of South American Blacks." *Ethnic and Racial Studies* 8, no. 2 (1985): 233-49.

Williams, Raymond. *Marxism and Literature.* Oxford: Oxford University Press, 1977.

Willig, Ann C. "A Meta-Analysis of Selected Studies on Effectiveness of Bilingual Education." *Review of Educational Research* 55, no. 3 (1985): 269-317.

Wilson, William Julius. "The Black Community in the 1980s: Questions of Race, Class, and Public Policy." In *Majority and Minority: The Dynamics of Race and Ethnicity in American Life,* edited by Norman R. Yetman, 490-522. Boston: Allyn and Bacon, 1985.

Woll, Allen. "Bandits and Lovers: Hispanic Images in American Film." In *The Kaleidoscopic Lens: How Hollywood Views Ethnic Groups,* edited by Richard Miller, 54-71. New York: J. S. Ozer, 1980.

Yankelovich, Skelly & White. *Spanish America: A Study of the Hispanic Market.* New York: SIN, Inc., 1984.

Yetman, Norman R., ed. *Majority and Minority: The Dynamics of Race and Ethnicity in American Life.* Boston: Allyn and Bacon, 1985.

Young Lords Party and Michael Abramson. *Palante: The Young Lords Party.* New York: McGraw Hill, 1971.

Zavella, Patricia. *Women's Work and Chicano Families: Cannery Workers of the Santa Clara Valley.* Ithaca, N.Y.: Cornell University Press, 1987.

Zea, Leopoldo, ed. *América Latína en sus ideas.* Mexico City: Siglo XXI Editores/UNESCO, 1987.

Zentella, Ana Celia. "Language Politics in the U.S.A.: The English Only Movement." In *Literature, Language and Politics,* edited by Betty Jean Craige, 39-51. Athens: University of Georgia Press, 1988.

Zinn, Howard. *A People's History of the United States.* New York: Harper and Row, 1980.

Index

Compiled by Eileen Quam and Theresa Wolner

Suzanne Oboler, a Peruvian American, is currently assistant professor in the Department of American Civilization at Brown University, where she teaches courses on Latino/Latina studies and the literature and cultures of the Americas. Her current research is on race, citizenship, and identity formation in the Americas. She has taught courses on Latin American literature and culture and on Latinos in the United States at Eugene Lang College, the New School for Social Research, and the Institute for Puerto Rican Urban Studies, a cross-cultural research and training institute. She has also directed worker education programs in New York City and has taught literature to adults in popular education classes in Brazil.